"THE SNOWMEN PLOT"

PART ONE

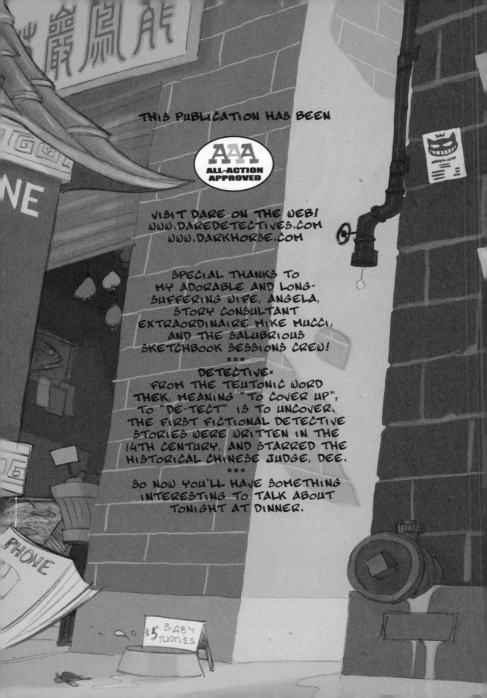

THIS PUBLICATION HAS BEEN

AAA
ALL-ACTION
APPROVED

VISIT DARE ON THE WEB!
WWW.DAREDETECTIVES.COM
WWW.DARKHORSE.COM

SPECIAL THANKS TO
MY ADORABLE AND LONG-
SUFFERING WIFE, ANGELA,
STORY CONSULTANT
EXTRAORDINAIRE MIKE MUCCI,
AND THE SALUBRIOUS
SKETCHBOOK SESSIONS CREW!

***

DETECTIVE=
FROM THE TEUTONIC WORD
THEK, MEANING "TO COVER UP",
TO "DE-TECT" IS TO UNCOVER.
THE FIRST FICTIONAL DETECTIVE
STORIES WERE WRITTEN IN THE
14TH CENTURY, AND STARRED THE
HISTORICAL CHINESE JUDGE, DEE.

***

SO NOW YOU'LL HAVE SOMETHING
INTERESTING TO TALK ABOUT
TONIGHT AT DINNER.

PHONE

$5 BABY
TURTLES

THE DARE! DETECTIVES™

VOLUME ONE
"THE SNOWPEA PLOT"

STORY AND ART BY
BEN CALDWELL

DARK HORSE BOOKS™

PUBLISHER
MIKE RICHARDSON

EDITOR
CHRIS WARNER

THE FONT USED FOR THIS BOOK IS "ARIS"
"ARIS" ©2004 GILLES ARIS
HTTP://FOUDEBD.FREE.FR/

THE DARE DETECTIVES! VOL. 1:
"THE SNOW PEA PLOT"

PUBLISHED BY
DARK HORSE BOOKS
A DIVISION OF DARK HORSE COMICS, INC.
10956 S.E. MAIN STREET
MILWAUKIE, OR 97222

DARKHORSE.COM
DAREDETECTIVES.COM

TALK ABOUT THIS BOOK ONLINE!
DARKHORSE.COM/COMMUNITY/BOARDS

TO FIND A COMICS SHOP IN YOUR AREA,
CALL THE COMIC SHOP LOCATOR SERVICE
TOLL-FREE AT 1-888-266-4226

FIRST EDITION: OCTOBER 2004
ISBN: 1-59307-176-0

1 3 5 7 9 10 8 6 4 2
PRINTED IN CANADA

NO BUNNIES WERE HARMED
IN MAKING THIS BOOK

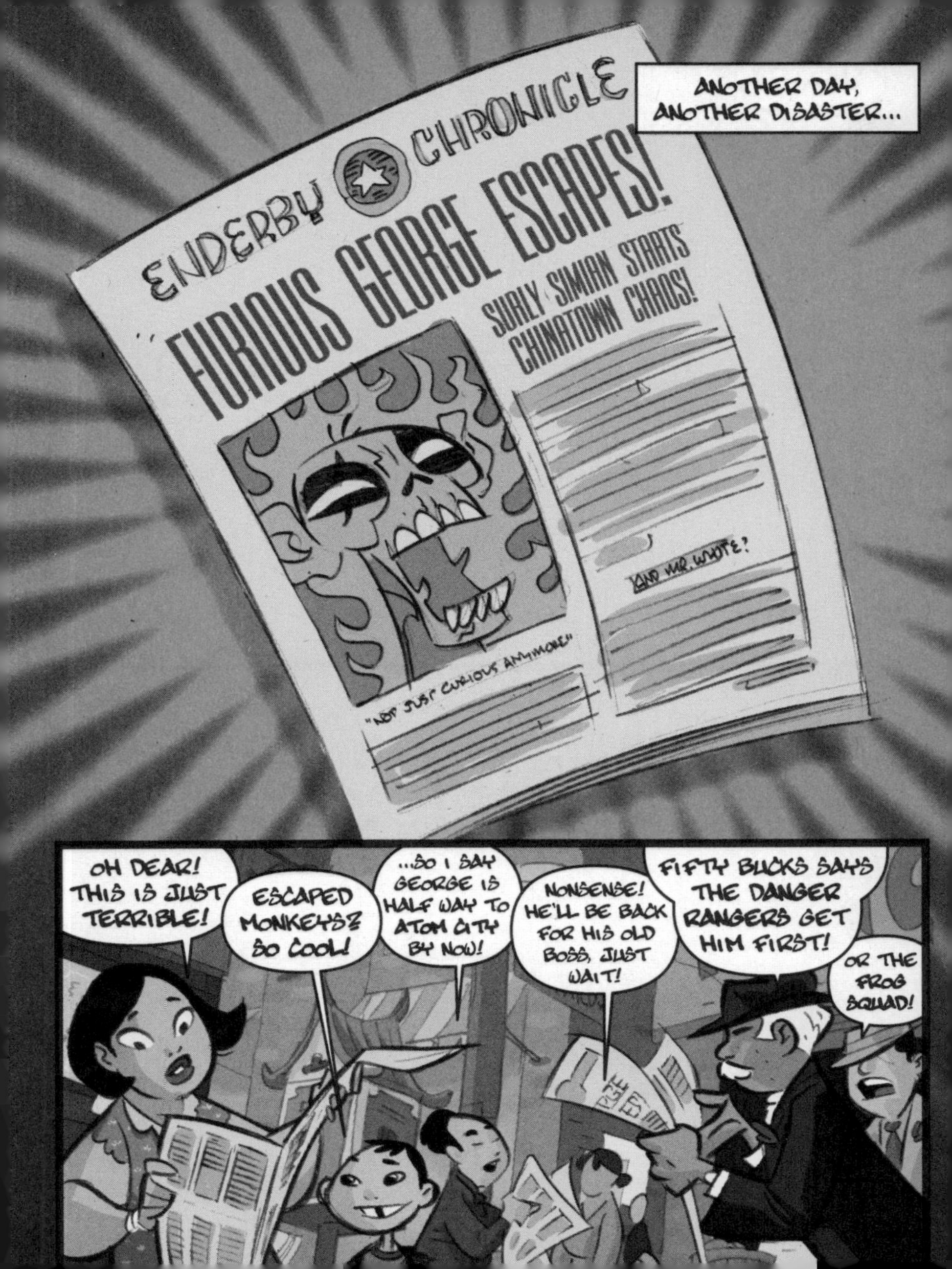
ANOTHER DAY, ANOTHER DISASTER...
ENDERBY CHRONICLE
FURIOUS GEORGE ESCAPES!
SURLY SIMIAN STARTS CHINATOWN CHAOS!
"NOT JUST CURIOUS ANYMORE"
OH DEAR! THIS IS JUST TERRIBLE!
ESCAPED MONKEYS? SO COOL!
...SO I SAY GEORGE IS HALF WAY TO ATOM CITY BY NOW!
NONSENSE! HE'LL BE BACK FOR HIS OLD BOSS, JUST WAIT!
FIFTY BUCKS SAYS THE DANGER RANGERS GET HIM FIRST!
OR THE FROG SQUAD!

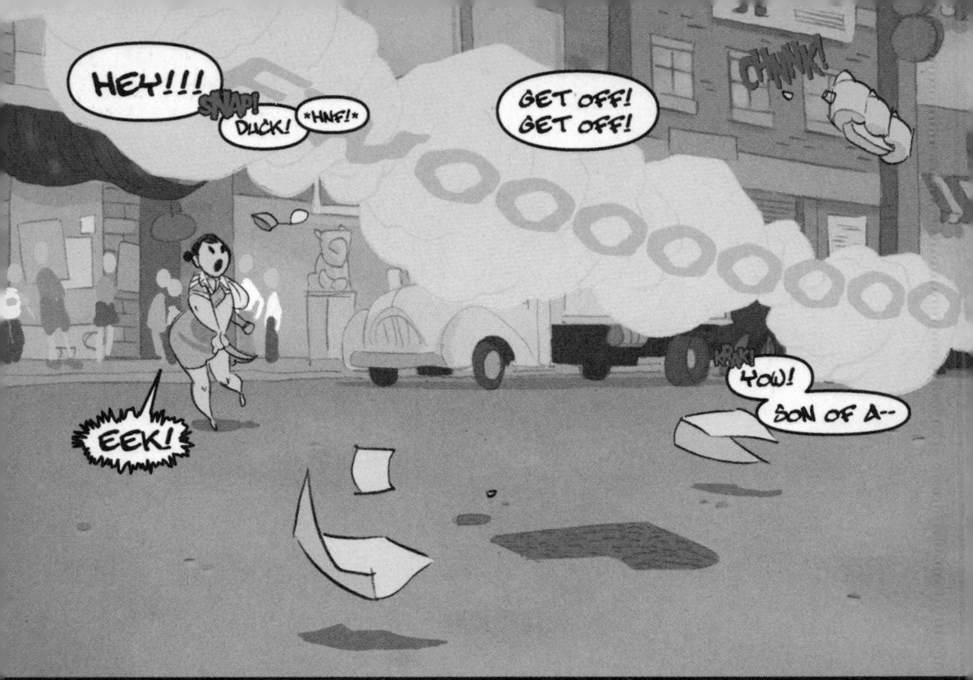
HEY!!!
SNAP!
DUCK!
HNF!
GET OFF! GET OFF!
CHINK!
EEK!
YOW!
SON OF A--

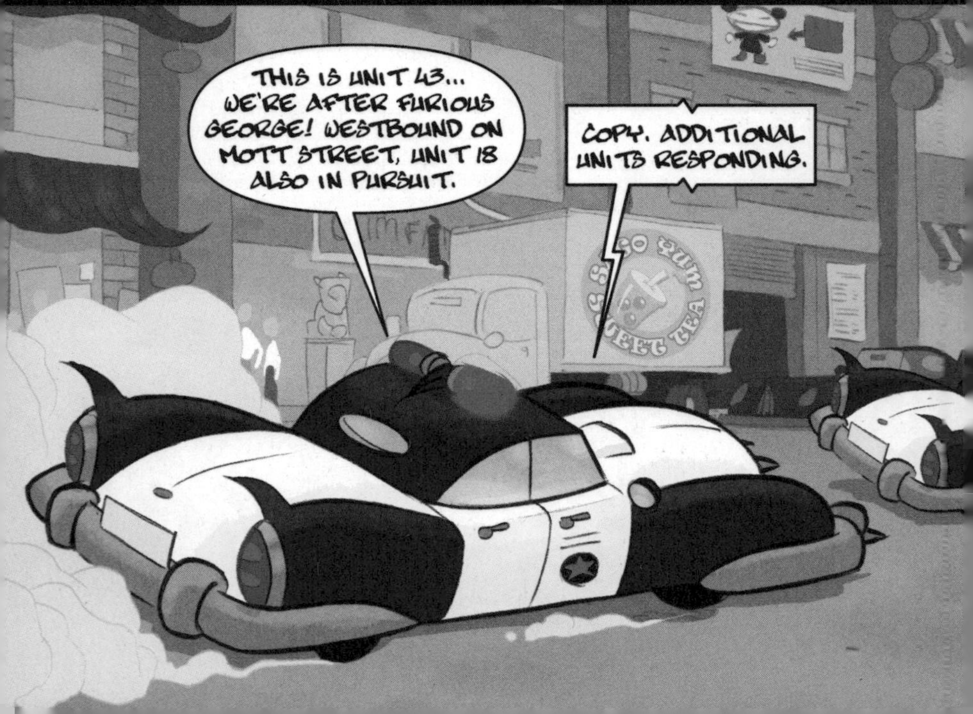
THIS IS UNIT 43... WE'RE AFTER FURIOUS GEORGE! WESTBOUND ON MOTT STREET, UNIT 18 ALSO IN PURSUIT.
COPY. ADDITIONAL UNITS RESPONDING.
SO YUM SWEET TEA

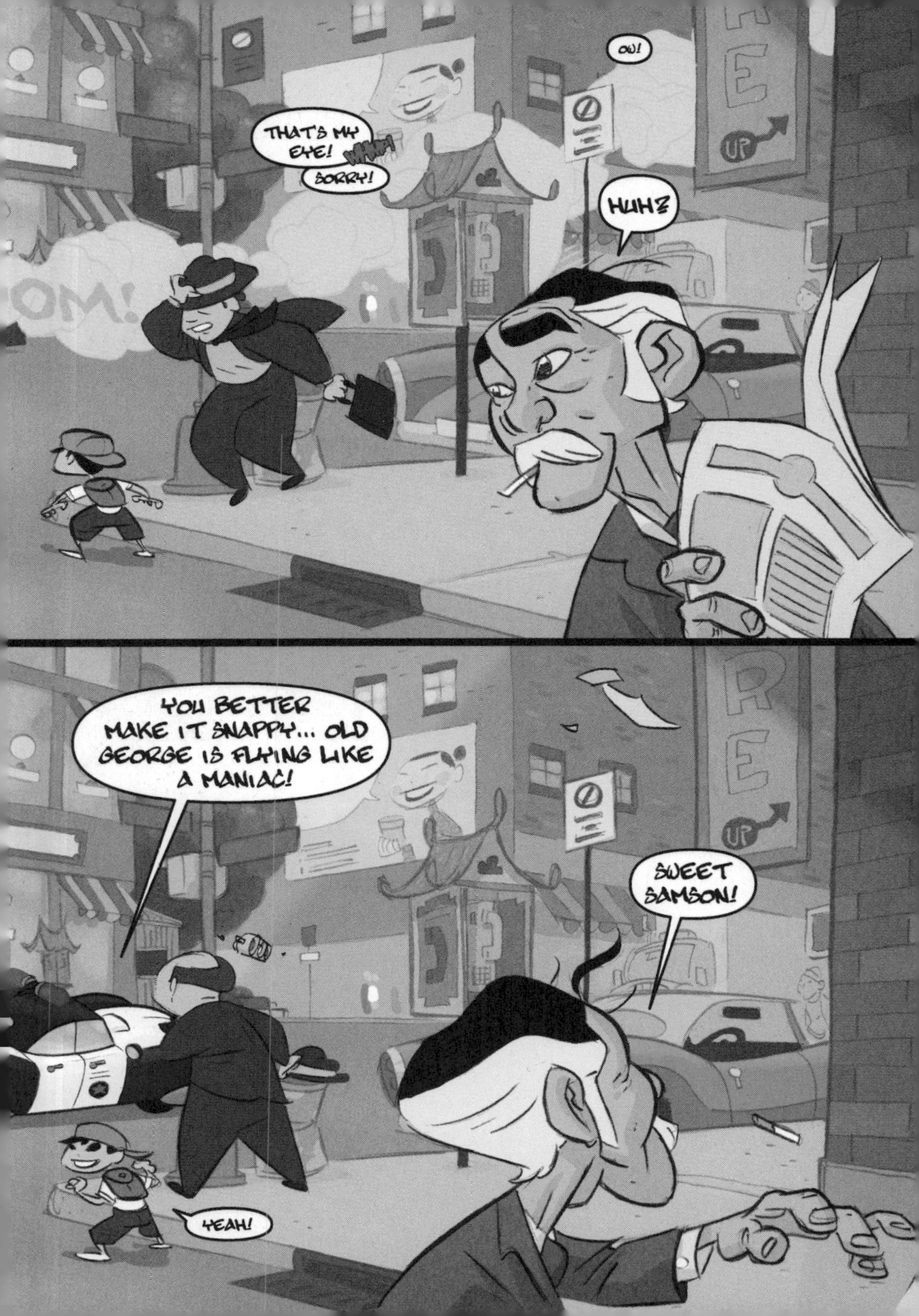
THAT'S MY EYE!
SORRY!
OW!
HUH?
YOU BETTER MAKE IT SNAPPY... OLD GEORGE IS FLYING LIKE A MANIAC!
SWEET SAMSON!
YEAH!

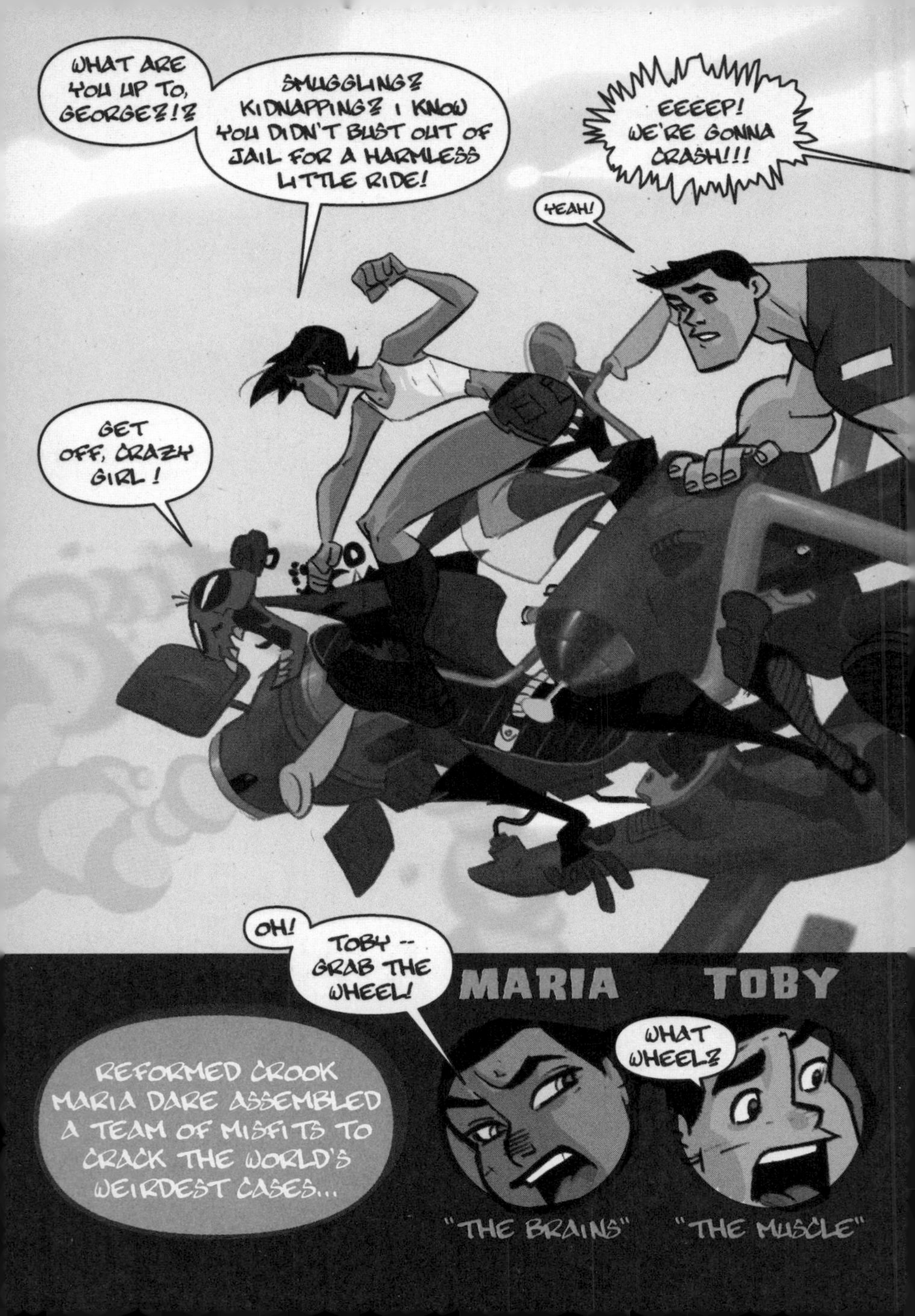
WHAT ARE YOU UP TO, GEORGE?!?
SMUGGLING? KIDNAPPING? I KNOW YOU DIDN'T BUST OUT OF JAIL FOR A HARMLESS LITTLE RIDE!
EEEEP! WE'RE GONNA CRASH!!!
YEAH!
GET OFF, CRAZY GIRL!
OH!
TOBY -- GRAB THE WHEEL!
MARIA
TOBY
WHAT WHEEL?
REFORMED CROOK MARIA DARE ASSEMBLED A TEAM OF MISFITS TO CRACK THE WORLD'S WEIRDEST CASES...
"THE BRAINS"
"THE MUSCLE"

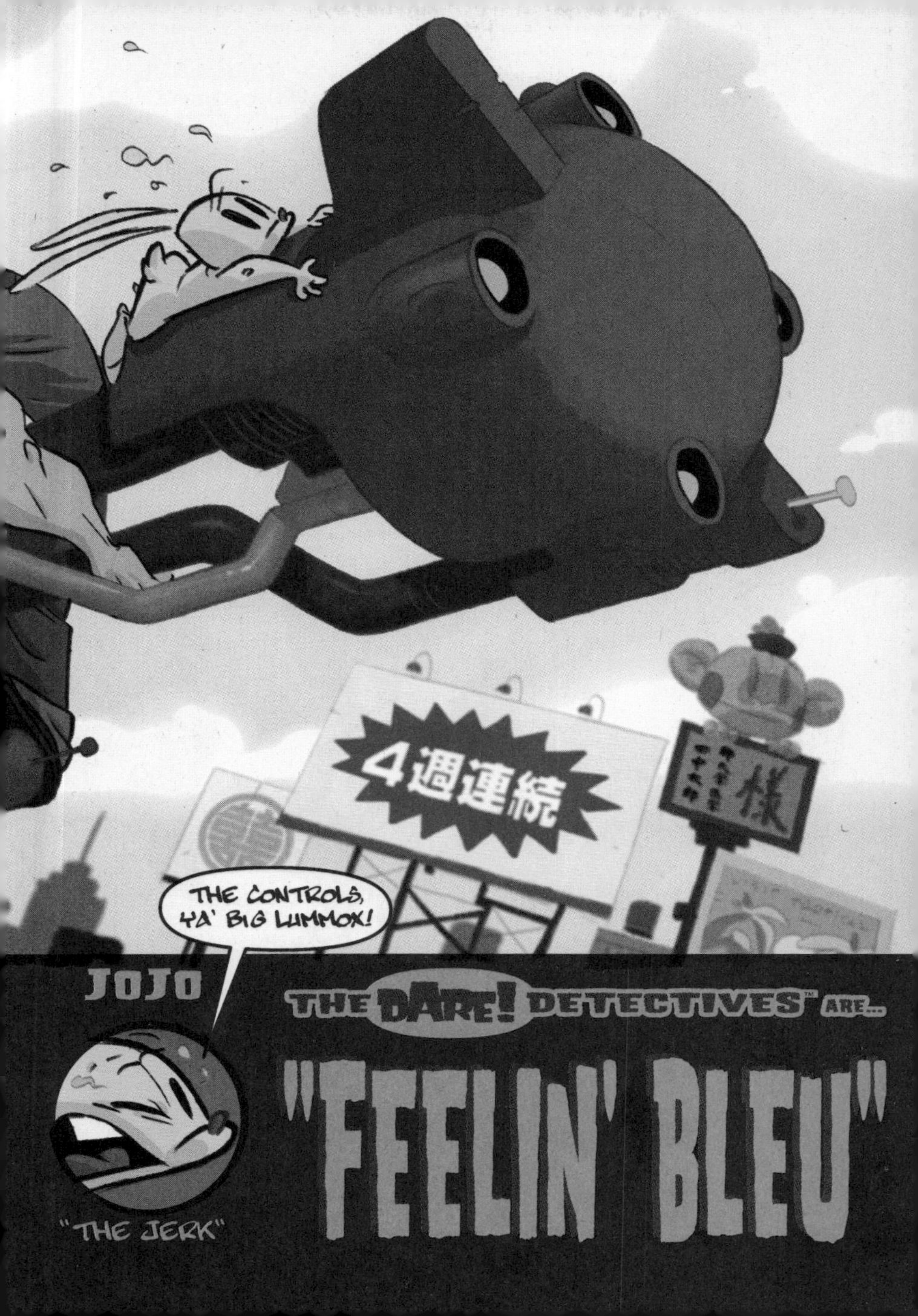
4週連続
THE CONTROLS, YA' BIG LUMMOX!
JOJO
"THE JERK"
THE DARE! DETECTIVES™ ARE...
"FEELIN' BLEU"

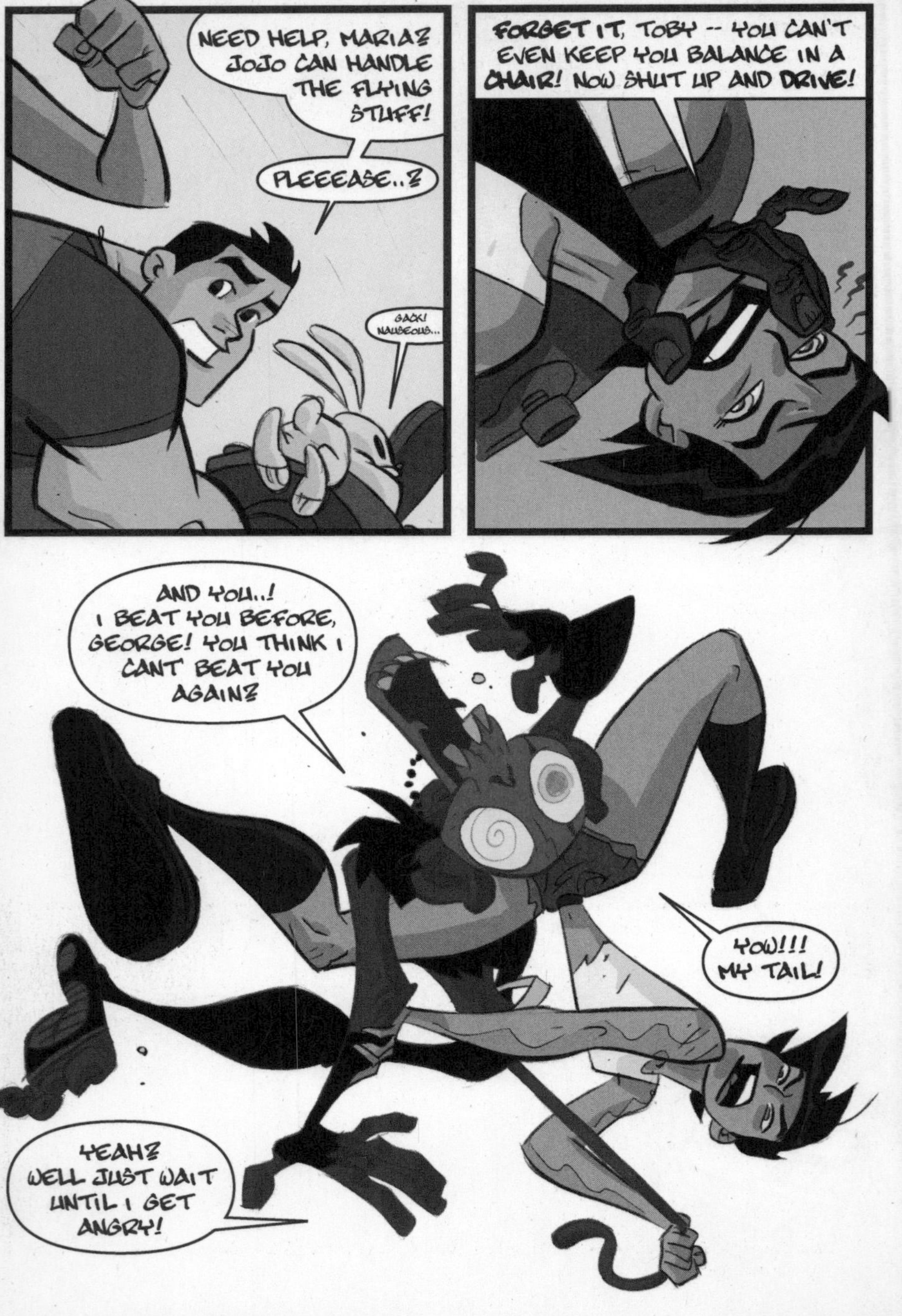
NEED HELP, MARIA? JOJO CAN HANDLE THE FLYING STUFF!
PLEEEASE..?
GACK! NAUSEOUS...
FORGET IT, TOBY -- YOU CAN'T EVEN KEEP YOU BALANCE IN A CHAIR! NOW SHUT UP AND DRIVE!
AND YOU..! I BEAT YOU BEFORE, GEORGE! YOU THINK I CANT BEAT YOU AGAIN?
YOW!!! MY TAIL!
YEAH? WELL JUST WAIT UNTIL I GET ANGRY!

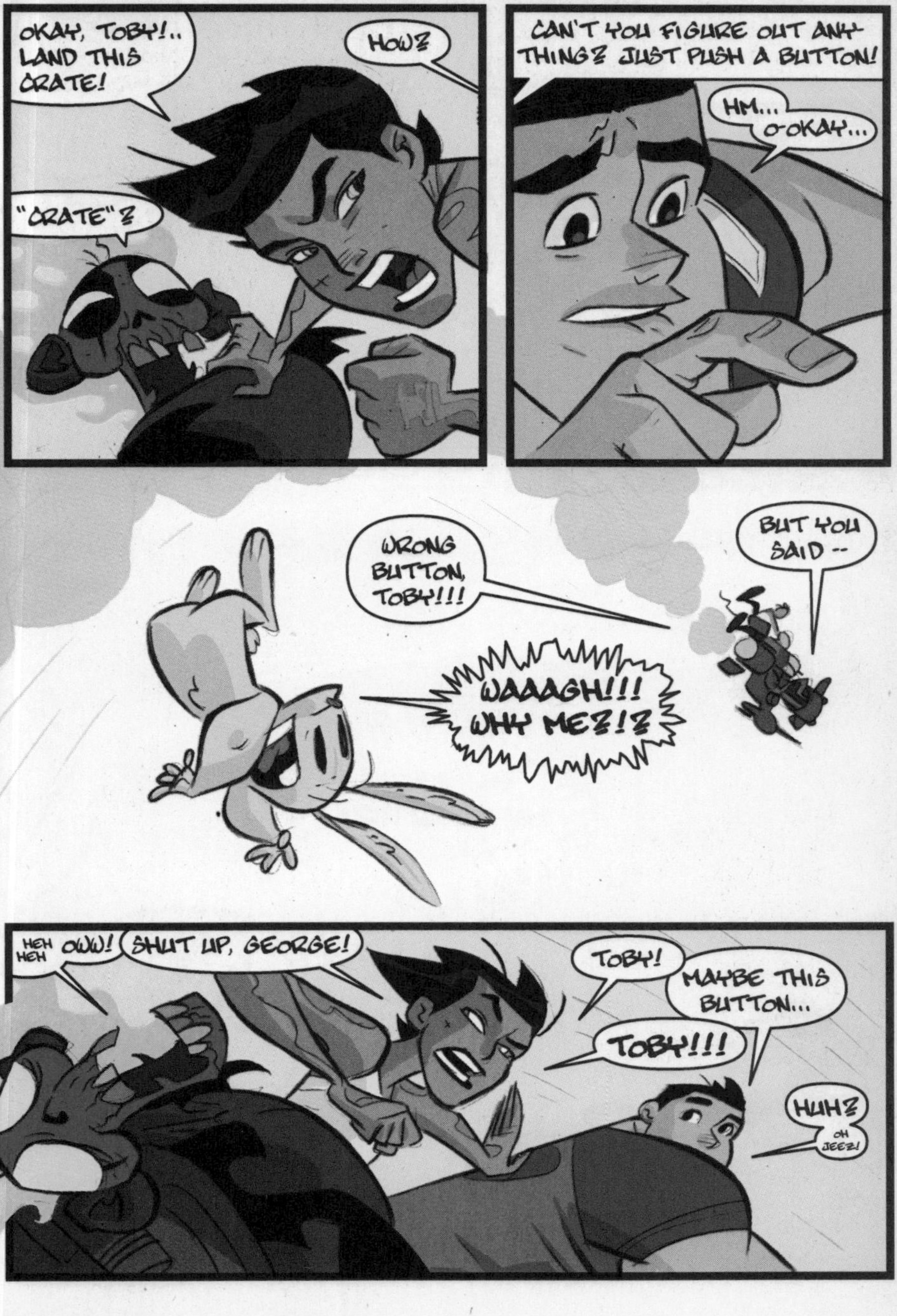
OKAY, TOBY!.. LAND THIS CRATE!
HOW?
"CRATE"?
CAN'T YOU FIGURE OUT ANYTHING? JUST PUSH A BUTTON!
HM... O-OKAY...
WRONG BUTTON, TOBY!!!
BUT YOU SAID --
WAAAGH!!! WHY ME?!?
HEH HEH
OWW!
SHUT UP, GEORGE!
TOBY!
MAYBE THIS BUTTON...
TOBY!!!
HUH?
OH JEEZ!

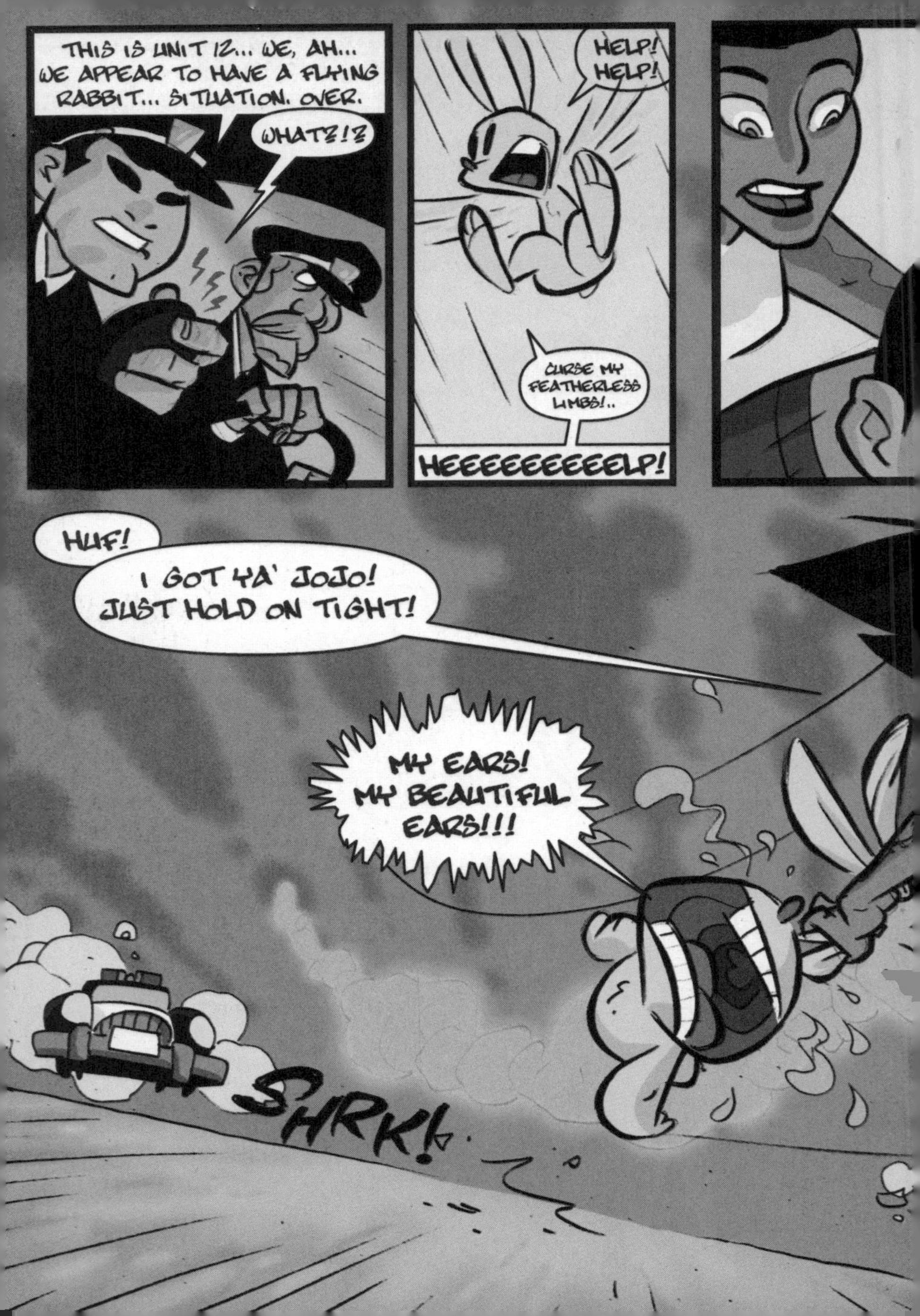
THIS IS UNIT 12... WE, AH... WE APPEAR TO HAVE A FLYING RABBIT... SITUATION. OVER.
WHAT?!?
HELP! HELP!
CURSE MY FEATHERLESS LIMBS!..
HEEEEEEEEEELP!
HUF!
I GOT YA' JOJO! JUST HOLD ON TIGHT!
MY EARS! MY BEAUTIFUL EARS!!!
SHRK!

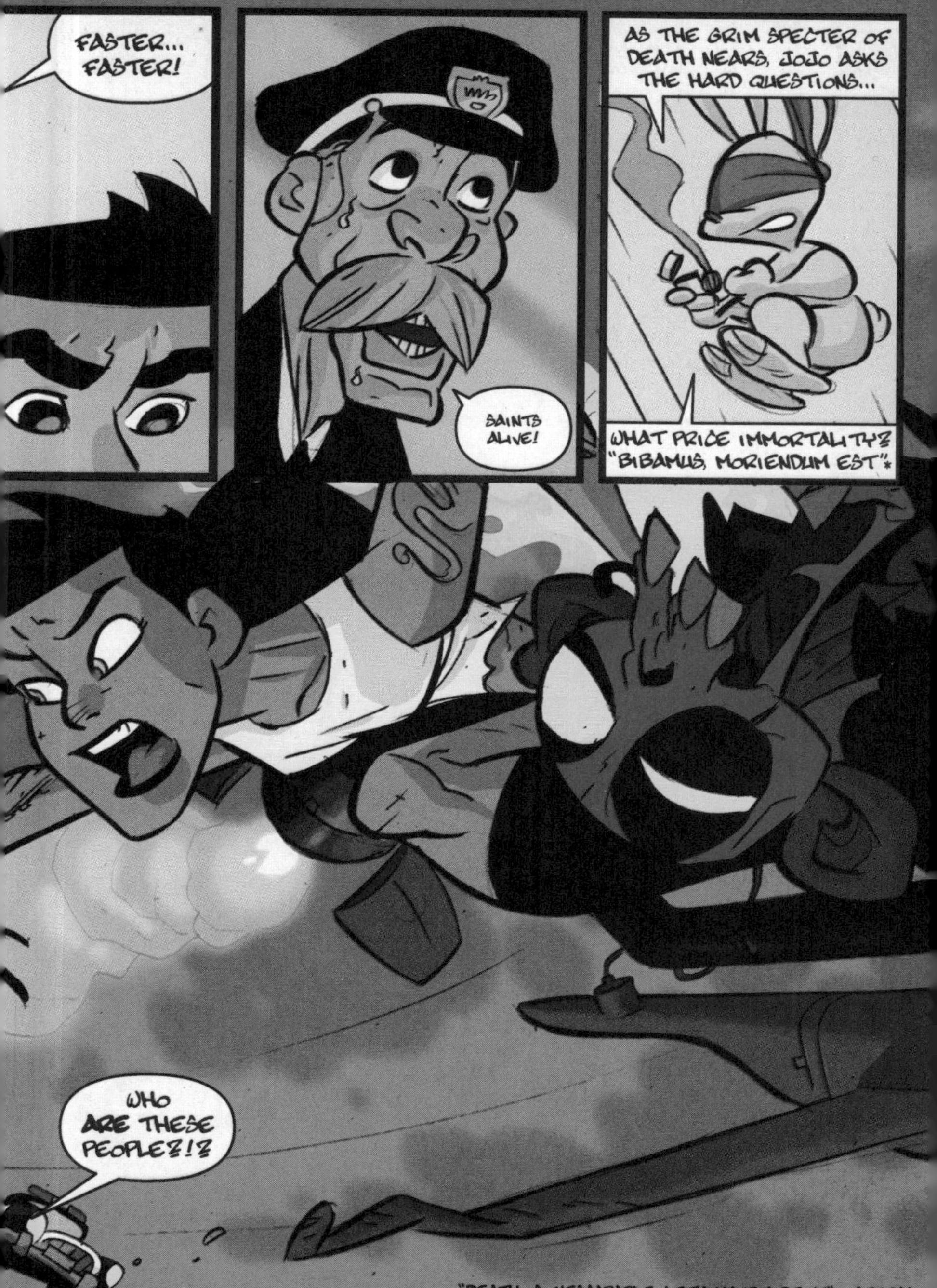
FASTER... FASTER!
SAINTS ALIVE!
AS THE GRIM SPECTER OF DEATH NEARS, JOJO ASKS THE HARD QUESTIONS...
WHAT PRICE IMMORTALITY? "BIBAMUS, MORIENDUM EST"*
WHO ARE THESE PEOPLE?!?
*"DEATH IS INESCAPABLE, LET'S HAVE A DRINK" - SENECA

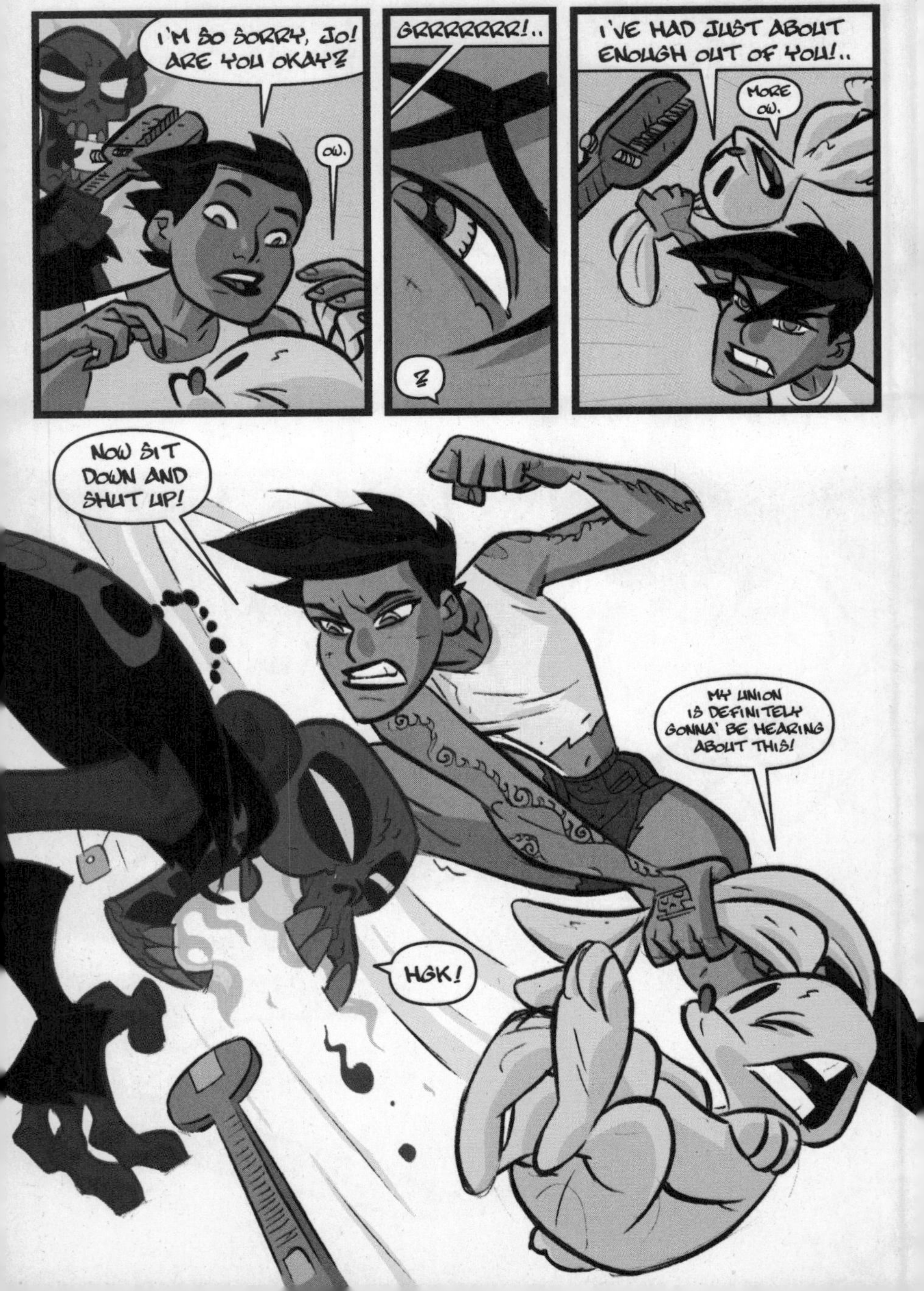
I'M SO SORRY, JO! ARE YOU OKAY?
OW.
GRRRRRRRR!..
Z
I'VE HAD JUST ABOUT ENOUGH OUT OF YOU!..
MORE OW.
NOW SIT DOWN AND SHUT UP!
MY UNION IS DEFINITELY GONNA' BE HEARING ABOUT THIS!
HGK!

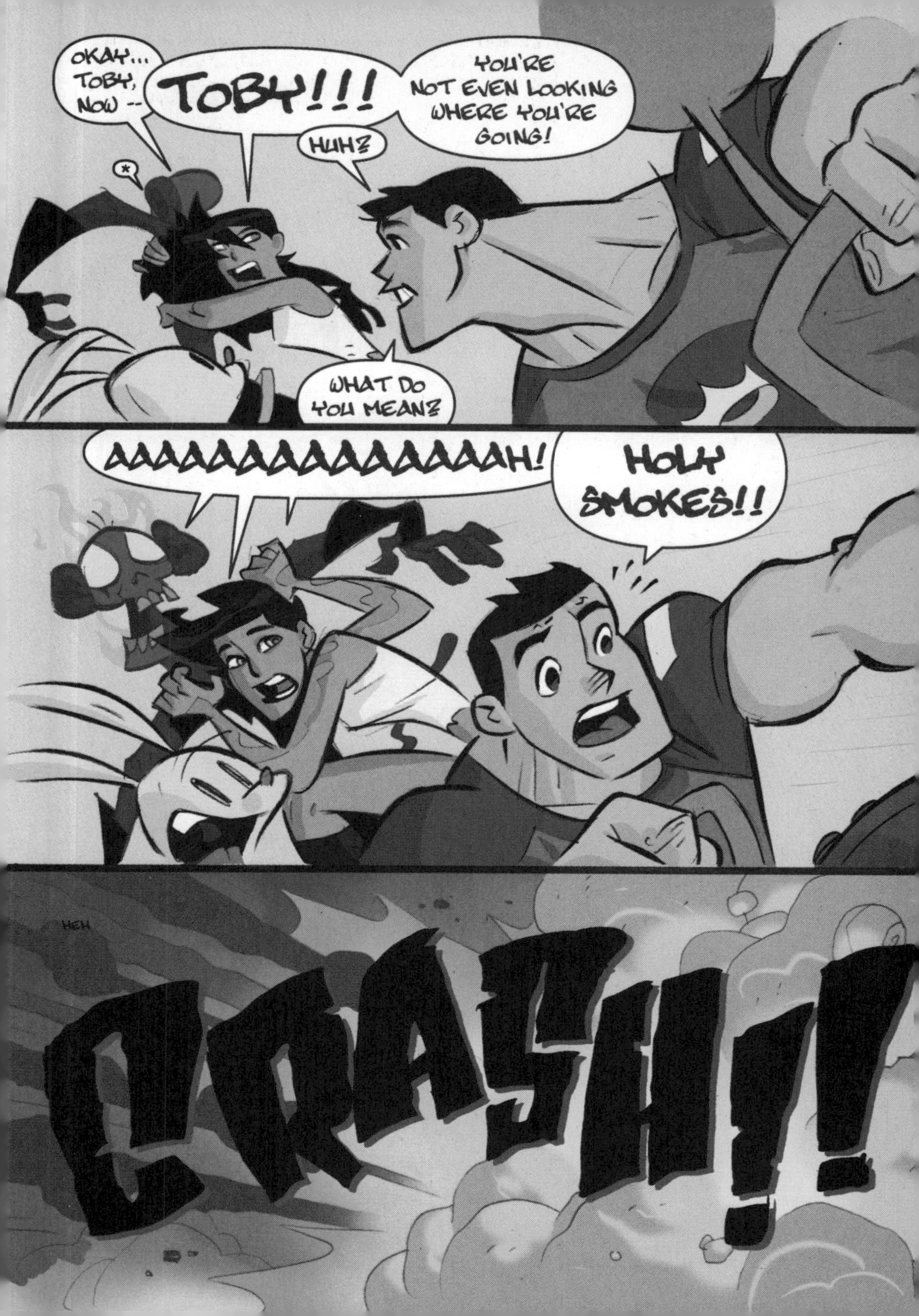

OKAY... TOBY, NOW --
TOBY!!!
HUH?
YOU'RE NOT EVEN LOOKING WHERE YOU'RE GOING!
*
WHAT DO YOU MEAN?
AAAAAAAAAAAAAAAH!
HOLY SMOKES!!
HEH
CRASH!!

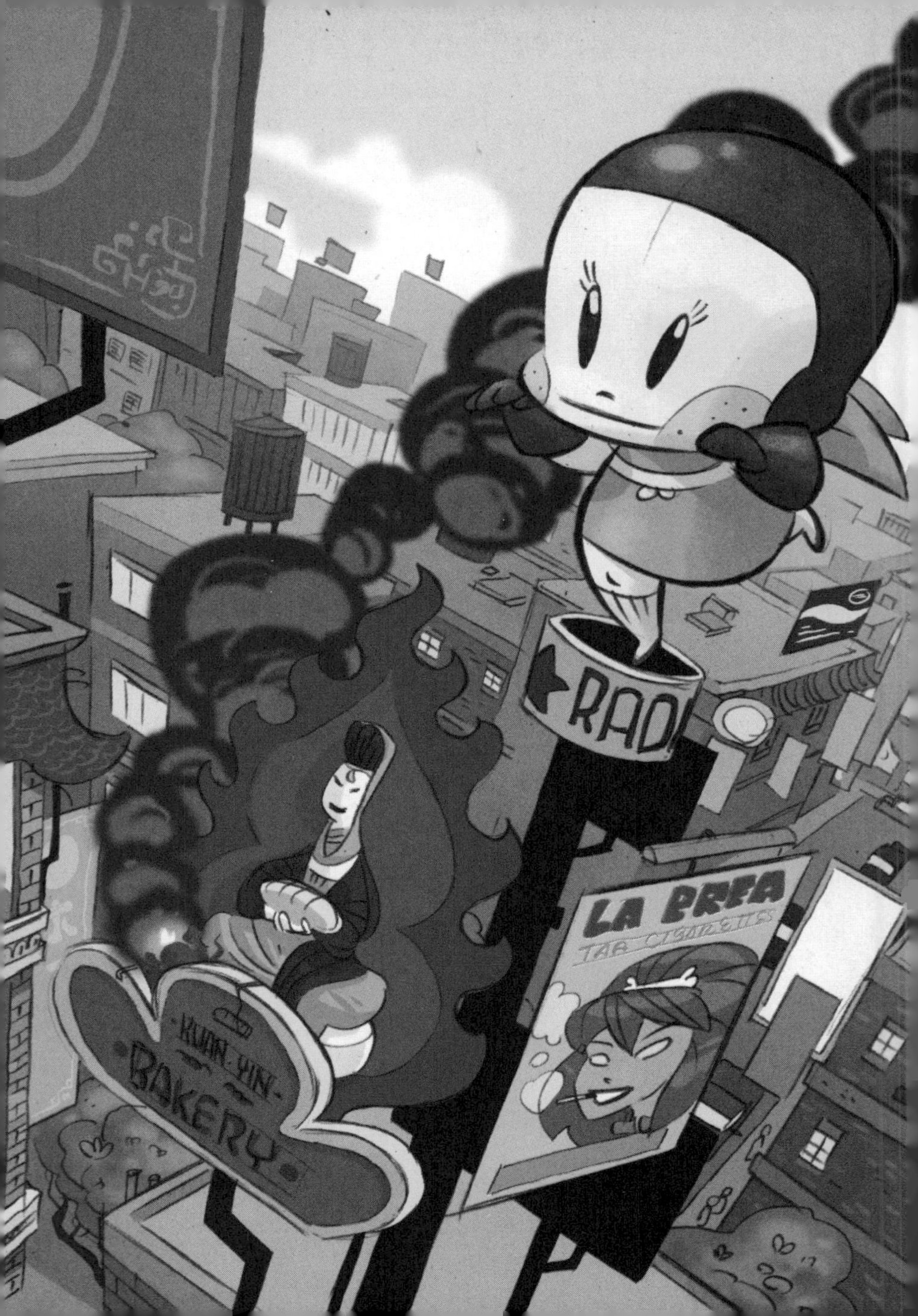
RAD
LA BREA
TAR CIGARETTES
KUAN YIN
BAKERY

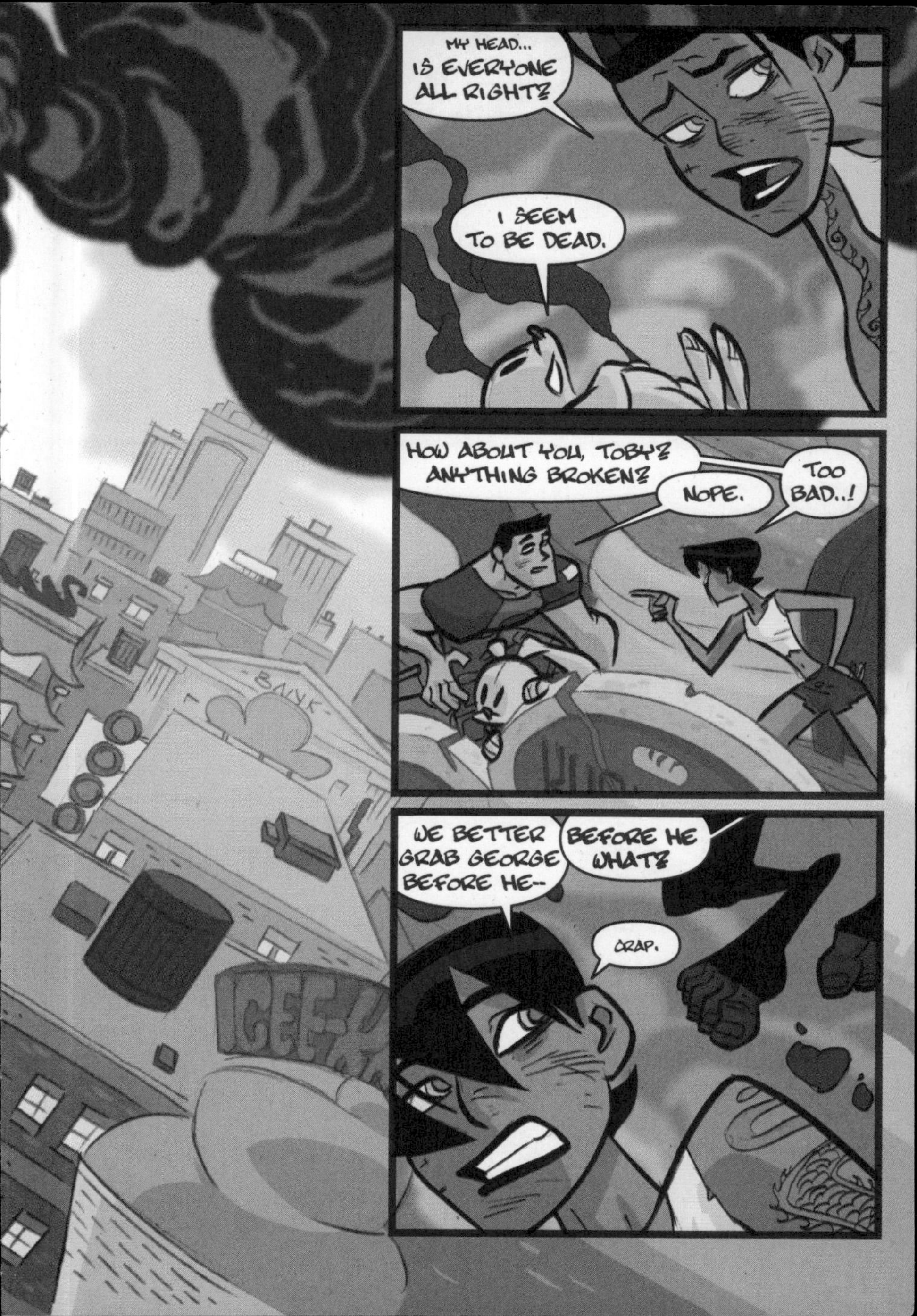
MY HEAD...
IS EVERYONE ALL RIGHT?
I SEEM TO BE DEAD.
HOW ABOUT YOU, TOBY? ANYTHING BROKEN?
NOPE.
TOO BAD..!
WE BETTER GRAB GEORGE BEFORE HE--
BEFORE HE WHAT?
CRAP.
BANK
ICE

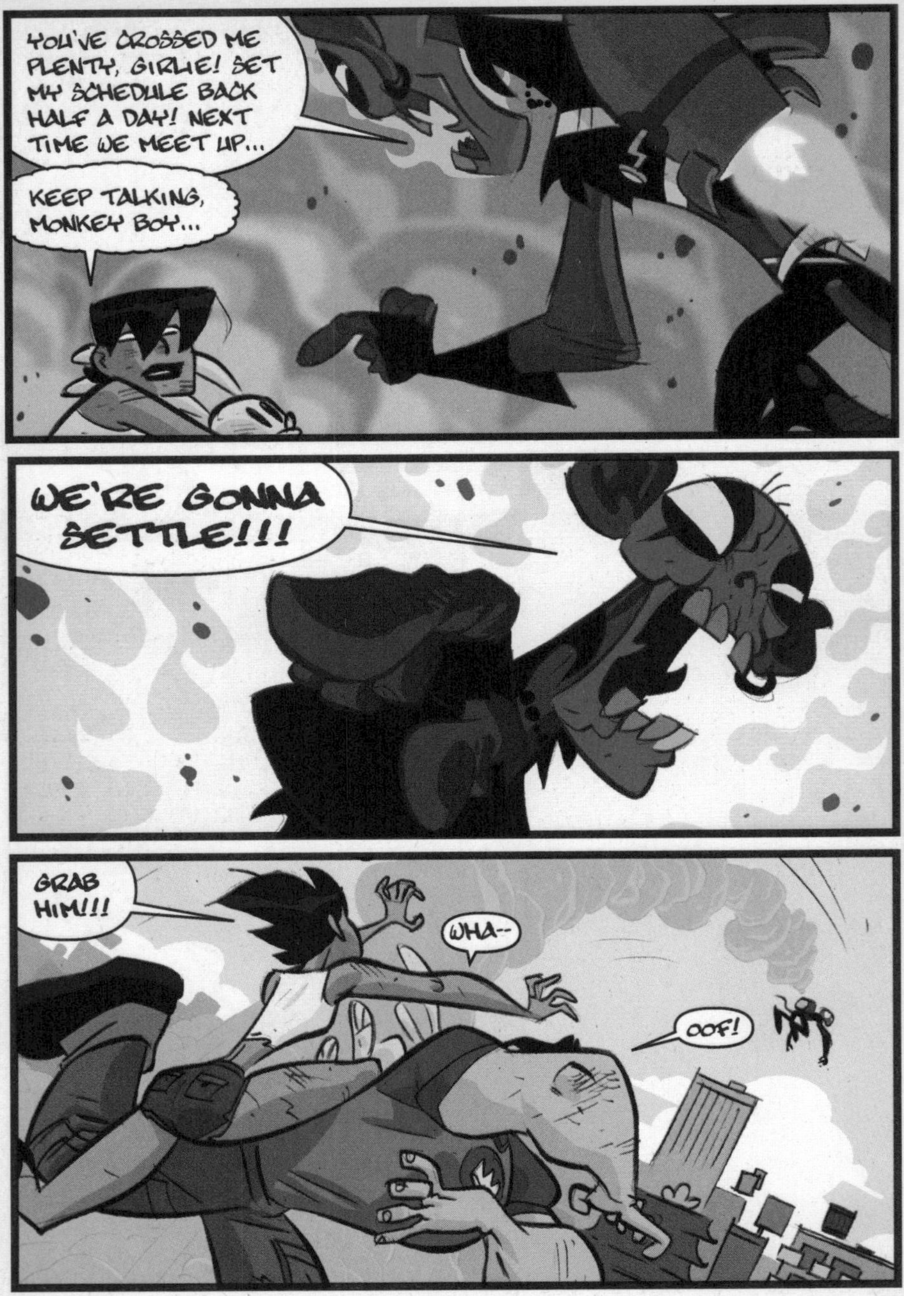
YOU'VE CROSSED ME PLENTY, GIRLIE! SET MY SCHEDULE BACK HALF A DAY! NEXT TIME WE MEET UP...
KEEP TALKING, MONKEY BOY...
WE'RE GONNA SETTLE!!!
GRAB HIM!!!
WHA--
OOF!

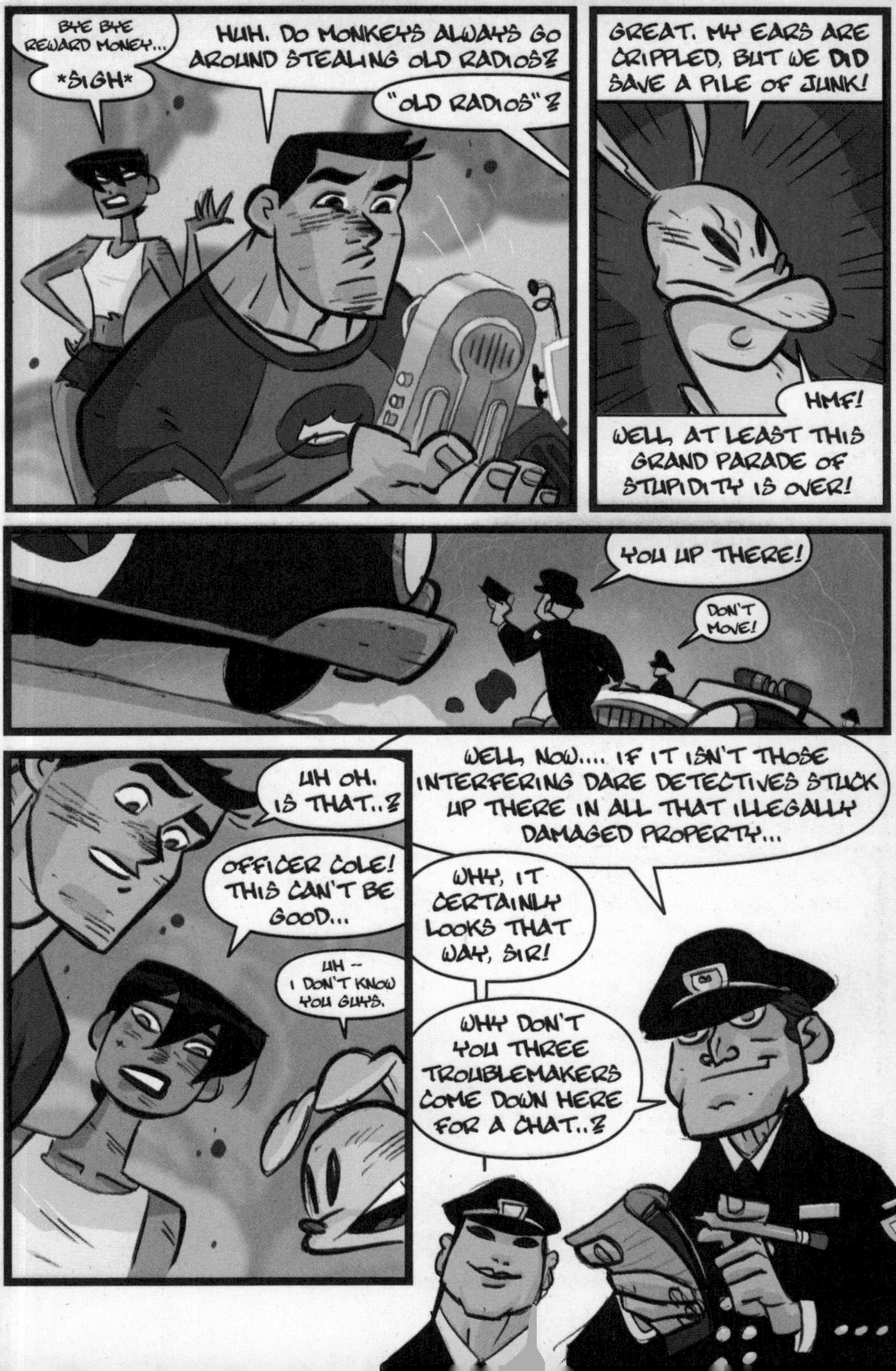
BYE BYE REWARD MONEY...
SIGH
HUH. DO MONKEYS ALWAYS GO AROUND STEALING OLD RADIOS?
"OLD RADIOS"?
GREAT. MY EARS ARE CRIPPLED, BUT WE DID SAVE A PILE OF JUNK!
HMF!
WELL, AT LEAST THIS GRAND PARADE OF STUPIDITY IS OVER!
YOU UP THERE!
DON'T MOVE!
UH OH. IS THAT..?
WELL, NOW.... IF IT ISN'T THOSE INTERFERING DARE DETECTIVES STUCK UP THERE IN ALL THAT ILLEGALLY DAMAGED PROPERTY...
OFFICER COLE! THIS CAN'T BE GOOD...
WHY, IT CERTAINLY LOOKS THAT WAY, SIR!
UH -- I DON'T KNOW YOU GUYS.
WHY DON'T YOU THREE TROUBLEMAKERS COME DOWN HERE FOR A CHAT..?

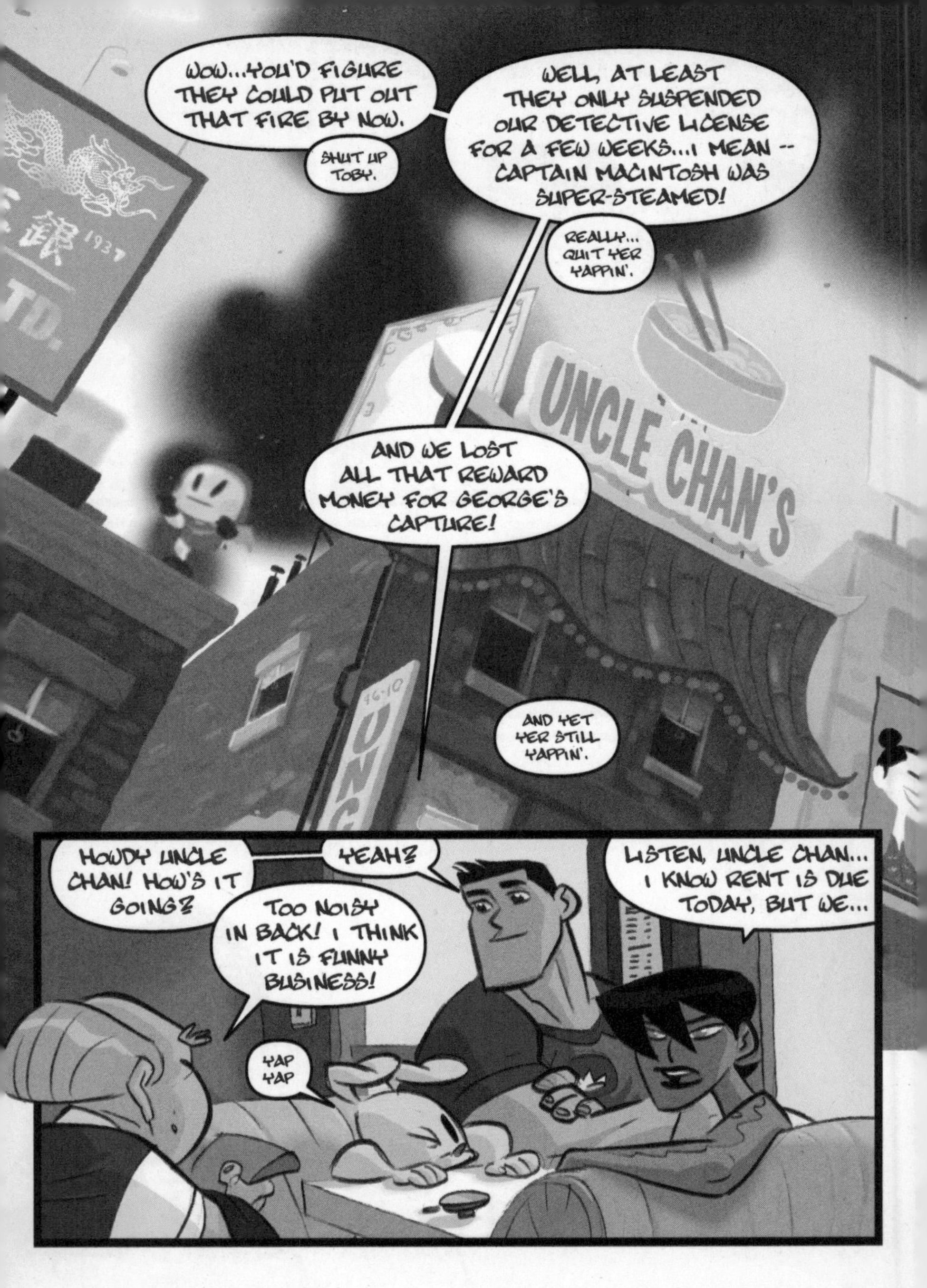
WOW...YOU'D FIGURE THEY COULD PUT OUT THAT FIRE BY NOW.
SHUT UP TOBY.
WELL, AT LEAST THEY ONLY SUSPENDED OUR DETECTIVE LICENSE FOR A FEW WEEKS...I MEAN -- CAPTAIN MACINTOSH WAS SUPER-STEAMED!
REALLY... QUIT YER YAPPIN'.
UNCLE CHAN'S
AND WE LOST ALL THAT REWARD MONEY FOR GEORGE'S CAPTURE!
AND YET YER STILL YAPPIN'.
HOWDY UNCLE CHAN! HOW'S IT GOING?
YEAH?
TOO NOISY IN BACK! I THINK IT IS FUNNY BUSINESS!
LISTEN, UNCLE CHAN... I KNOW RENT IS DUE TODAY, BUT WE...
YAP YAP

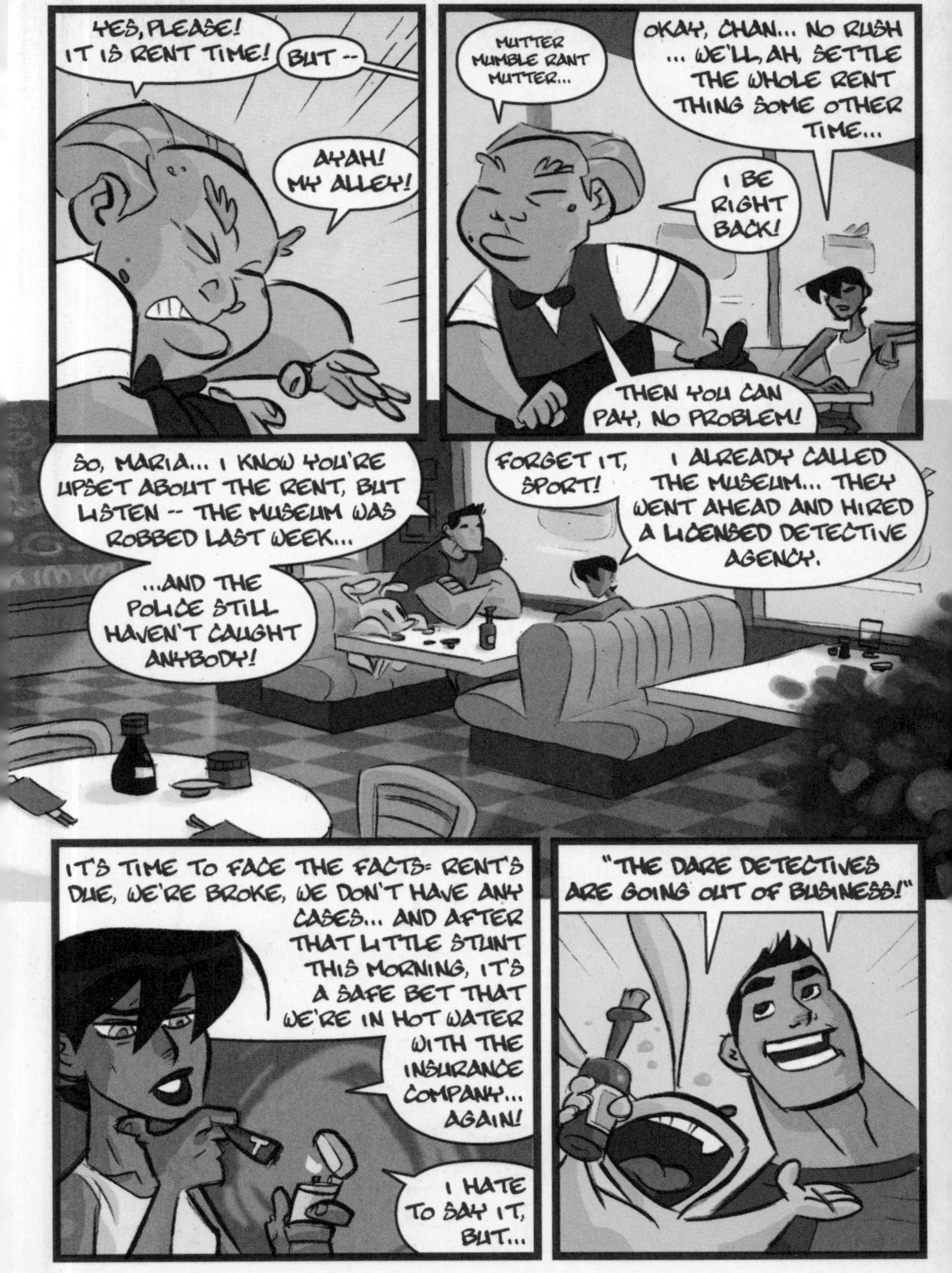
YES, PLEASE! IT IS RENT TIME!
BUT --
AYAH! MY ALLEY!
MUTTER MUMBLE RANT MUTTER...
OKAY, CHAN... NO RUSH ... WE'LL, AH, SETTLE THE WHOLE RENT THING SOME OTHER TIME...
I BE RIGHT BACK!
THEN YOU CAN PAY, NO PROBLEM!
SO, MARIA... I KNOW YOU'RE UPSET ABOUT THE RENT, BUT LISTEN -- THE MUSEUM WAS ROBBED LAST WEEK...
...AND THE POLICE STILL HAVEN'T CAUGHT ANYBODY!
FORGET IT, SPORT!
I ALREADY CALLED THE MUSEUM... THEY WENT AHEAD AND HIRED A LICENSED DETECTIVE AGENCY.
IT'S TIME TO FACE THE FACTS: RENT'S DUE, WE'RE BROKE, WE DON'T HAVE ANY CASES... AND AFTER THAT LITTLE STUNT THIS MORNING, IT'S A SAFE BET THAT WE'RE IN HOT WATER WITH THE INSURANCE COMPANY... AGAIN!
I HATE TO SAY IT, BUT...
"THE DARE DETECTIVES ARE GOING OUT OF BUSINESS!"

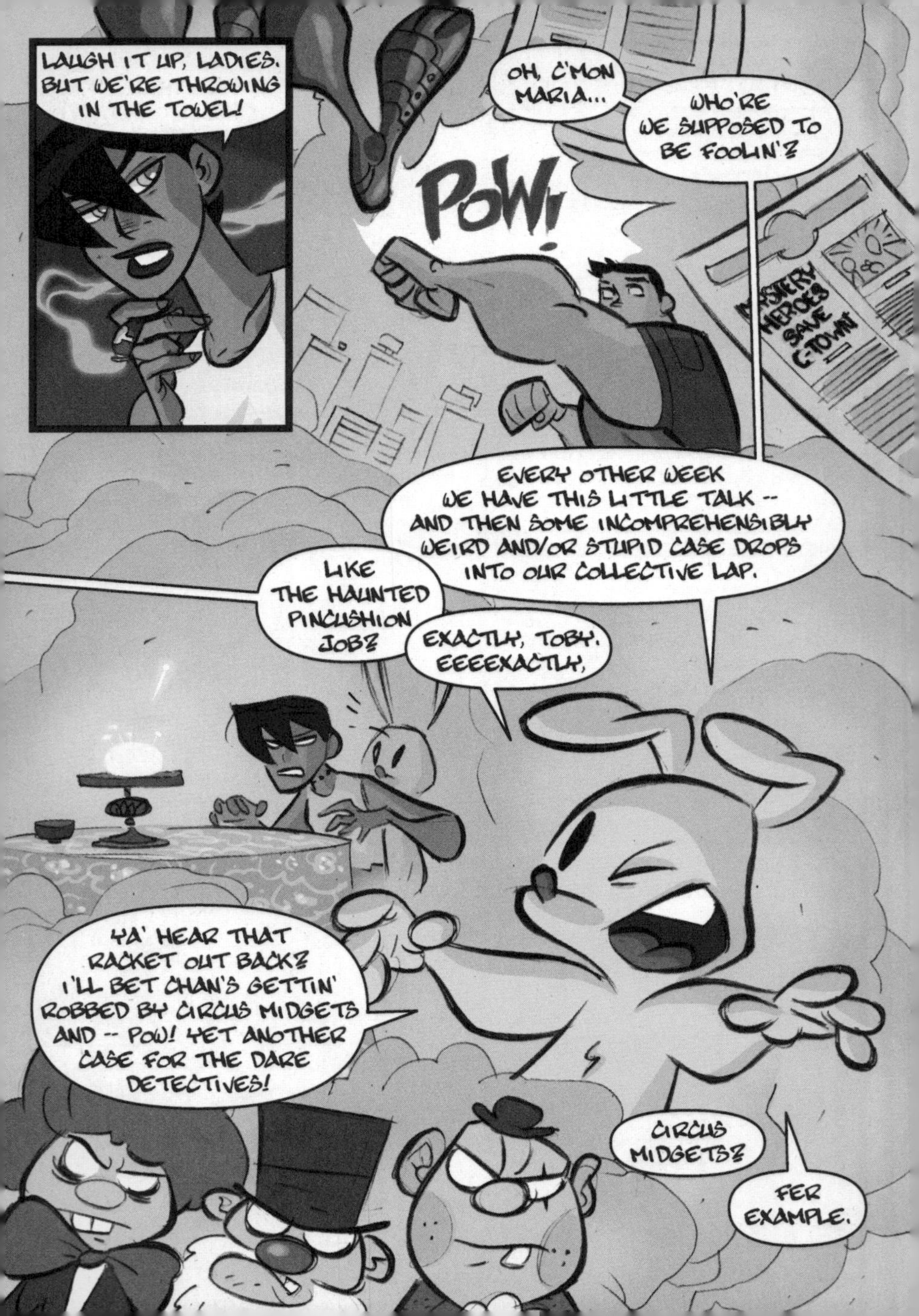
LAUGH IT UP, LADIES. BUT WE'RE THROWING IN THE TOWEL!
OH, C'MON MARIA...
WHO'RE WE SUPPOSED TO BE FOOLIN'?
POW!
MYSTERY HEROES SAVE C-TOWN
EVERY OTHER WEEK WE HAVE THIS LITTLE TALK -- AND THEN SOME INCOMPREHENSIBLY WEIRD AND/OR STUPID CASE DROPS INTO OUR COLLECTIVE LAP.
LIKE THE HAUNTED PINCUSHION JOB?
EXACTLY, TOBY. EEEEXACTLY.
YA' HEAR THAT RACKET OUT BACK? I'LL BET CHAN'S GETTIN' ROBBED BY CIRCUS MIDGETS AND -- POW! YET ANOTHER CASE FOR THE DARE DETECTIVES!
CIRCUS MIDGETS?
FER EXAMPLE.

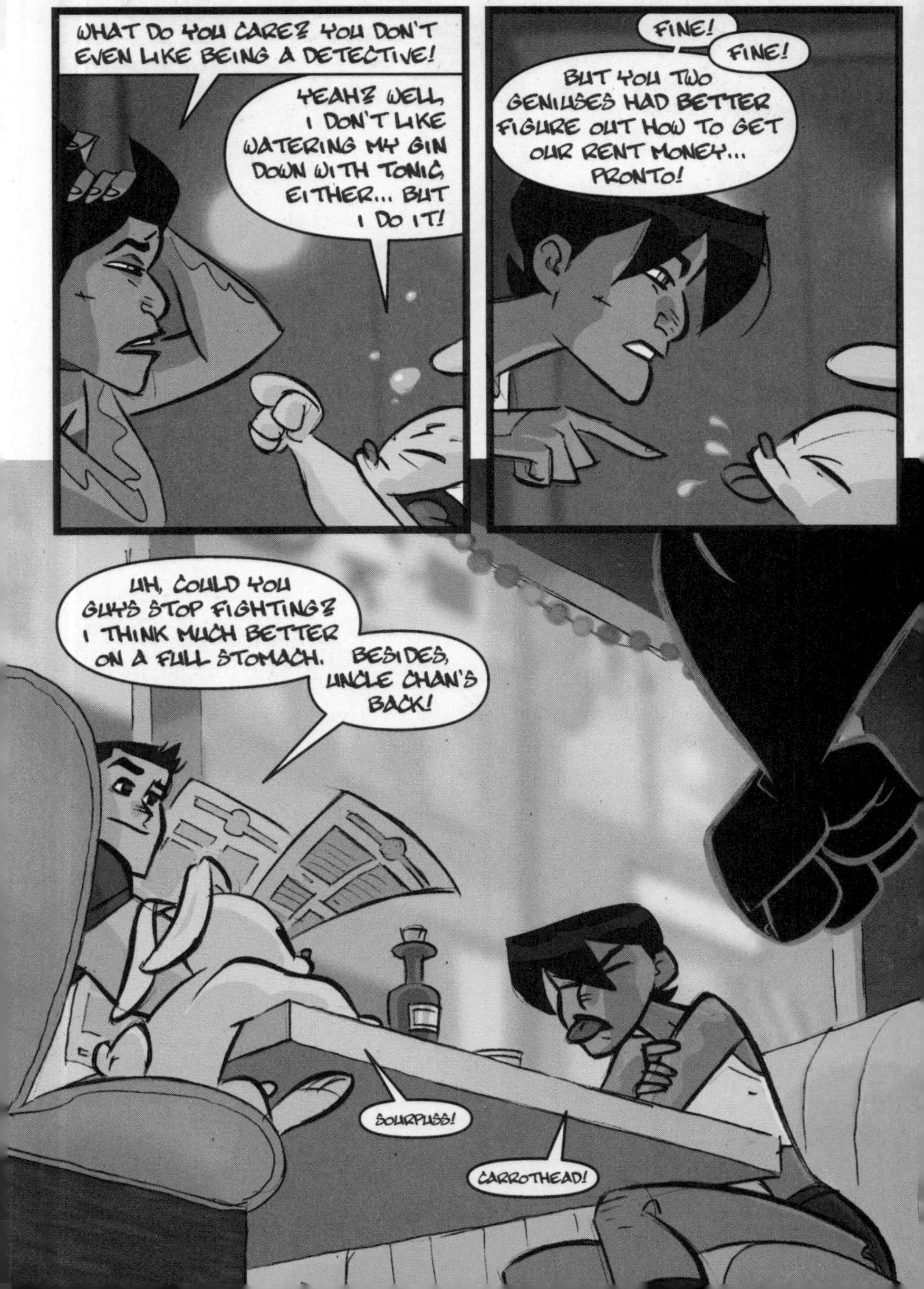
WHAT DO YOU CARE? YOU DON'T EVEN LIKE BEING A DETECTIVE!
YEAH? WELL, I DON'T LIKE WATERING MY GIN DOWN WITH TONIC, EITHER... BUT I DO IT!
FINE!
FINE!
BUT YOU TWO GENIUSES HAD BETTER FIGURE OUT HOW TO GET OUR RENT MONEY... PRONTO!
UH, COULD YOU GUYS STOP FIGHTING? I THINK MUCH BETTER ON A FULL STOMACH.
BESIDES, UNCLE CHAN'S BACK!
SOURPUSS!
CARROTHEAD!

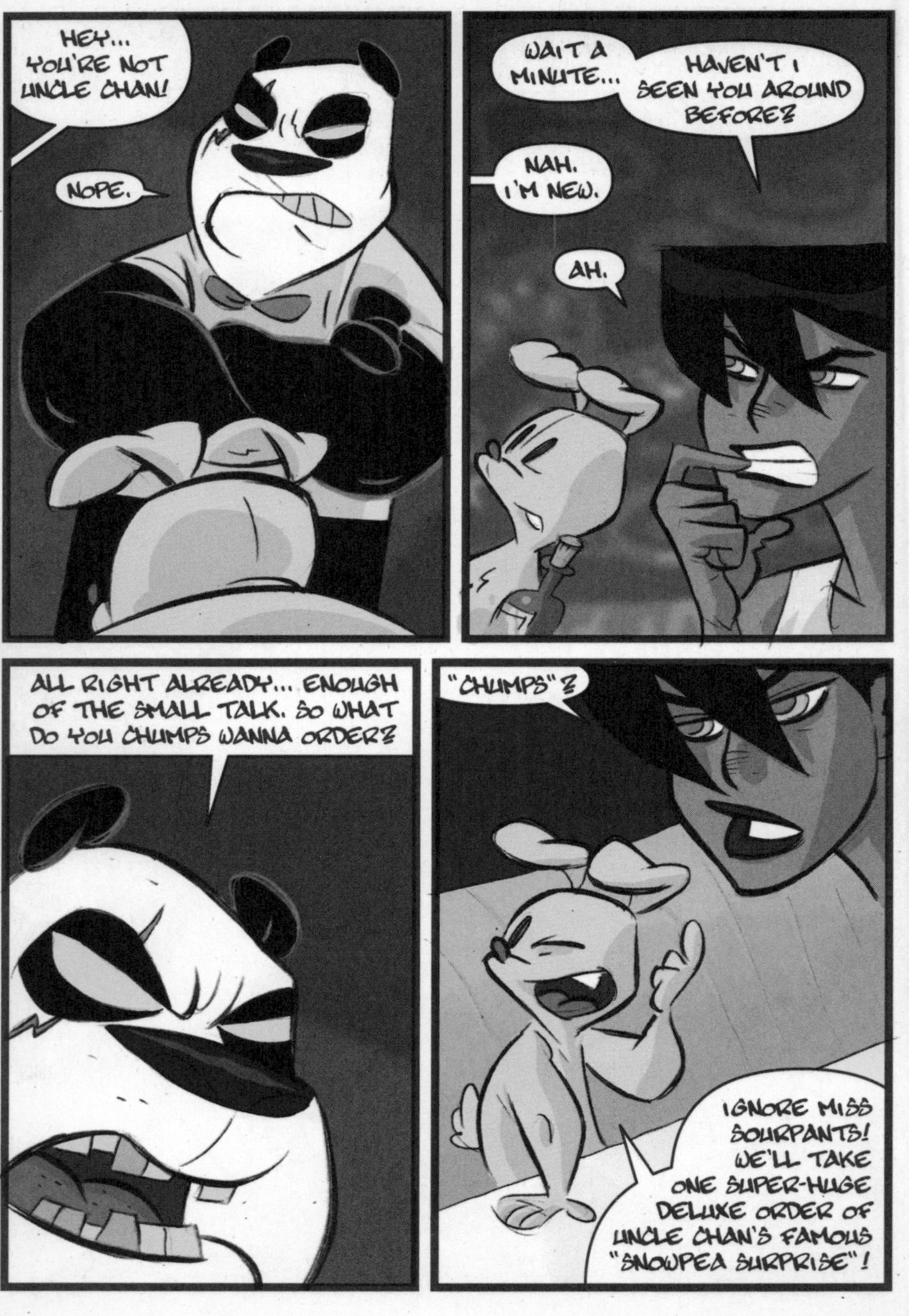
HEY... YOU'RE NOT UNCLE CHAN!
NOPE.
WAIT A MINUTE...
HAVEN'T I SEEN YOU AROUND BEFORE?
NAH. I'M NEW.
AH.
ALL RIGHT ALREADY... ENOUGH OF THE SMALL TALK. SO WHAT DO YOU CHUMPS WANNA ORDER?
"CHUMPS"?
IGNORE MISS SOURPANTS! WE'LL TAKE ONE SUPER-HUGE DELUXE ORDER OF UNCLE CHAN'S FAMOUS "SNOWPEA SURPRISE"!

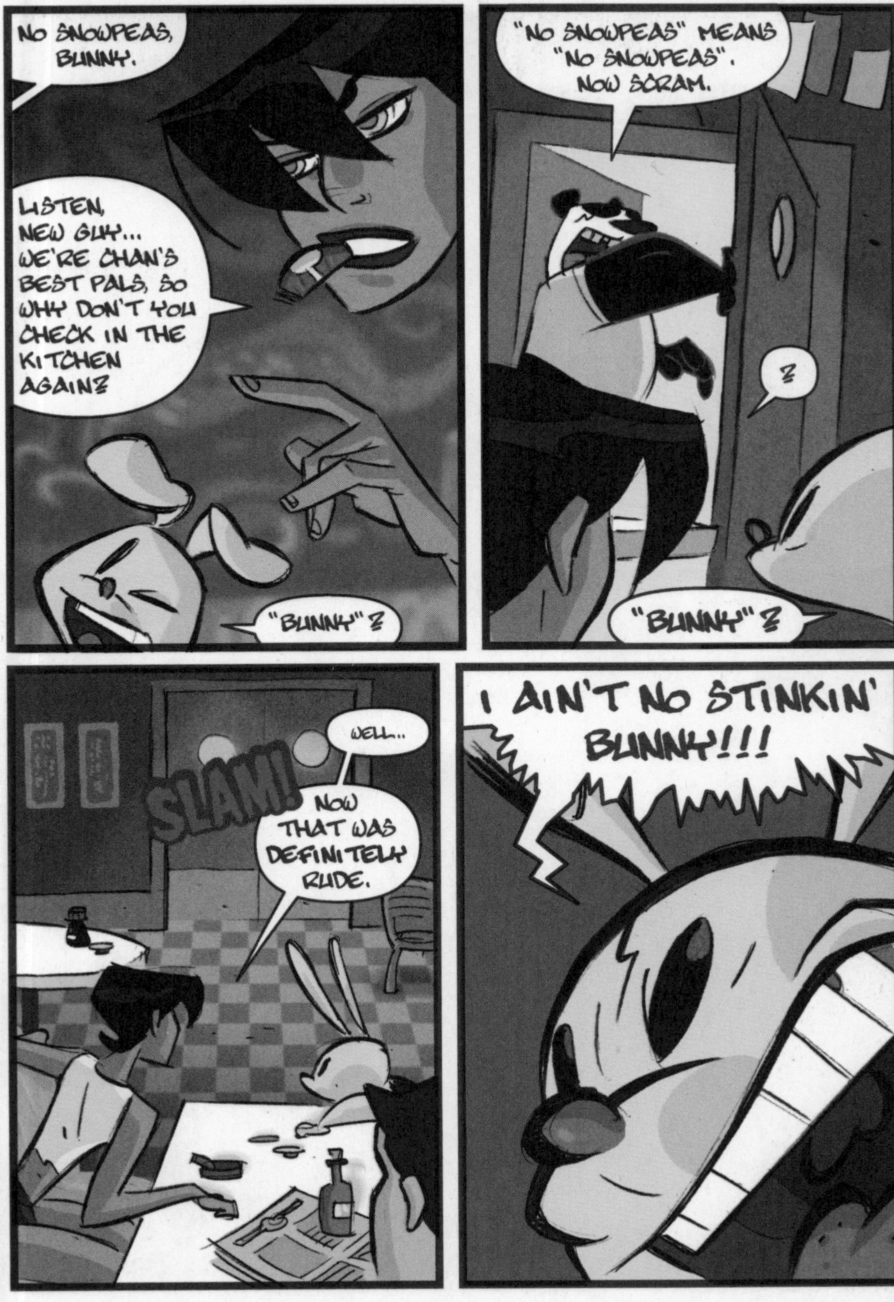
NO SNOWPEAS, BUNNY.
LISTEN, NEW GUY... WE'RE CHAN'S BEST PALS, SO WHY DON'T YOU CHECK IN THE KITCHEN AGAIN?
"BUNNY"?
"NO SNOWPEAS" MEANS "NO SNOWPEAS". NOW SCRAM.
?
"BUNNY"?
SLAM!
WELL...
NOW THAT WAS DEFINITELY RUDE.
I AIN'T NO STINKIN' BUNNY!!!

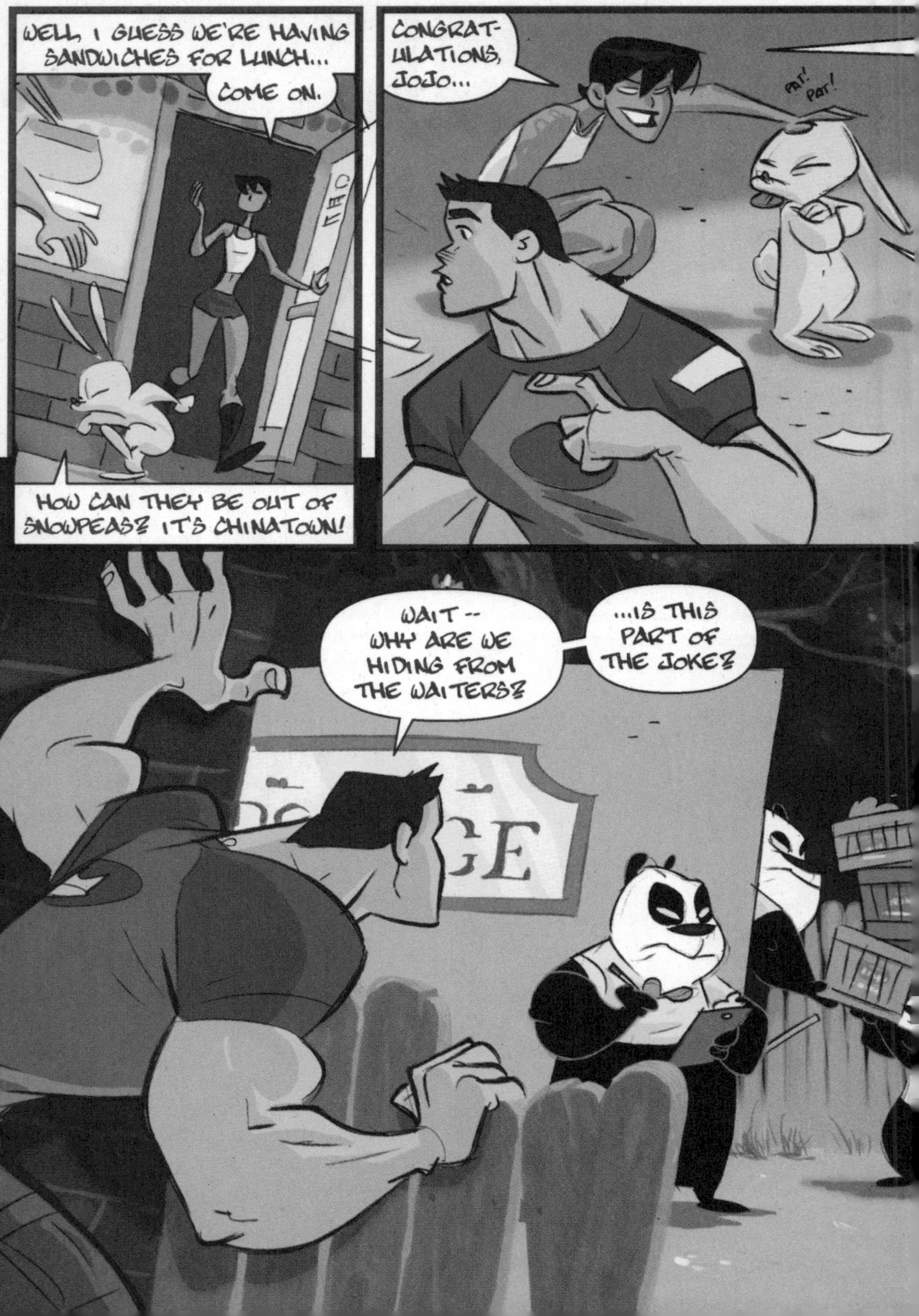
WELL, I GUESS WE'RE HAVING SANDWICHES FOR LUNCH...
COME ON.
HOW CAN THEY BE OUT OF SNOWPEAS? IT'S CHINATOWN!
CONGRAT-ULATIONS, JOJO...
PAT! PAT!
WAIT -- WHY ARE WE HIDING FROM THE WAITERS?
...IS THIS PART OF THE JOKE?

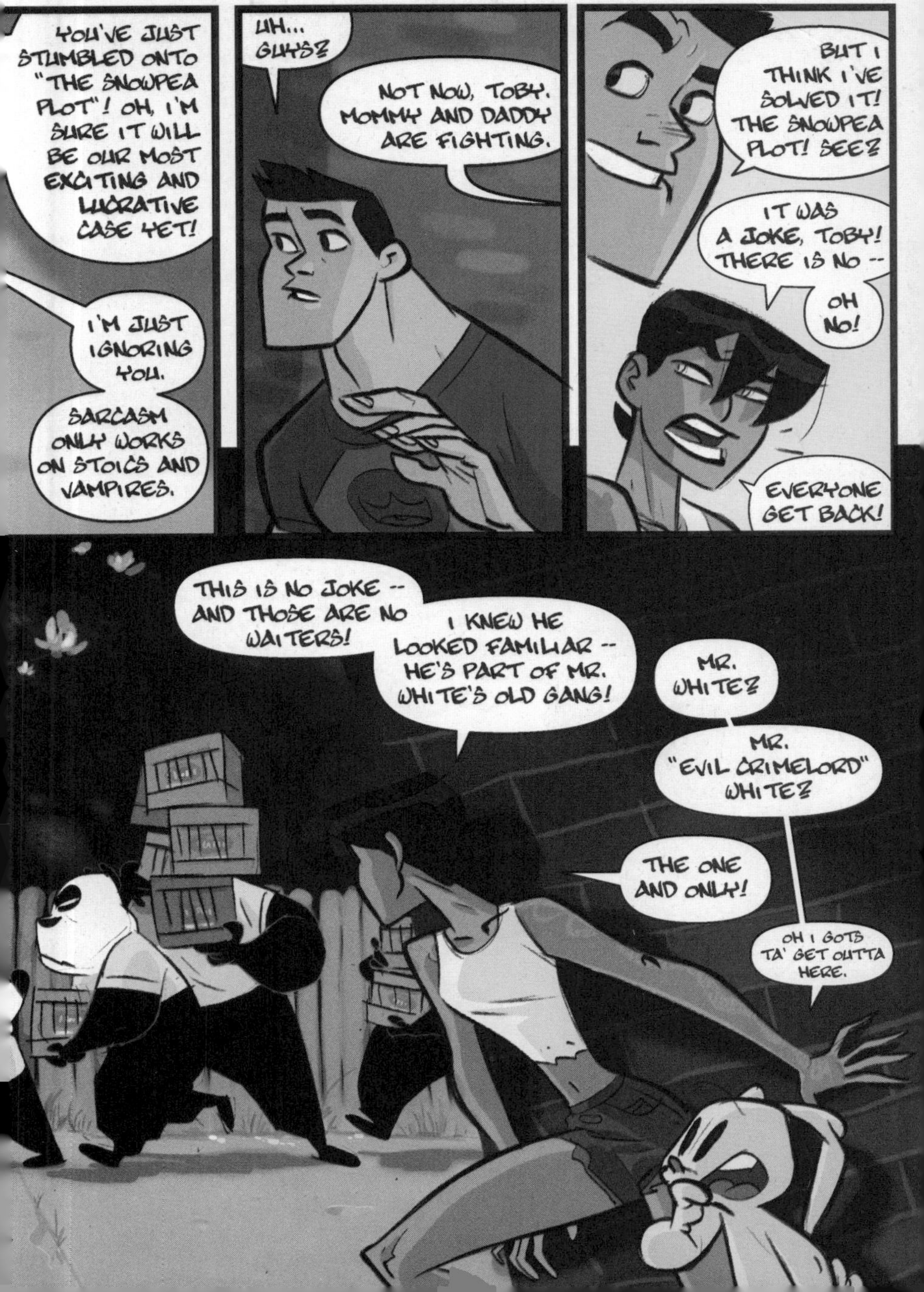

YOU'VE JUST STUMBLED ONTO "THE SNOWPEA PLOT"! OH, I'M SURE IT WILL BE OUR MOST EXCITING AND LUCRATIVE CASE YET!
I'M JUST IGNORING YOU.
SARCASM ONLY WORKS ON STOICS AND VAMPIRES.
UH... GUYS?
NOT NOW, TOBY. MOMMY AND DADDY ARE FIGHTING.
BUT I THINK I'VE SOLVED IT! THE SNOWPEA PLOT! SEE?
IT WAS A JOKE, TOBY! THERE IS NO --
OH NO!
EVERYONE GET BACK!
THIS IS NO JOKE -- AND THOSE ARE NO WAITERS!
I KNEW HE LOOKED FAMILIAR -- HE'S PART OF MR. WHITE'S OLD GANG!
MR. WHITE?
MR. "EVIL CRIMELORD" WHITE?
THE ONE AND ONLY!
OH I GOTS TA' GET OUTTA HERE.

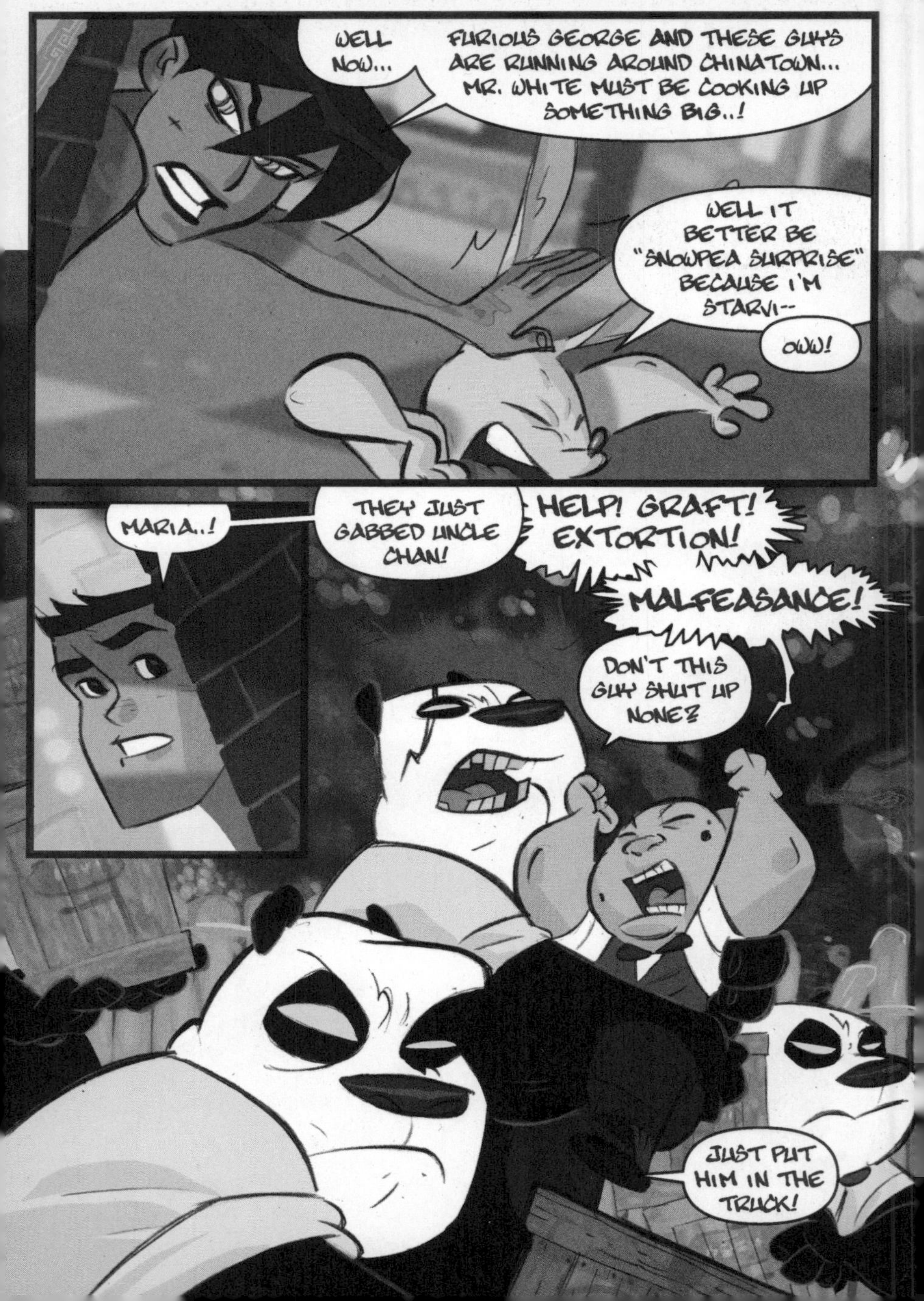
WELL NOW...
FURIOUS GEORGE AND THESE GUYS ARE RUNNING AROUND CHINATOWN... MR. WHITE MUST BE COOKING UP SOMETHING BIG..!
WELL IT BETTER BE "SNOWPEA SURPRISE" BECAUSE I'M STARVI--
OWW!
MARIA..!
THEY JUST GABBED UNCLE CHAN!
HELP! GRAFT! EXTORTION!
MALFEASANCE!
DON'T THIS GUY SHUT UP NONE?
JUST PUT HIM IN THE TRUCK!

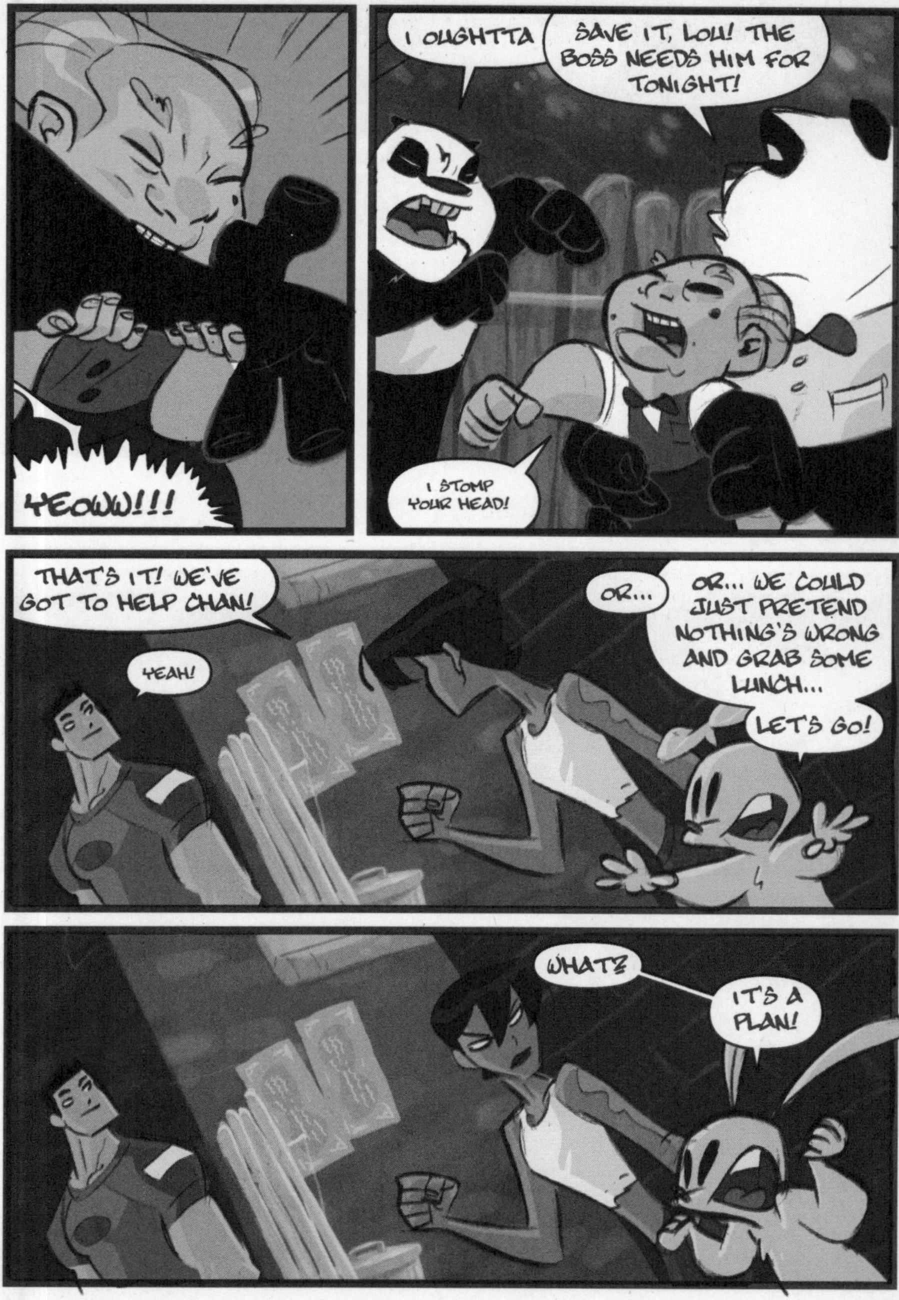
YEOWW!!!
I OUGHTTA
SAVE IT, LOU! THE BOSS NEEDS HIM FOR TONIGHT!
I STOMP YOUR HEAD!
THAT'S IT! WE'VE GOT TO HELP CHAN!
YEAH!
OR...
OR... WE COULD JUST PRETEND NOTHING'S WRONG AND GRAB SOME LUNCH...
LET'S GO!
WHAT?
IT'S A PLAN!

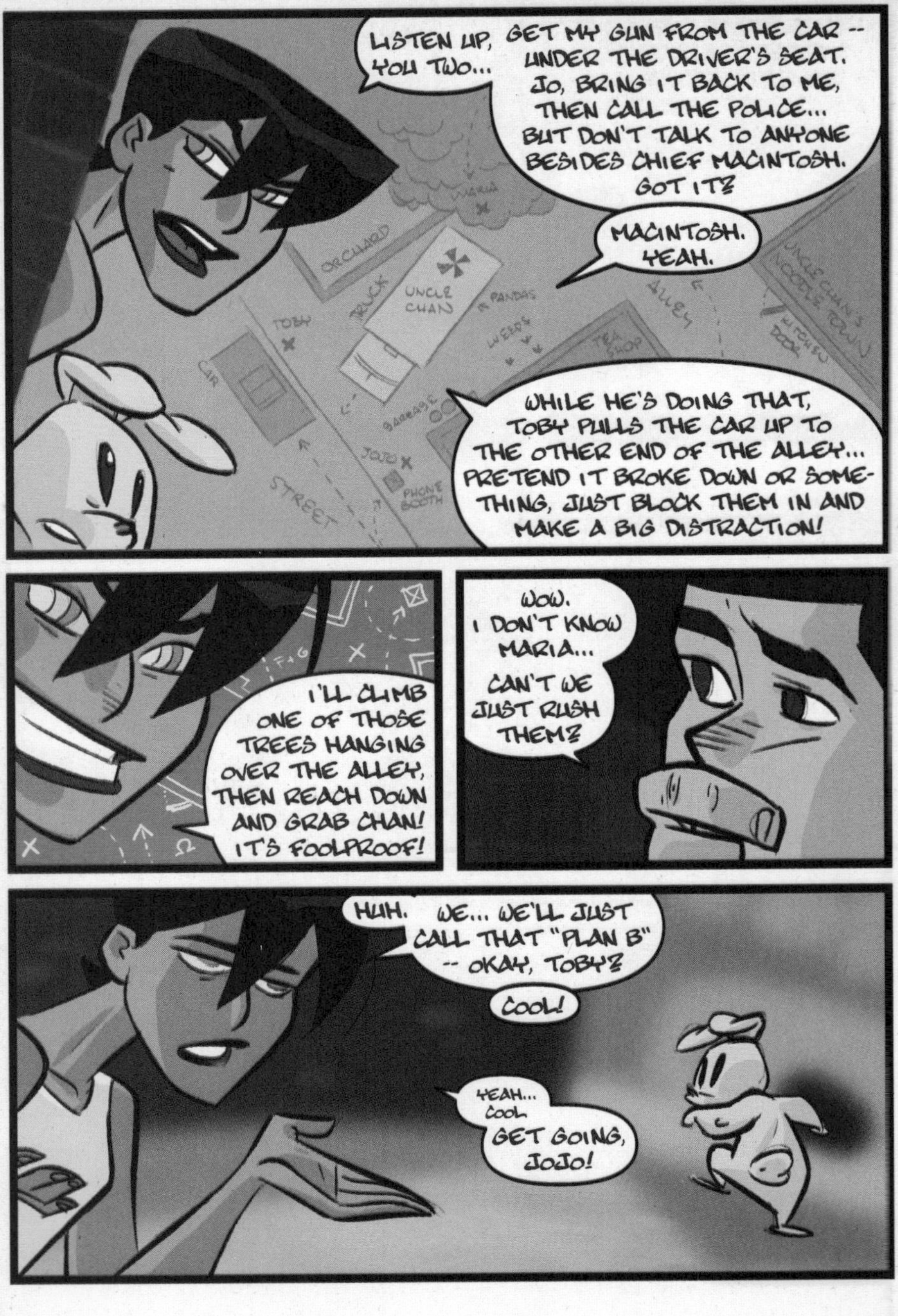
LISTEN UP, YOU TWO...
GET MY GUN FROM THE CAR -- UNDER THE DRIVER'S SEAT. JO, BRING IT BACK TO ME, THEN CALL THE POLICE... BUT DON'T TALK TO ANYONE BESIDES CHIEF MACINTOSH. GOT IT?
MACINTOSH. YEAH.
ORCHARD
MARIA
UNCLE CHAN
TRUCK
TOBY
CAR
PANDAS
WEEDS
TEA SHOP
ALLEY
UNCLE CHAN'S NOODLE TOWN
KITCHEN DOOR
GARBAGE
JOJO
PHONE BOOTH
STREET
WHILE HE'S DOING THAT, TOBY PULLS THE CAR UP TO THE OTHER END OF THE ALLEY... PRETEND IT BROKE DOWN OR SOME-THING, JUST BLOCK THEM IN AND MAKE A BIG DISTRACTION!
I'LL CLIMB ONE OF THOSE TREES HANGING OVER THE ALLEY, THEN REACH DOWN AND GRAB CHAN! IT'S FOOLPROOF!
WOW. I DON'T KNOW MARIA... CAN'T WE JUST RUSH THEM?
HUH.
WE... WE'LL JUST CALL THAT "PLAN B" -- OKAY, TOBY?
COOL!
YEAH... COOL
GET GOING, JOJO!

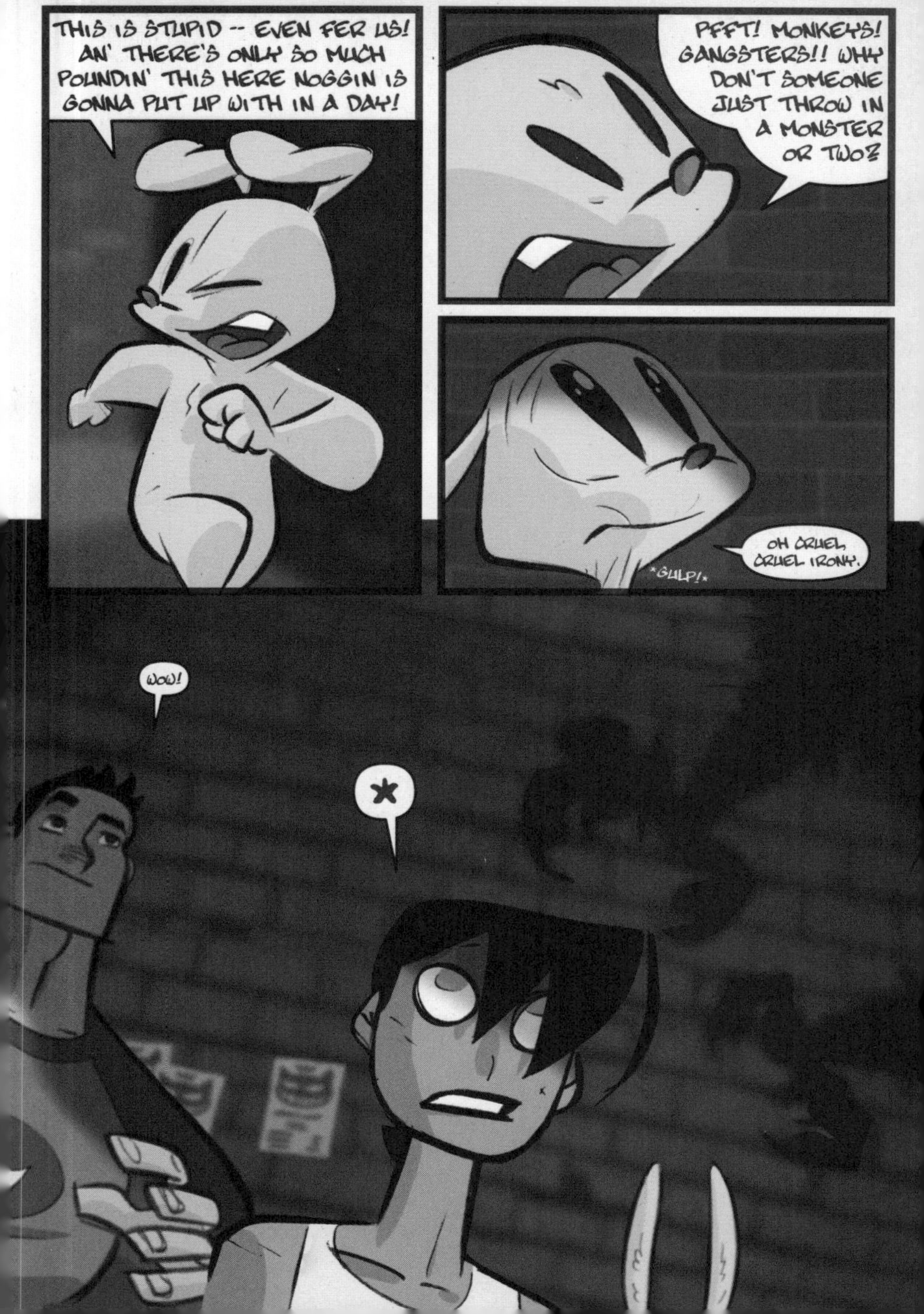
THIS IS STUPID -- EVEN FER US! AN' THERE'S ONLY SO MUCH POUNDIN' THIS HERE NOGGIN IS GONNA PUT UP WITH IN A DAY!
PFFT! MONKEYS! GANGSTERS!! WHY DON'T SOMEONE JUST THROW IN A MONSTER OR TWO?
GULP!
OH CRUEL, CRUEL IRONY.
WOW!
*

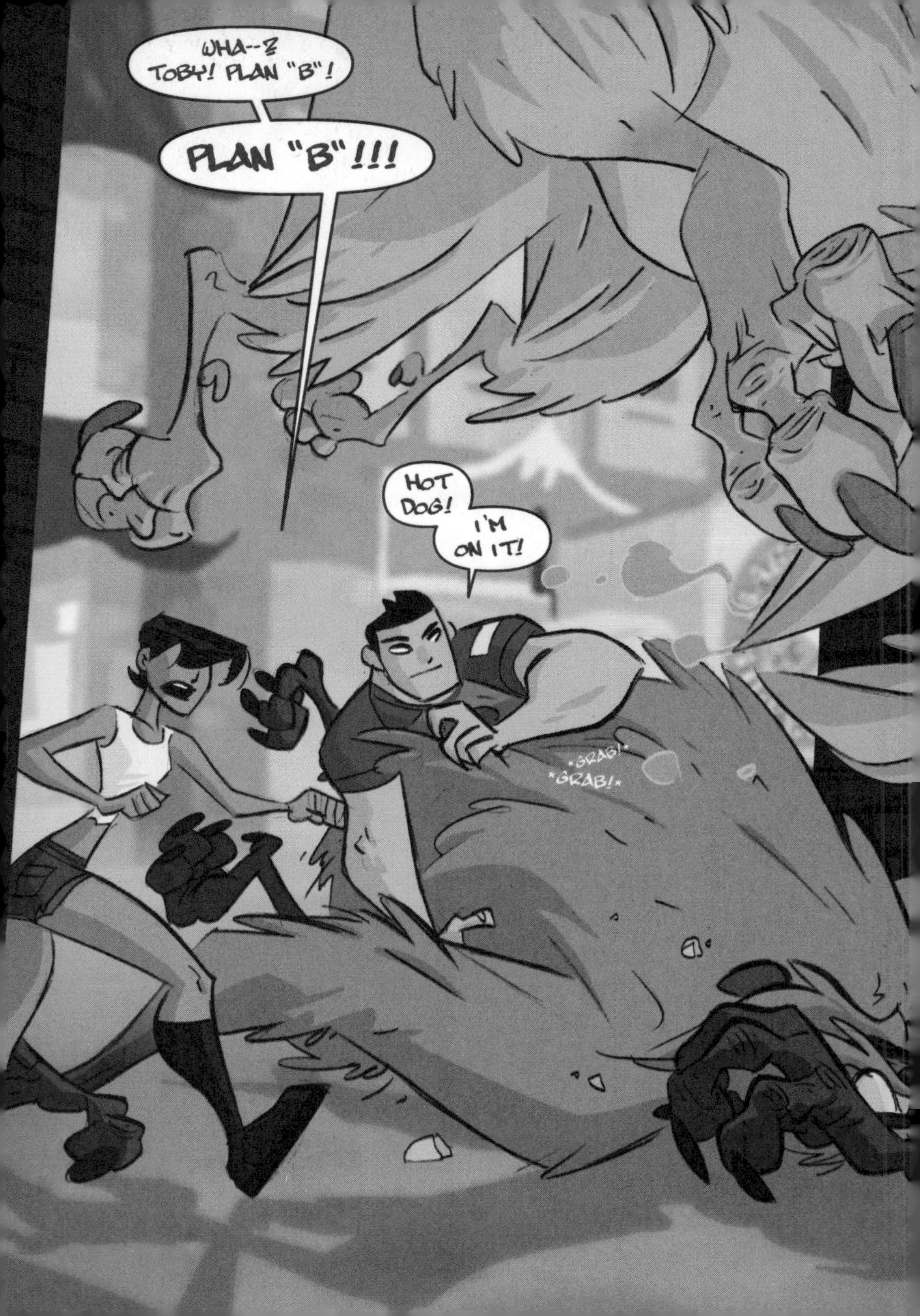
WHA--?
TOBY! PLAN "B"!
PLAN "B"!!!
HOT DOG!
I'M ON IT!
GRAB!
GRAB!

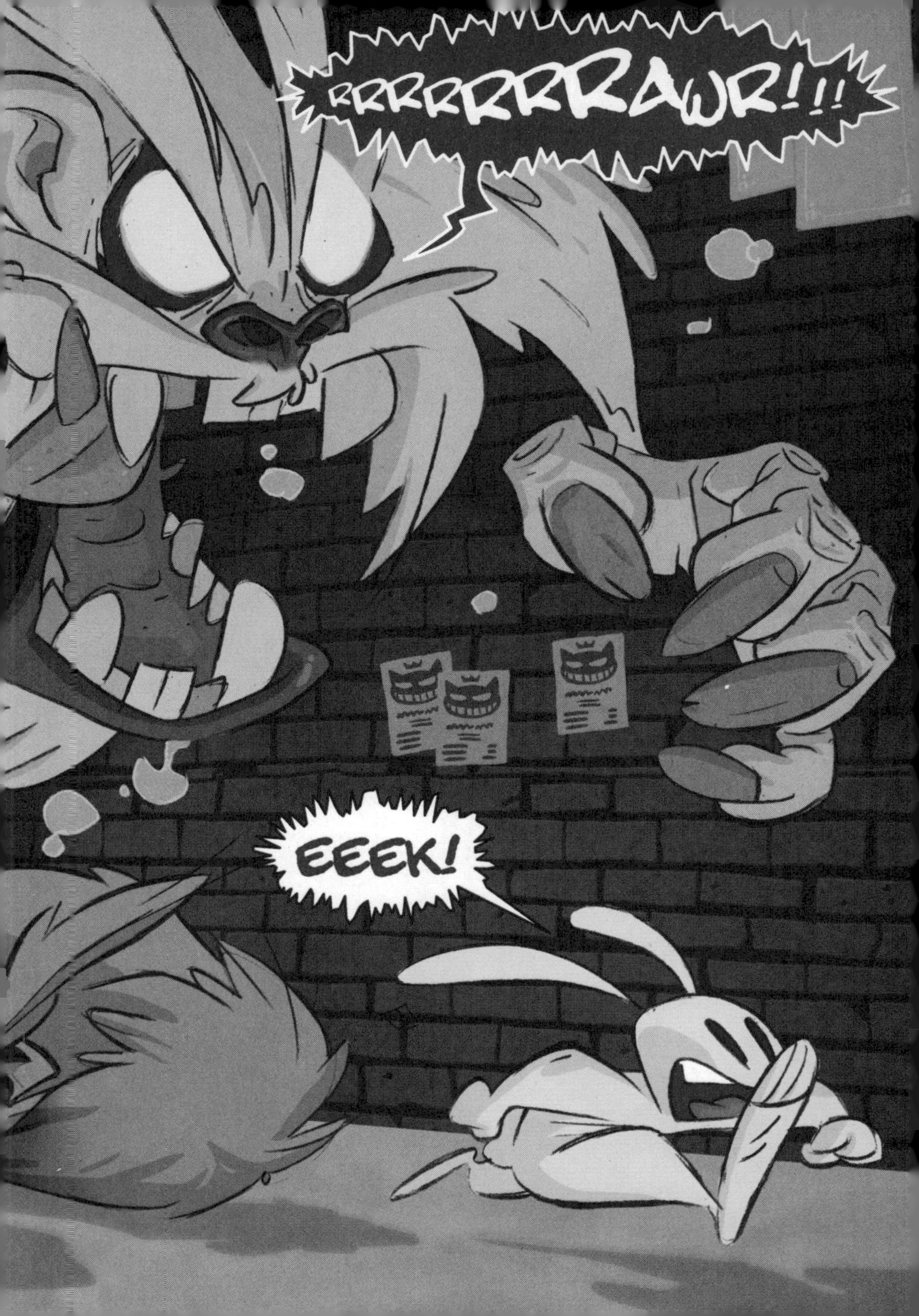
RRRRRRRRAWR!!!
EEEK!

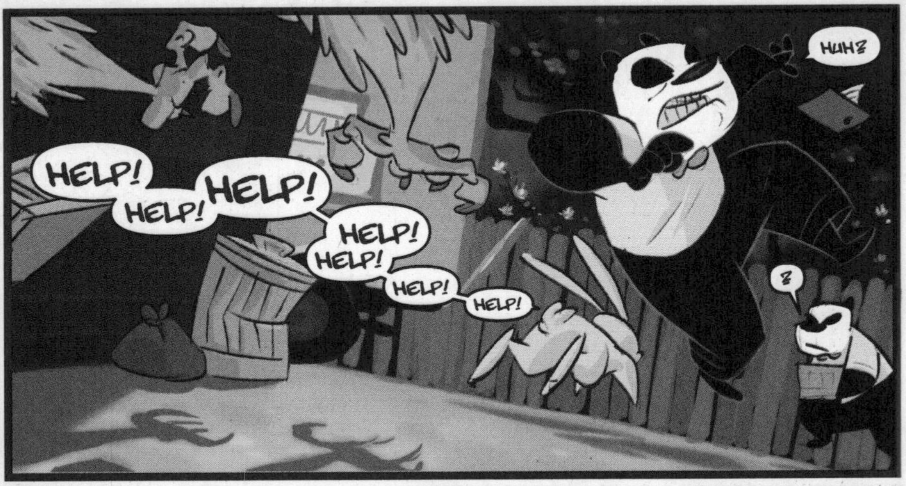
HELP!
HELP!
HELP!
HELP!
HELP!
HELP!
HELP!
HUH?
?

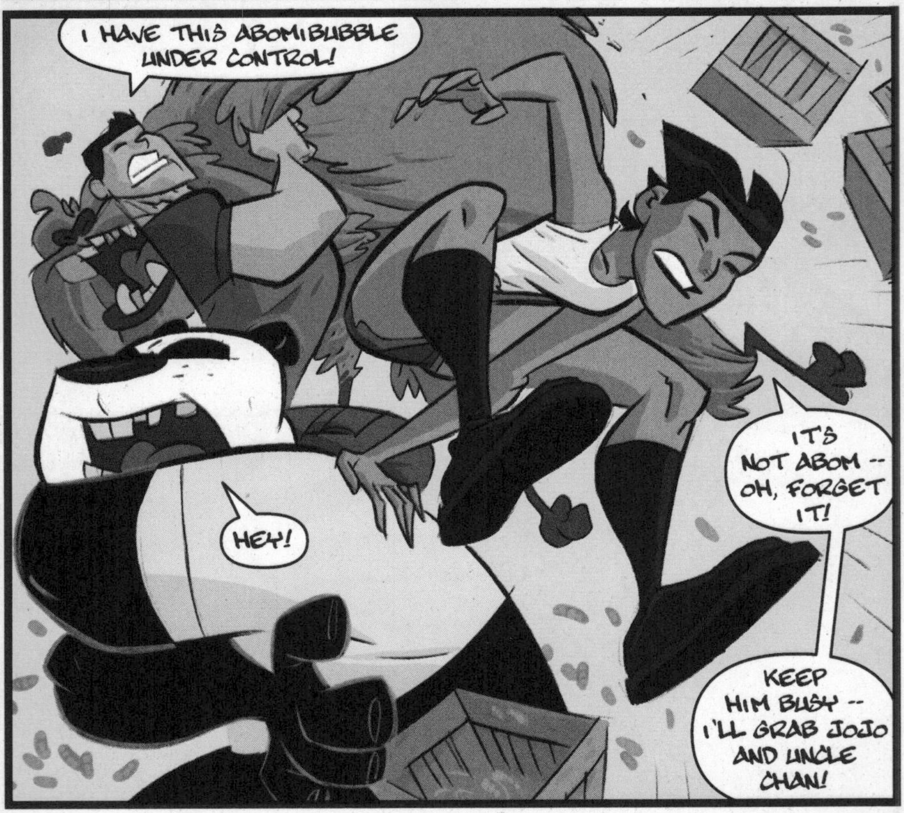
I HAVE THIS ABOMIBUBBLE UNDER CONTROL!
HEY!
IT'S NOT ABOM -- OH, FORGET IT!
KEEP HIM BUSY -- I'LL GRAB JOJO AND UNCLE CHAN!

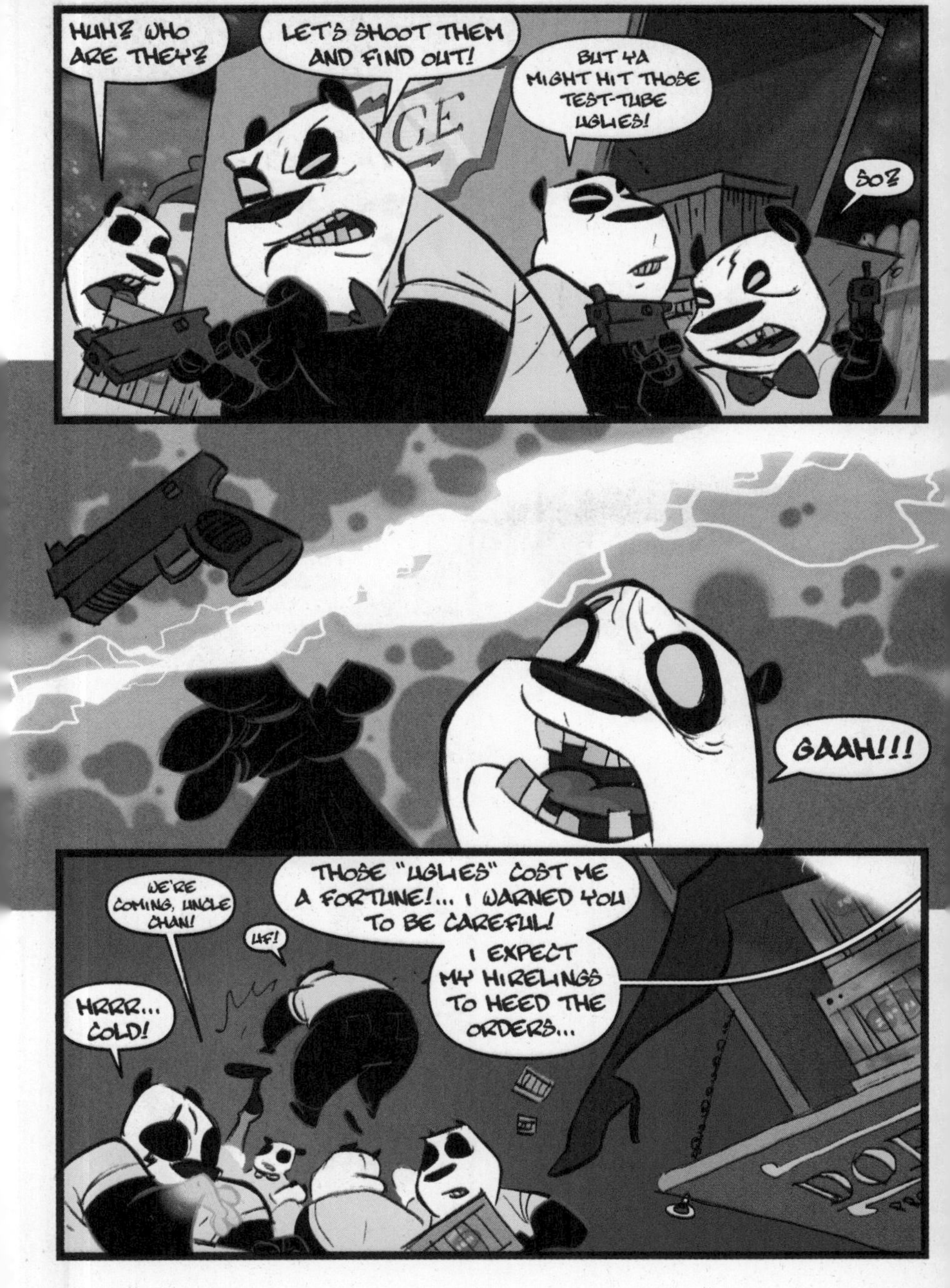
HUH? WHO ARE THEY?
LET'S SHOOT THEM AND FIND OUT!
BUT YA MIGHT HIT THOSE TEST-TUBE UGLIES!
SO?
GAAH!!!
WE'RE COMING, UNCLE CHAN!
UF!
THOSE "UGLIES" COST ME A FORTUNE!... I WARNED YOU TO BE CAREFUL!
I EXPECT MY HIRELINGS TO HEED THE ORDERS...
HRRR... COLD!

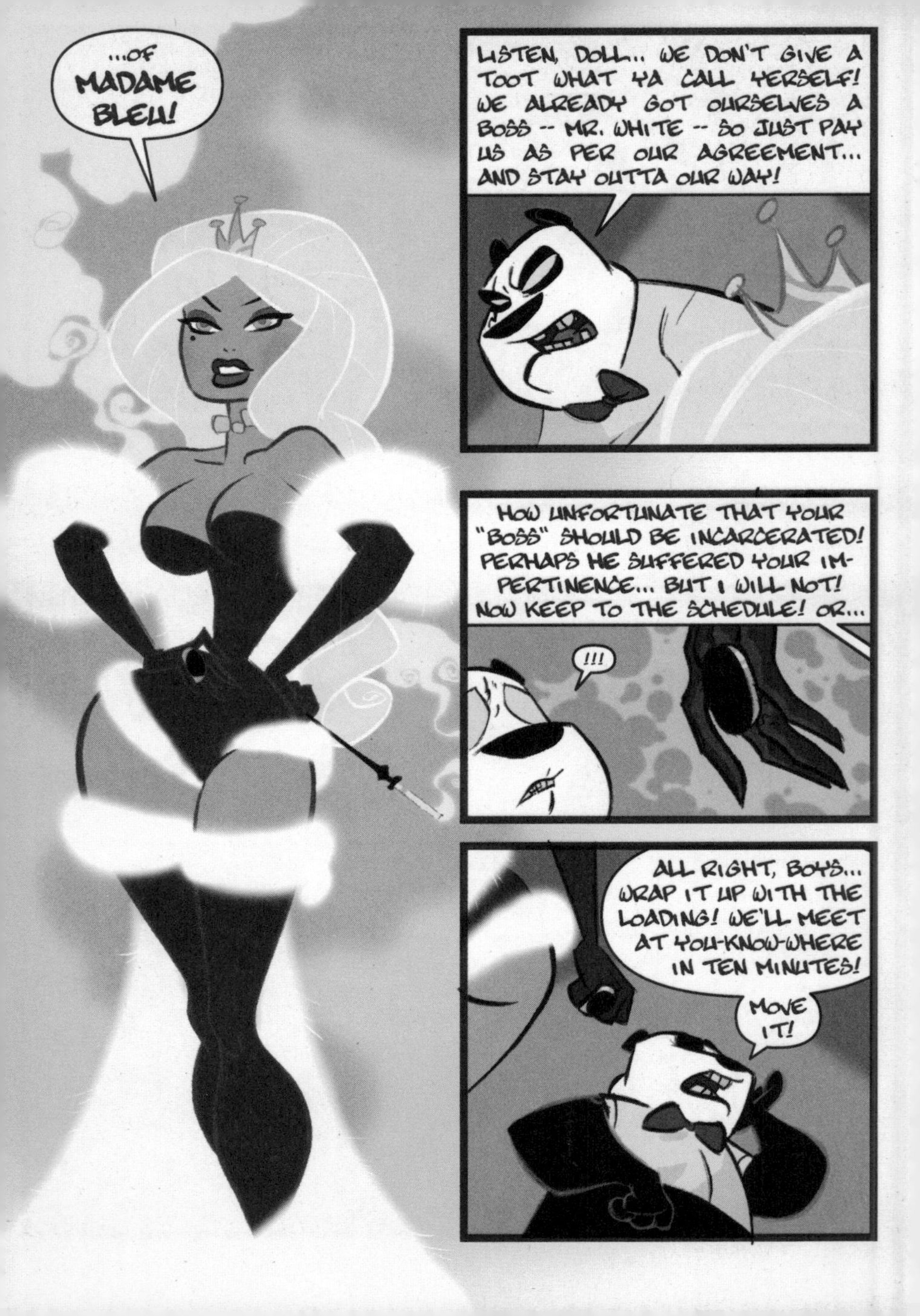
...OF MADAME BLEU!
LISTEN, DOLL... WE DON'T GIVE A TOOT WHAT YA CALL YERSELF! WE ALREADY GOT OURSELVES A BOSS -- MR. WHITE -- SO JUST PAY US AS PER OUR AGREEMENT... AND STAY OUTTA OUR WAY!
HOW UNFORTUNATE THAT YOUR "BOSS" SHOULD BE INCARCERATED! PERHAPS HE SUFFERED YOUR IMPERTINENCE... BUT I WILL NOT! NOW KEEP TO THE SCHEDULE! OR...
!!!
ALL RIGHT, BOYS... WRAP IT UP WITH THE LOADING! WE'LL MEET AT YOU-KNOW-WHERE IN TEN MINUTES!
MOVE IT!

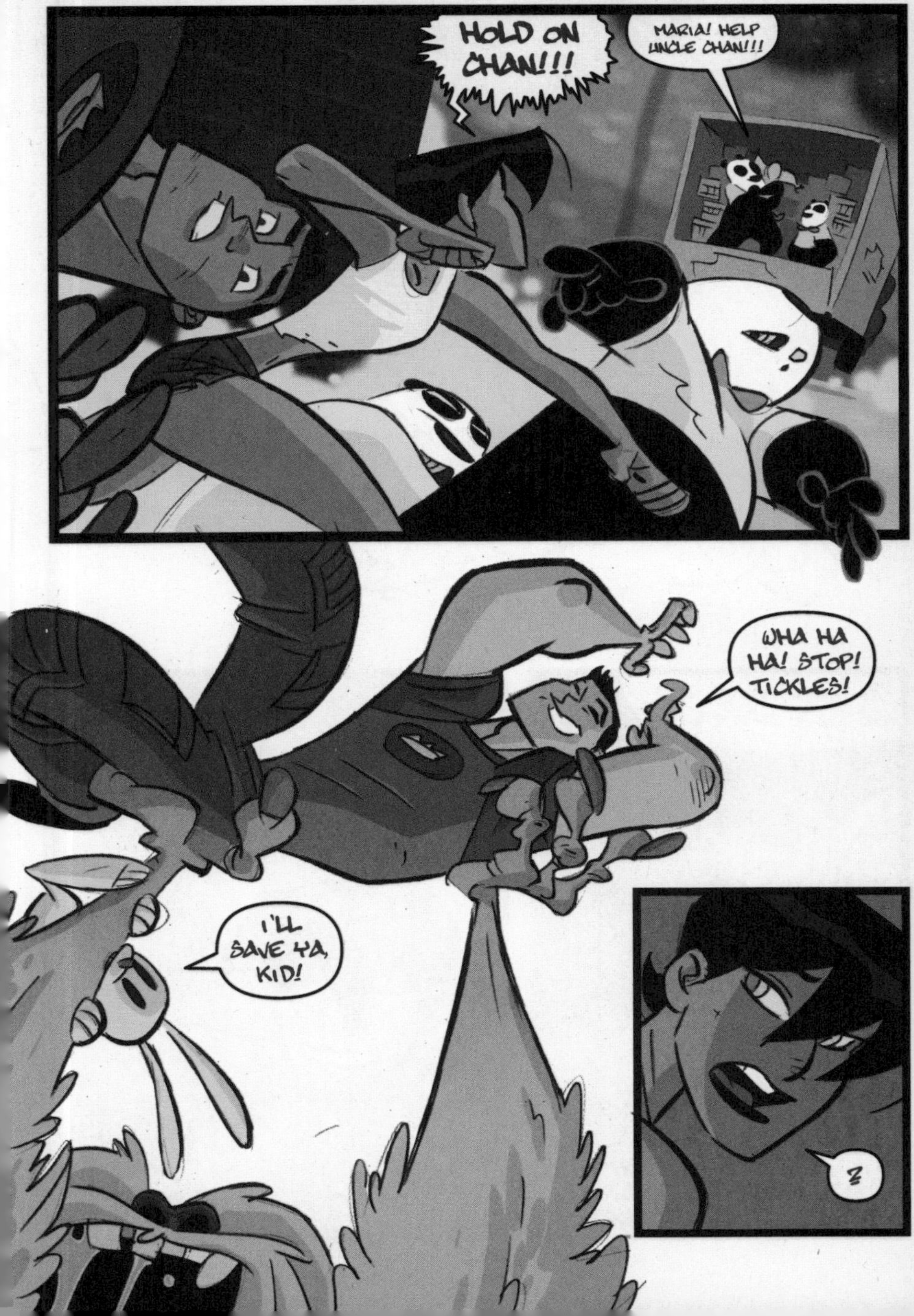
HOLD ON CHAN!!!
MARIA! HELP UNCLE CHAN!!!
WHA HA HA! STOP! TICKLES!
I'LL SAVE YA, KID!
?

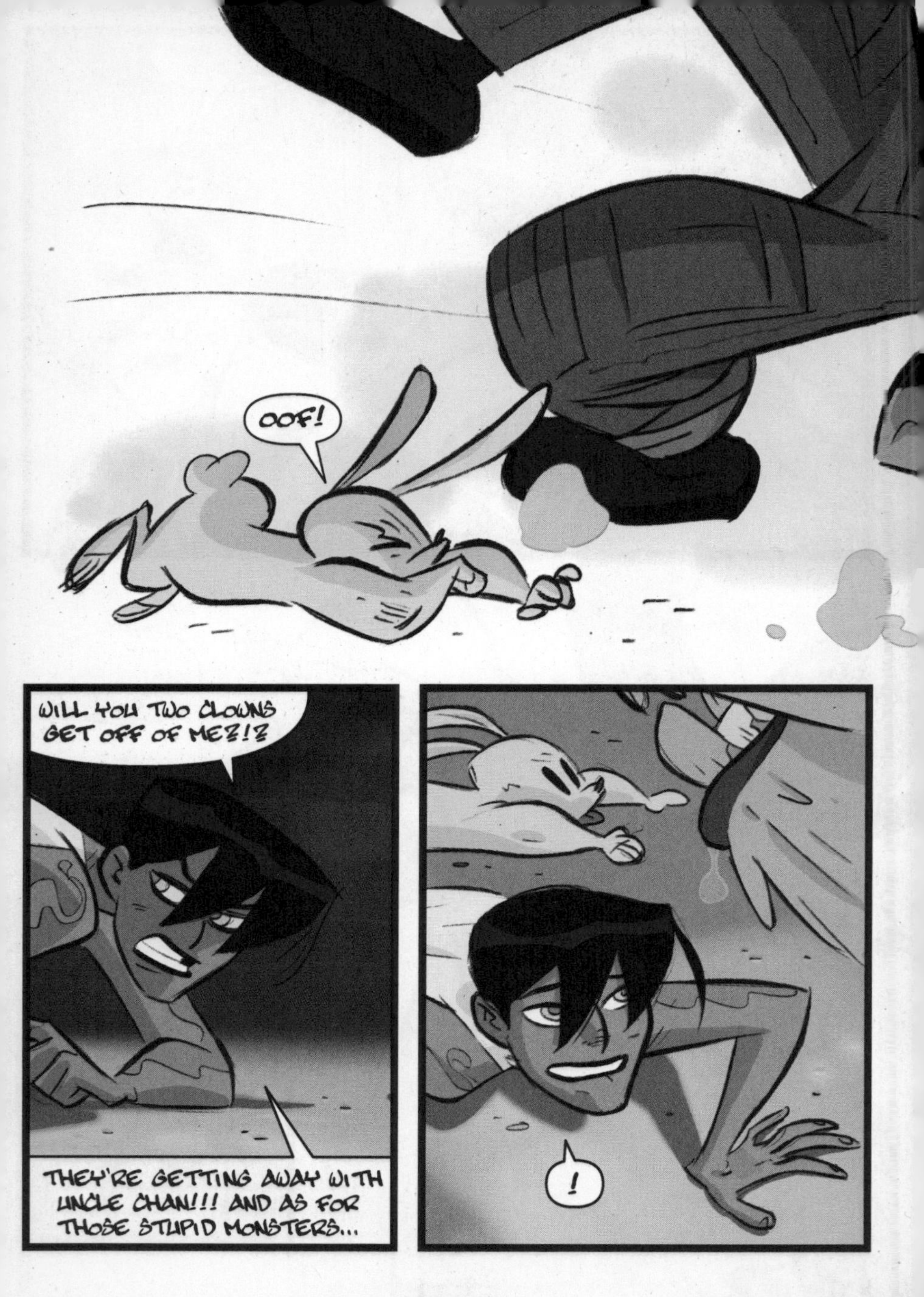
OOF!
WILL YOU TWO CLOWNS GET OFF OF ME?!?
THEY'RE GETTING AWAY WITH UNCLE CHAN!!! AND AS FOR THOSE STUPID MONSTERS...
!

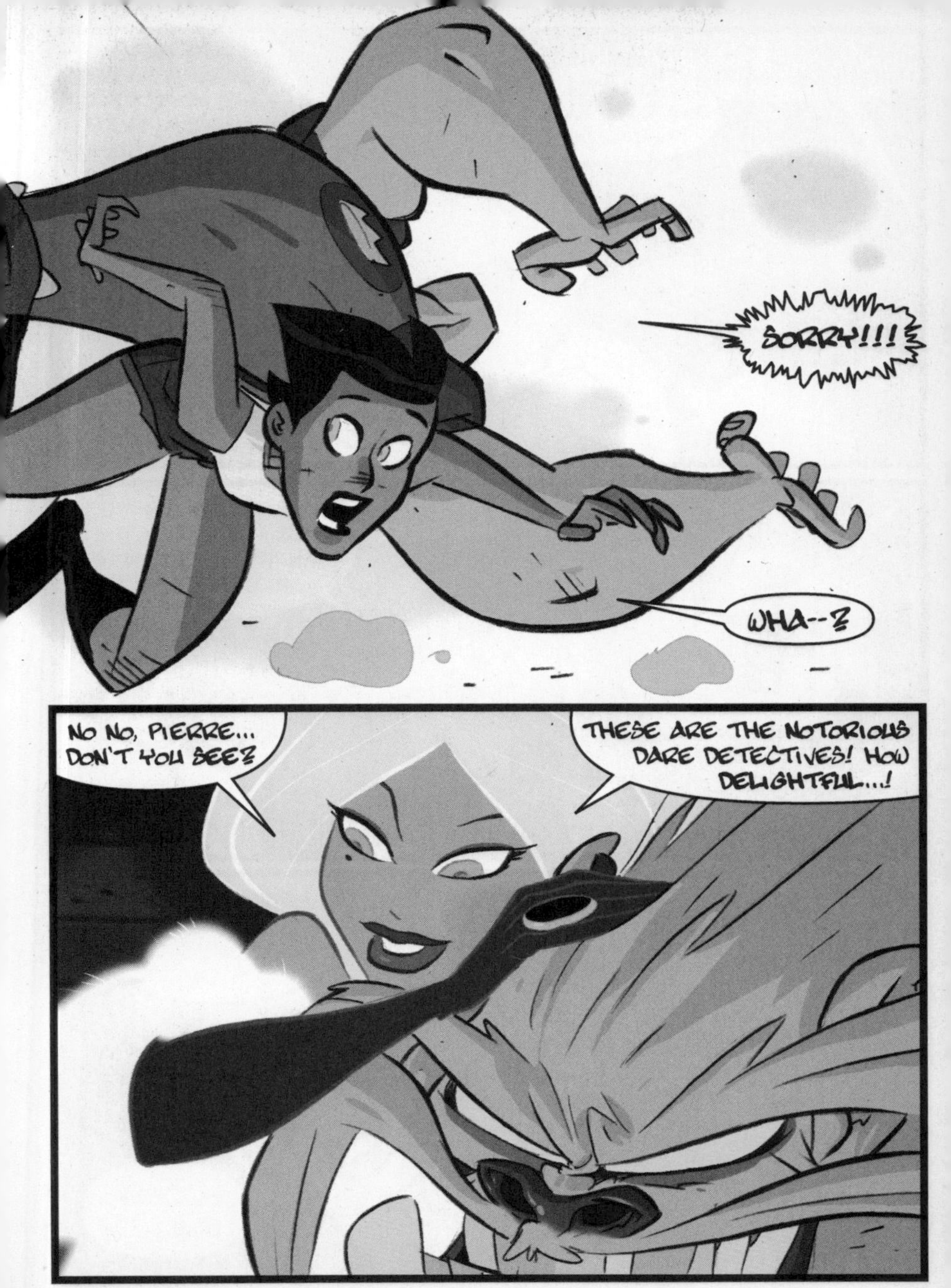
SORRY!!!
WHA--?
NO NO, PIERRE... DON'T YOU SEE?
THESE ARE THE NOTORIOUS DARE DETECTIVES! HOW DELIGHTFUL...!

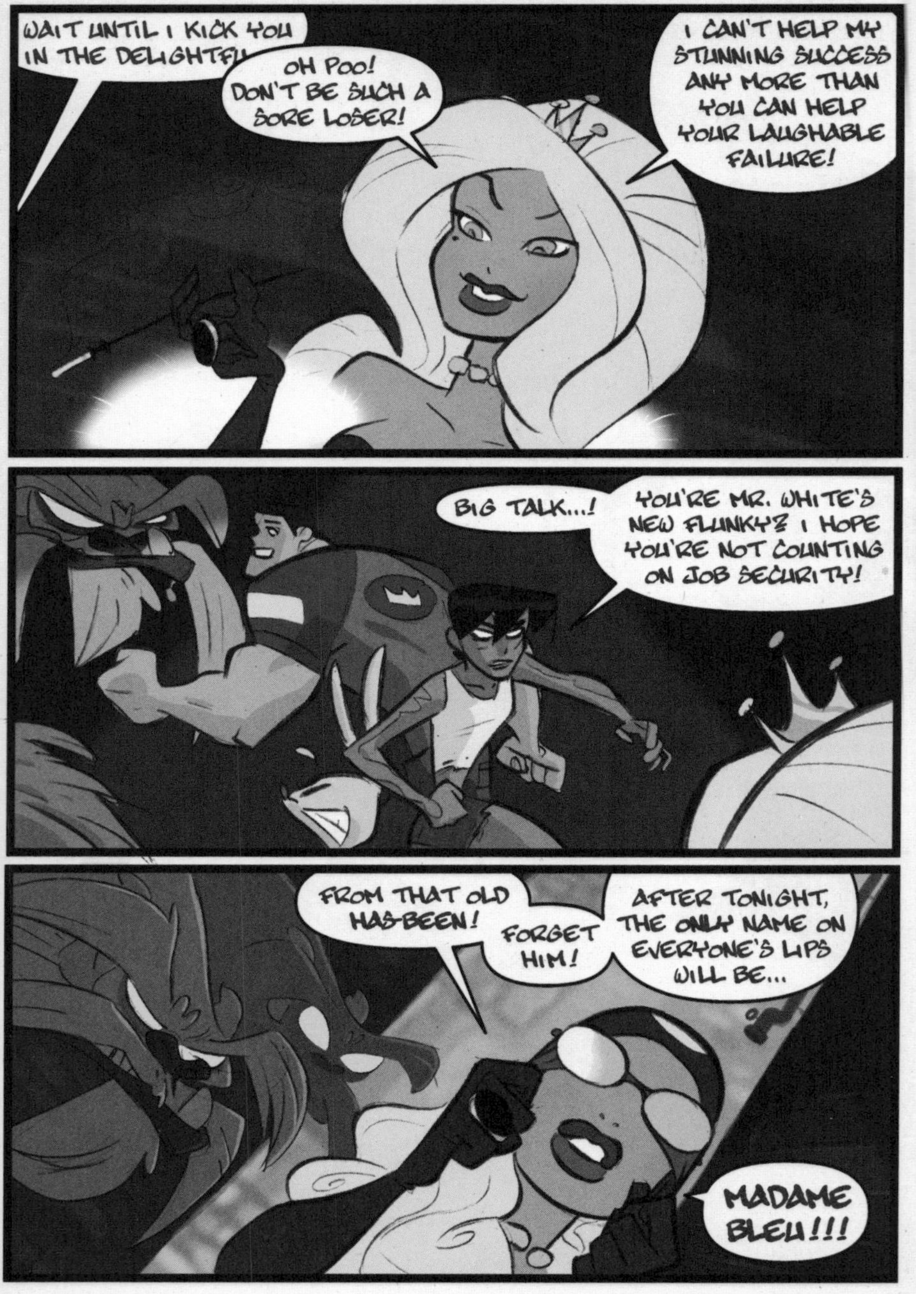

WAIT UNTIL I KICK YOU IN THE DELIGHTFU
OH POO! DON'T BE SUCH A SORE LOSER!
I CAN'T HELP MY STUNNING SUCCESS ANY MORE THAN YOU CAN HELP YOUR LAUGHABLE FAILURE!
BIG TALK...!
YOU'RE MR. WHITE'S NEW FLUNKY? I HOPE YOU'RE NOT COUNTING ON JOB SECURITY!
FROM THAT OLD HAS-BEEN!
FORGET HIM!
AFTER TONIGHT, THE ONLY NAME ON EVERYONE'S LIPS WILL BE...
MADAME BLEU!!!

OF COURSE, YOU'RE WELCOME TO TRY AND STOP ME...

IT'S SO DREARY HAVING EVERYTHING MY WAY...

HA! HA! HA! HA! HA! HA!

STUPID NAME BIG HAIR BIMBO HEAD

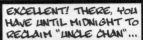

EXCELLENT! THERE, YOU HAVE UNTIL MIDNIGHT TO RECLAIM "UNCLE CHAN"...

BUT I AM AFRAID HE WON'T BE MUCH GOOD TO YOU... AFTER MIDNIGHT!

SO FOR NOW, IF YOU WILL EXCUSE ME...

POOF!

WHAAA--!

WOW! THAT IS COLD!!!

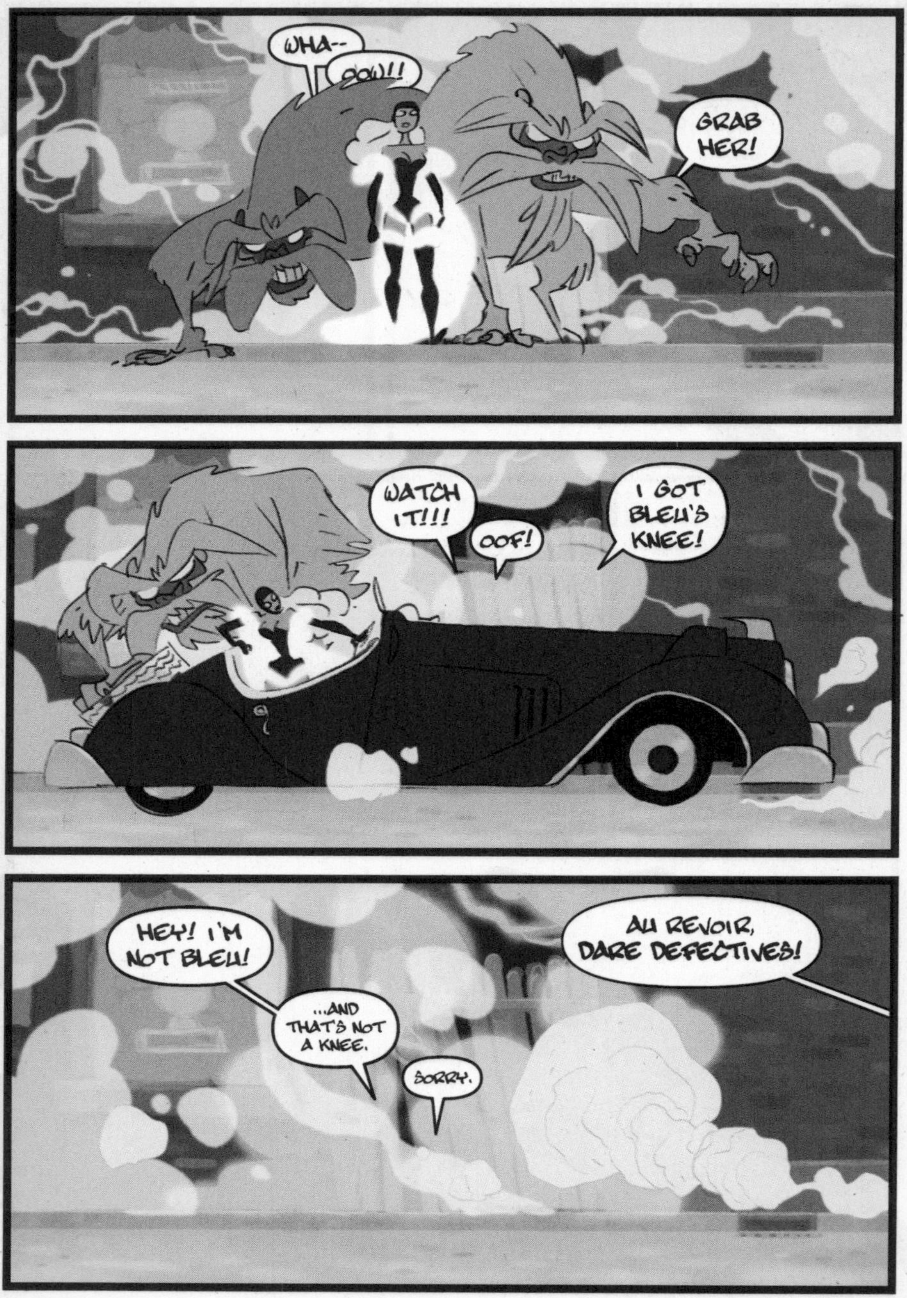
WHA--
OOW!!
GRAB HER!
WATCH IT!!!
OOF!
I GOT BLEU'S KNEE!
HEY! I'M NOT BLEU!
AU REVOIR, DARE DEFECTIVES!
...AND THAT'S NOT A KNEE.
SORRY.

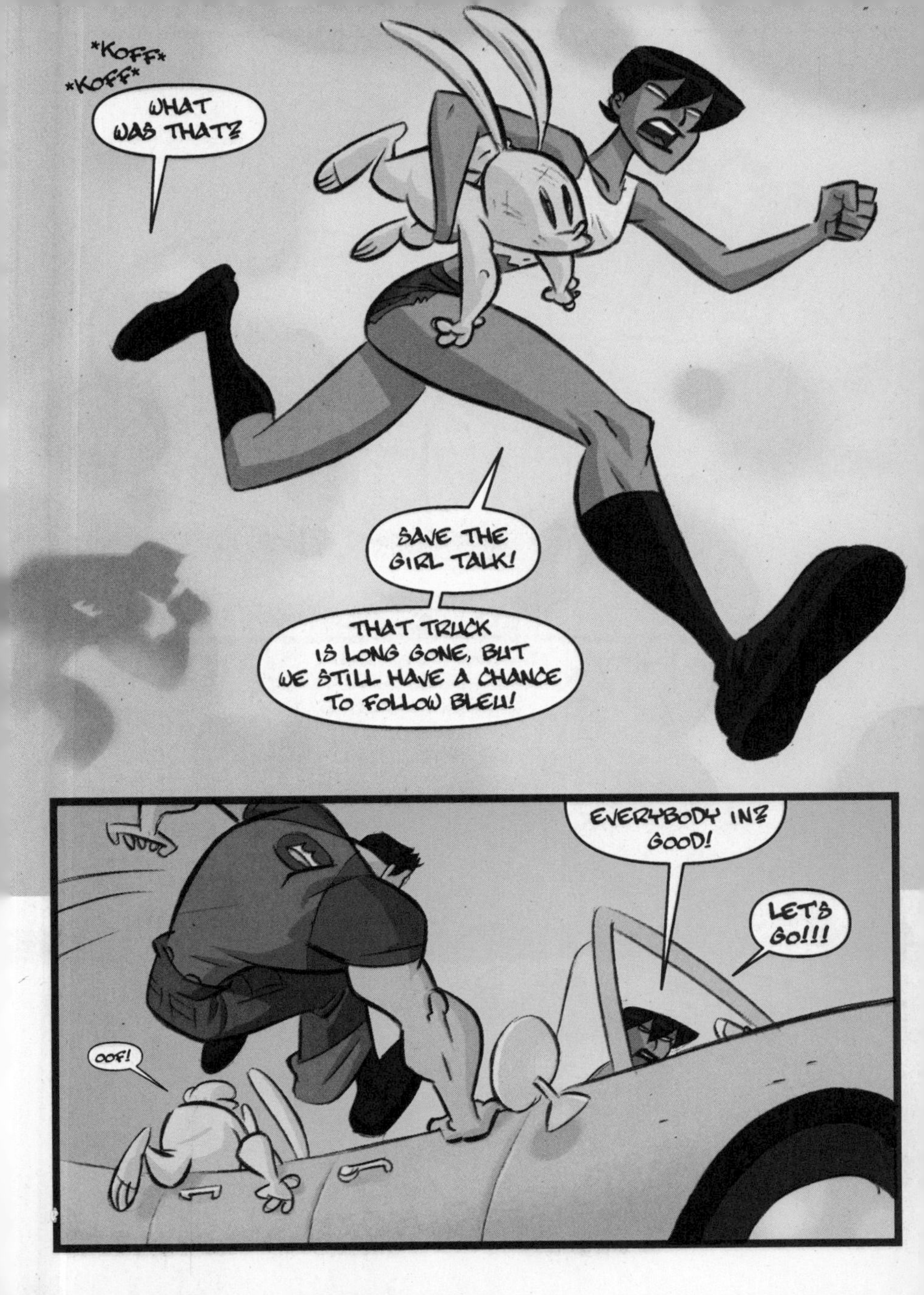
KOFF
KOFF
WHAT WAS THAT?
SAVE THE GIRL TALK!
THAT TRUCK IS LONG GONE, BUT WE STILL HAVE A CHANCE TO FOLLOW BLEU!
EVERYBODY IN? GOOD!
LET'S GO!!!
OOF!

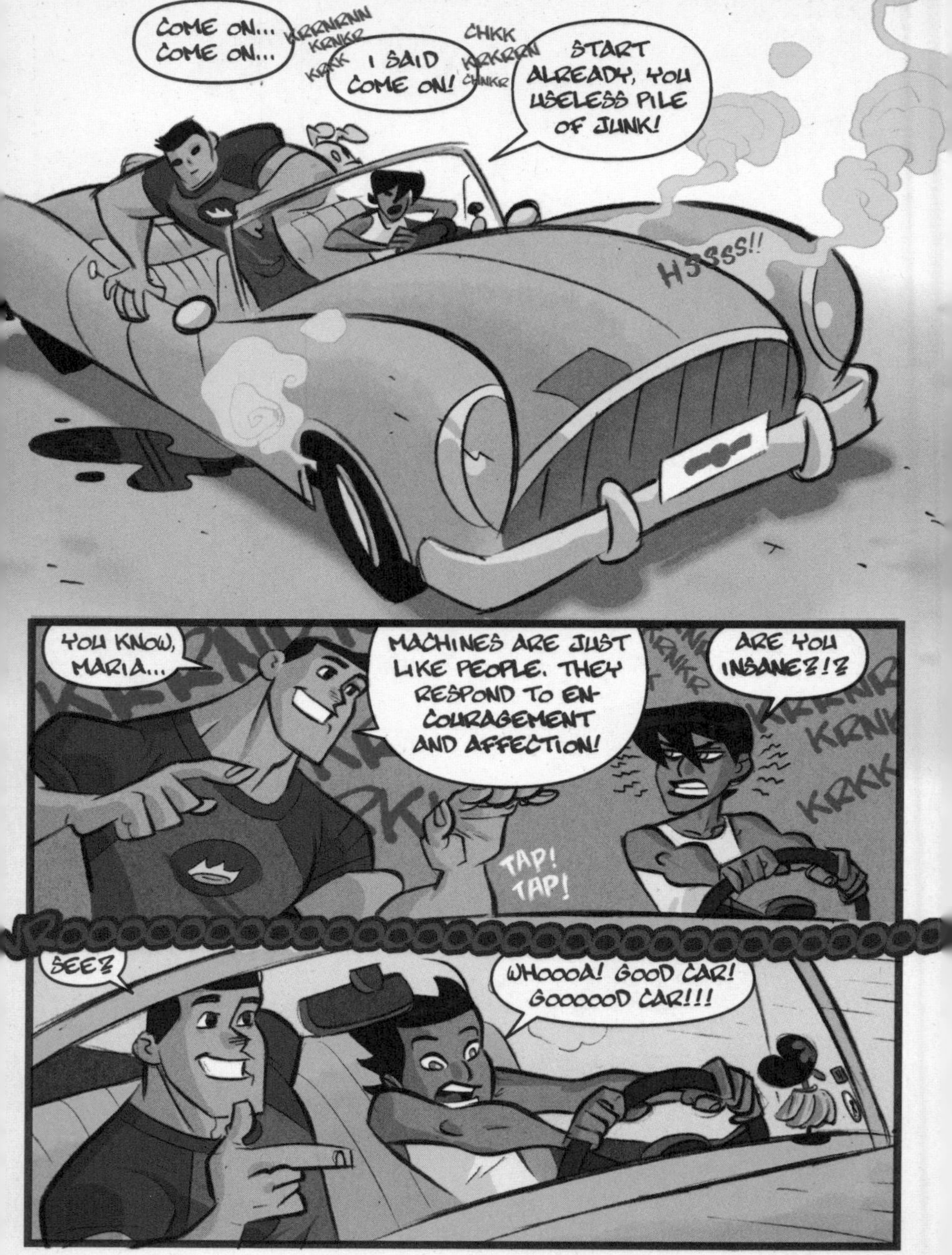
COME ON...
COME ON...
KRRNRNN
KRNKR
KRKK
I SAID
COME ON!
CHKK
KRKRRN
CHNKR
START
ALREADY, YOU
USELESS PILE
OF JUNK!
HSSSS!!
YOU KNOW,
MARIA...
MACHINES ARE JUST
LIKE PEOPLE. THEY
RESPOND TO EN-
COURAGEMENT
AND AFFECTION!
ARE YOU
INSANE?!?
TAP!
TAP!
VROOOOOOOOOOOOOOOOOOOOOOOOOOOOOOOOO
SEE?
WHOOOA! GOOD CAR!
GOOOOOD CAR!!!

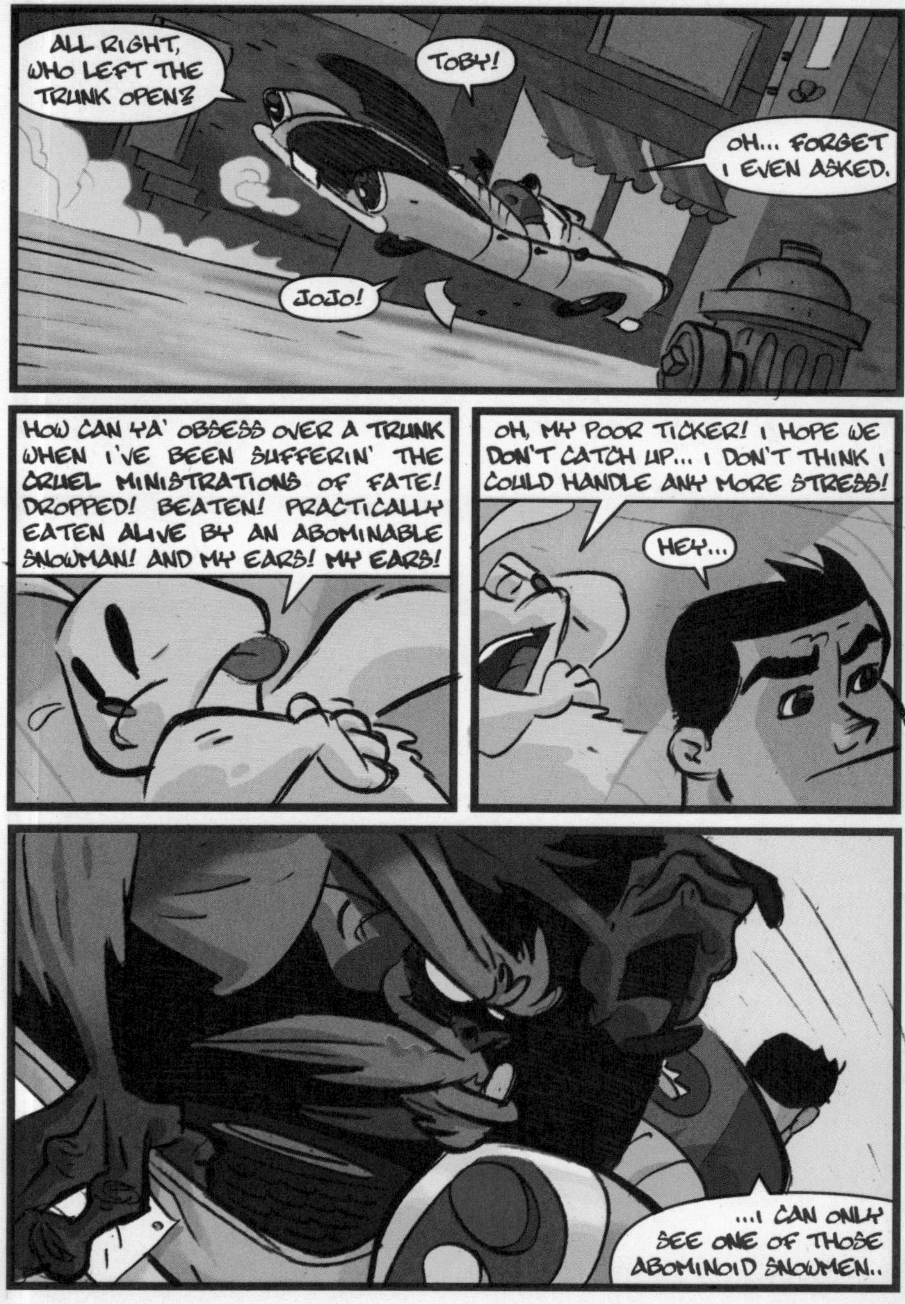
ALL RIGHT, WHO LEFT THE TRUNK OPEN?
TOBY!
JOJO!
OH... FORGET I EVEN ASKED.
HOW CAN YA' OBSESS OVER A TRUNK WHEN I'VE BEEN SUFFERIN' THE CRUEL MINISTRATIONS OF FATE! DROPPED! BEATEN! PRACTICALLY EATEN ALIVE BY AN ABOMINABLE SNOWMAN! AND MY EARS! MY EARS!
OH, MY POOR TICKER! I HOPE WE DON'T CATCH UP... I DON'T THINK I COULD HANDLE ANY MORE STRESS!
HEY...
...I CAN ONLY SEE ONE OF THOSE ABOMINOID SNOWMEN..

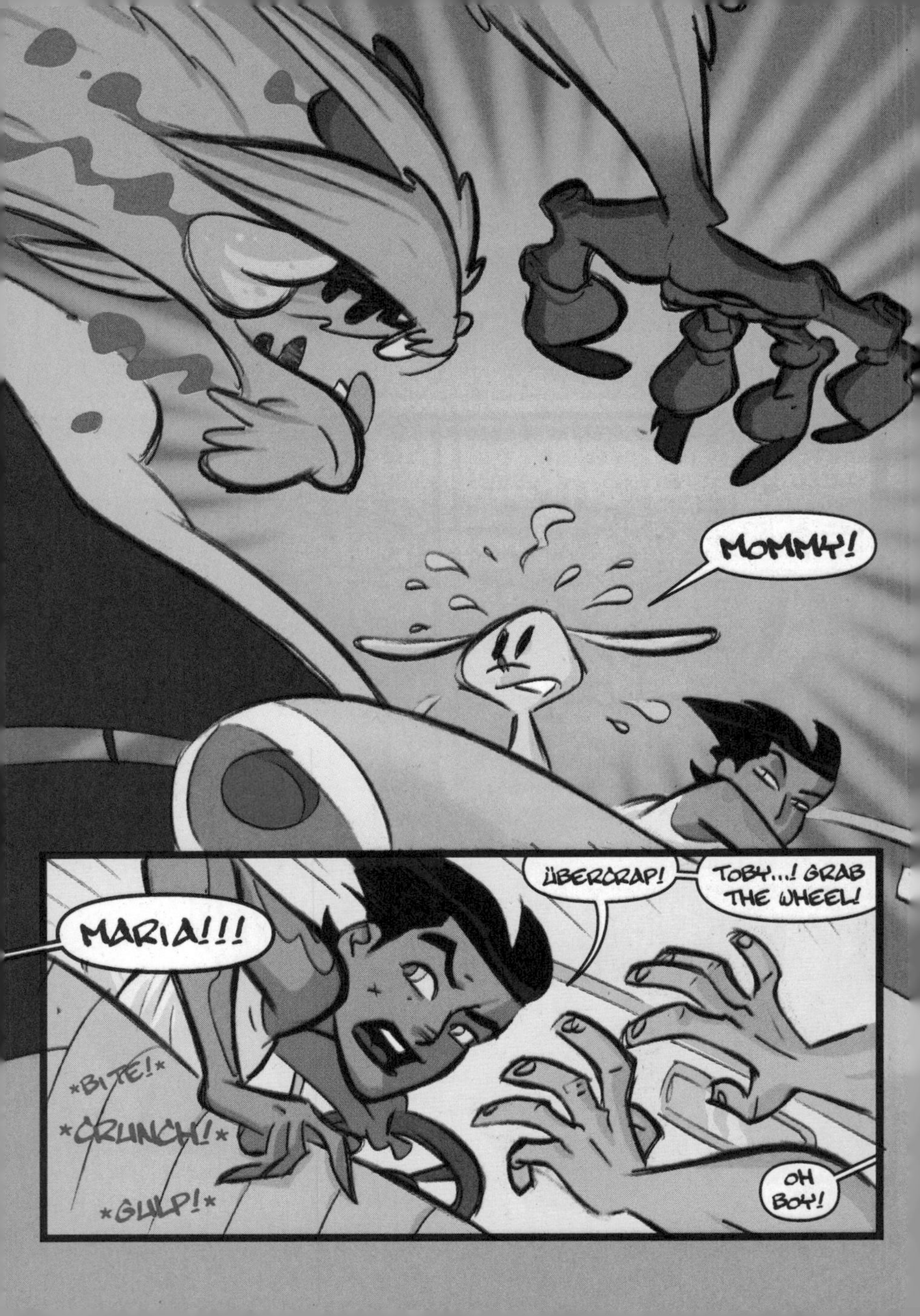
MOMMY!
MARIA!!!
ÜBERCRAP!
TOBY...! GRAB THE WHEEL!
BITE!
CRUNCH!
GULP!
OH BOY!

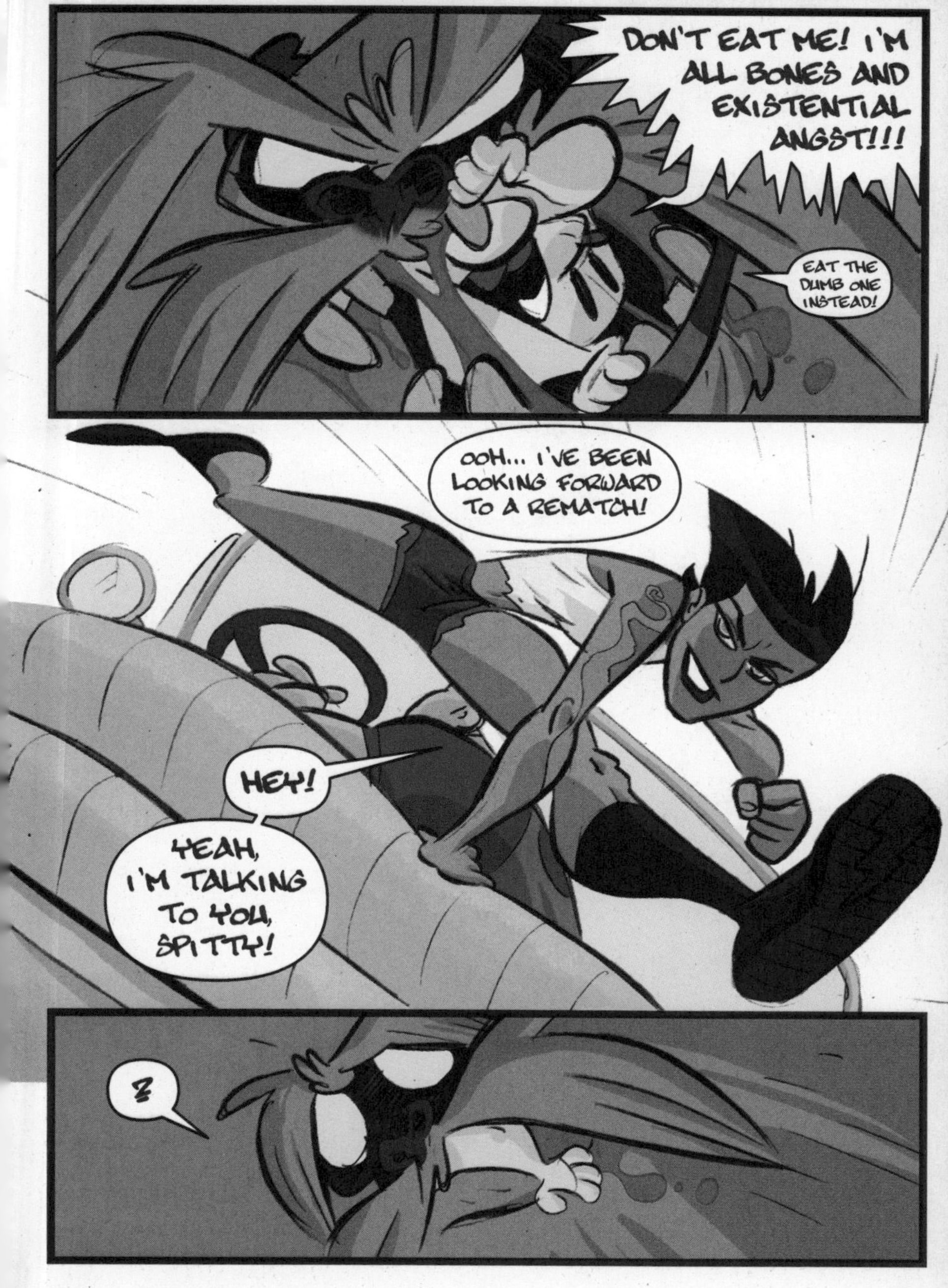
DON'T EAT ME! I'M ALL BONES AND EXISTENTIAL ANGST!!!
EAT THE DUMB ONE INSTEAD!
OOH... I'VE BEEN LOOKING FORWARD TO A REMATCH!
HEY!
YEAH, I'M TALKING TO YOU, SPITTY!
?

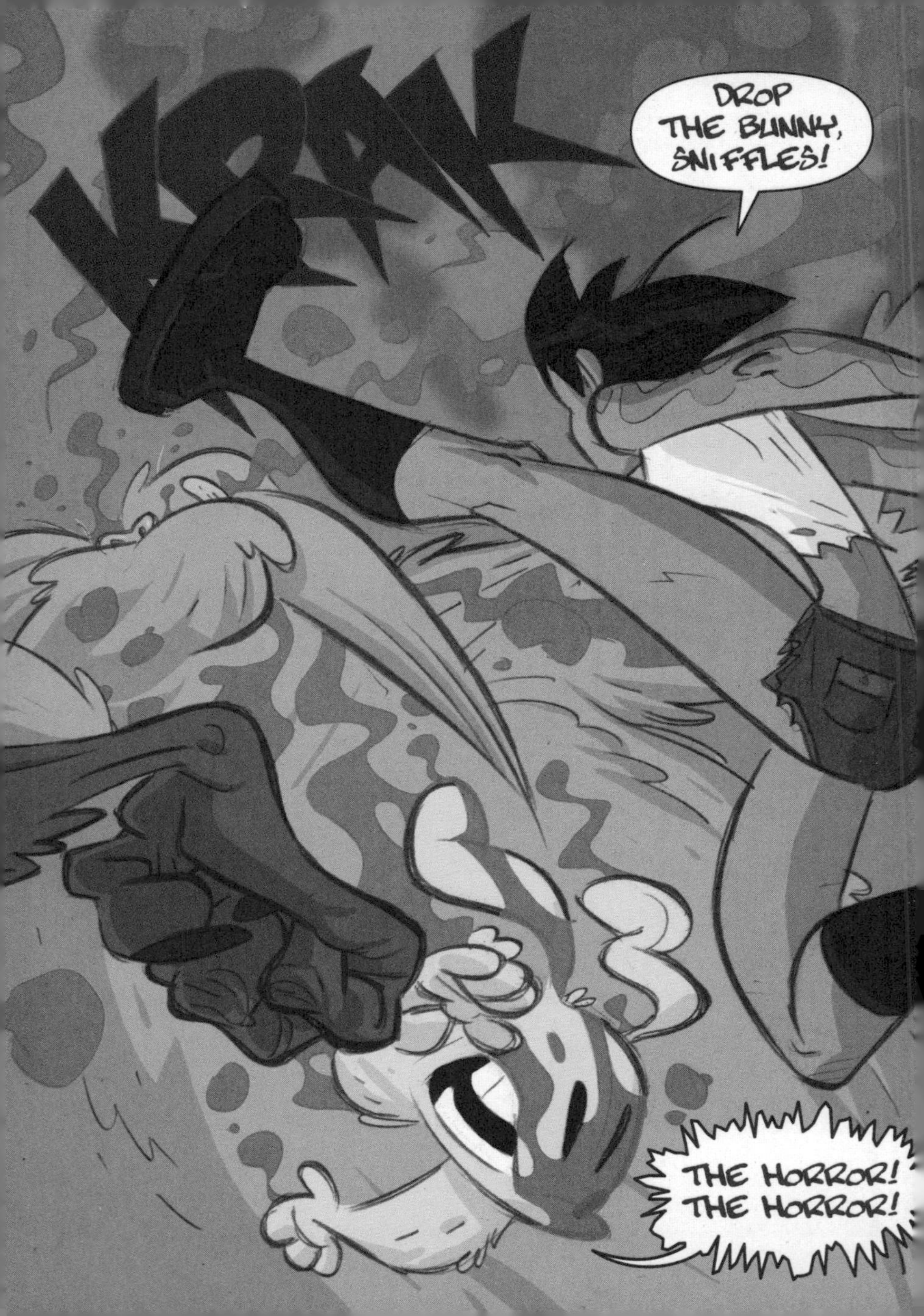
DROP THE BUNNY, SNIFFLES!
THE HORROR! THE HORROR!

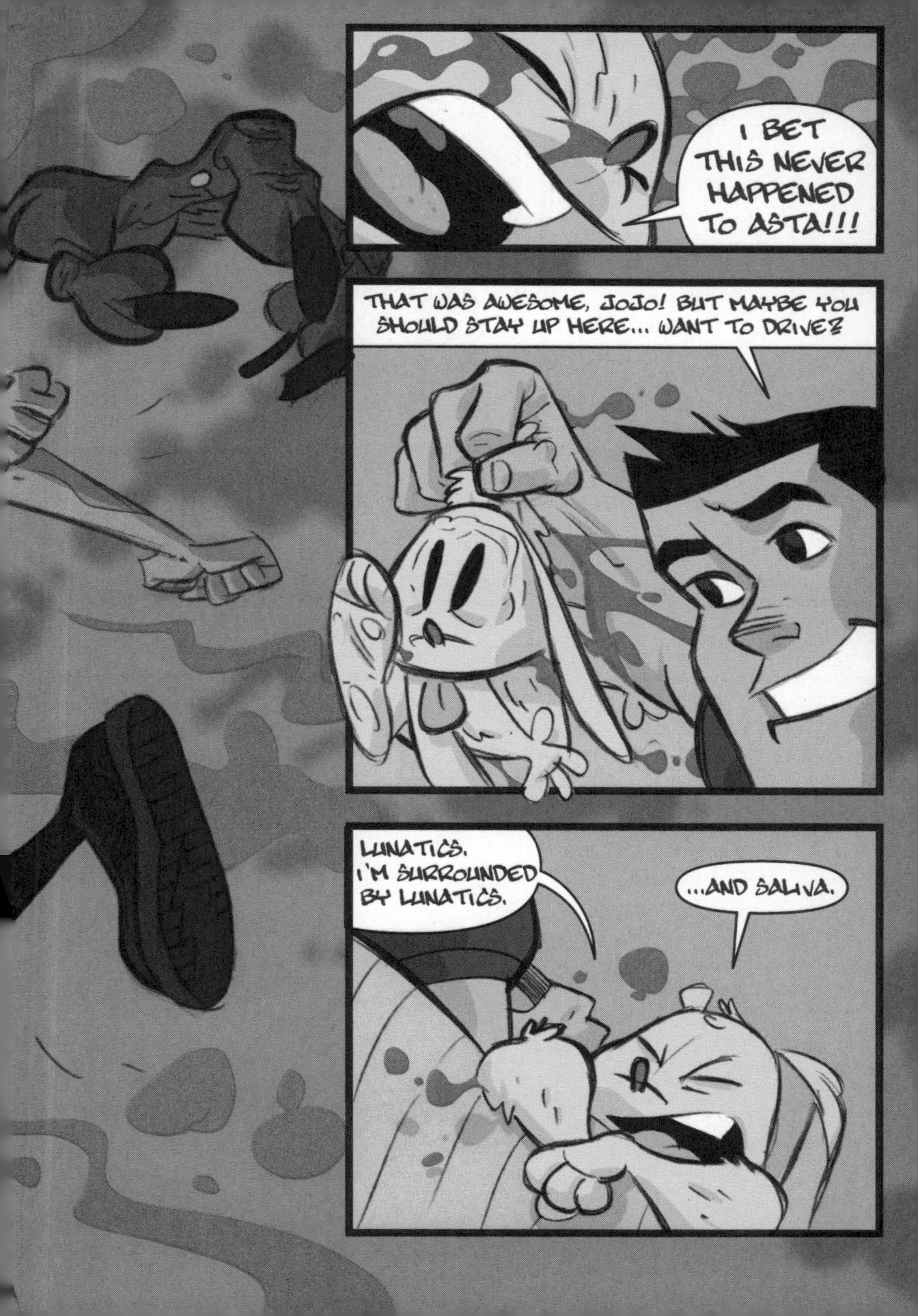
I BET THIS NEVER HAPPENED TO ASTA!!!
THAT WAS AWESOME, JOJO! BUT MAYBE YOU SHOULD STAY UP HERE... WANT TO DRIVE?
LUNATICS. I'M SURROUNDED BY LUNATICS.
...AND SALIVA.

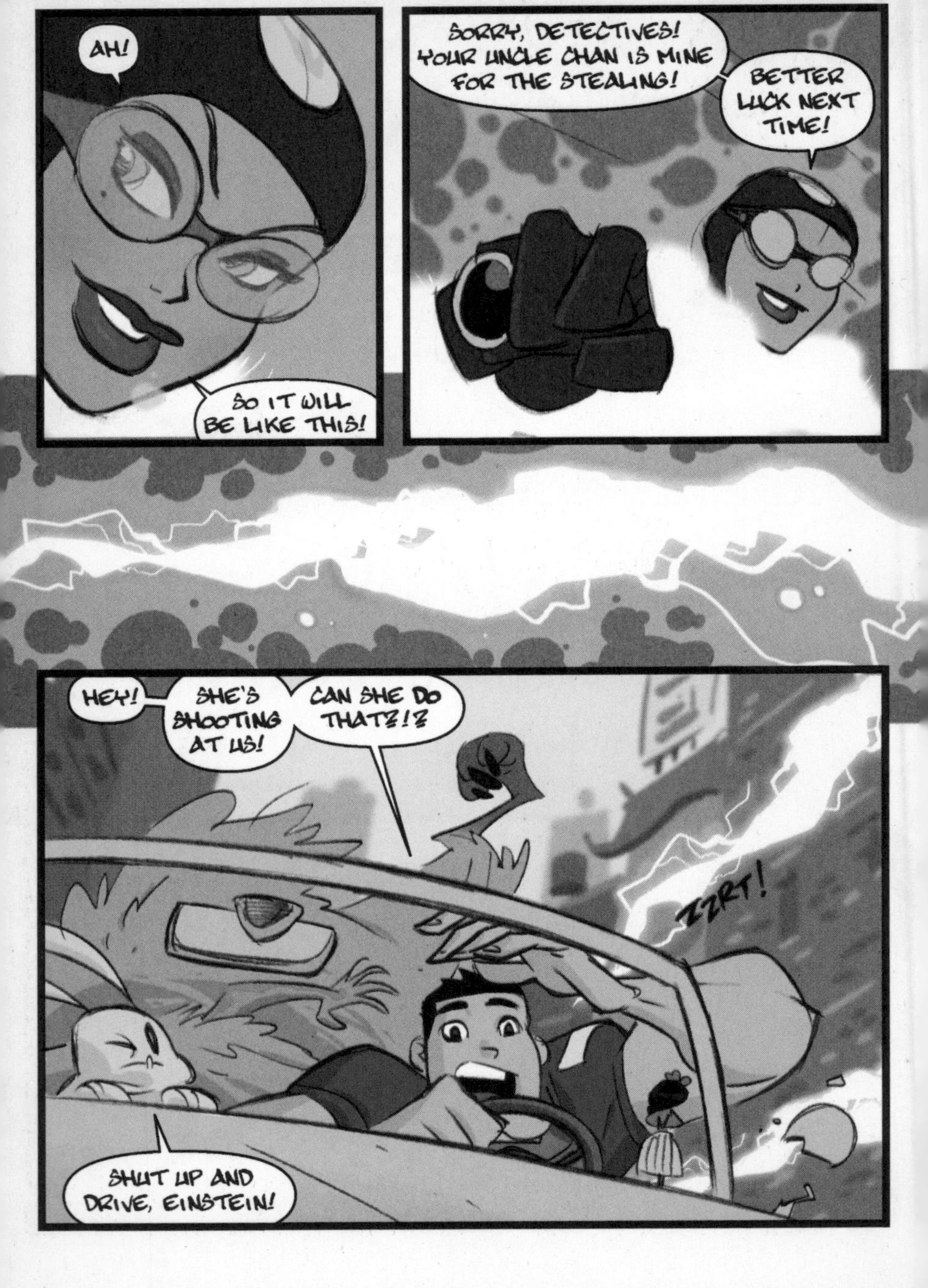
AH!
SO IT WILL BE LIKE THIS!
SORRY, DETECTIVES! YOUR UNCLE CHAN IS MINE FOR THE STEALING!
BETTER LUCK NEXT TIME!
HEY!
SHE'S SHOOTING AT US!
CAN SHE DO THAT?!?
ZZRT!
SHUT UP AND DRIVE, EINSTEIN!

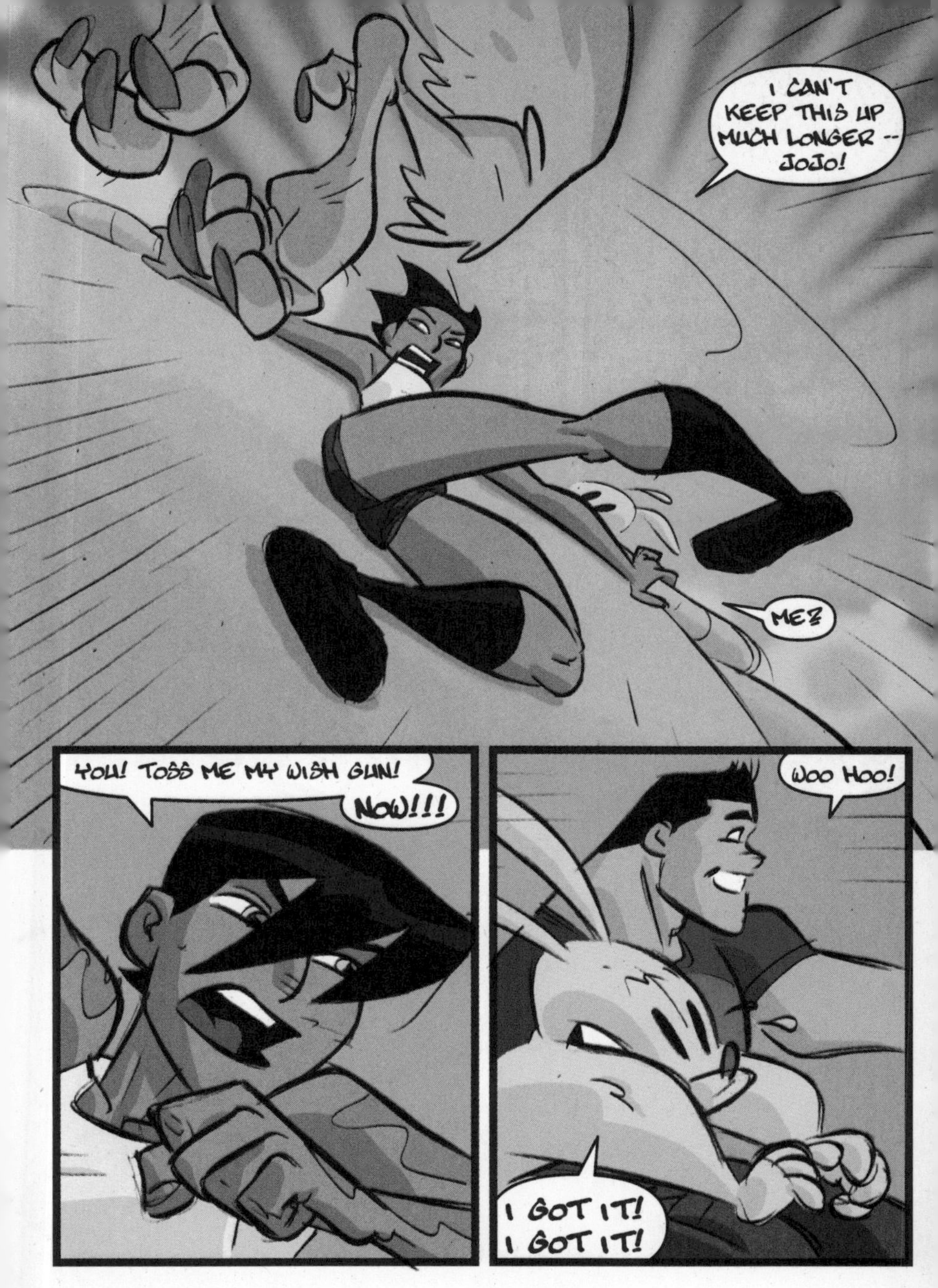
I CAN'T KEEP THIS UP MUCH LONGER -- JOJO!
ME?
YOU! TOSS ME MY WISH GUN!
NOW!!!
WOO HOO!
I GOT IT! I GOT IT!

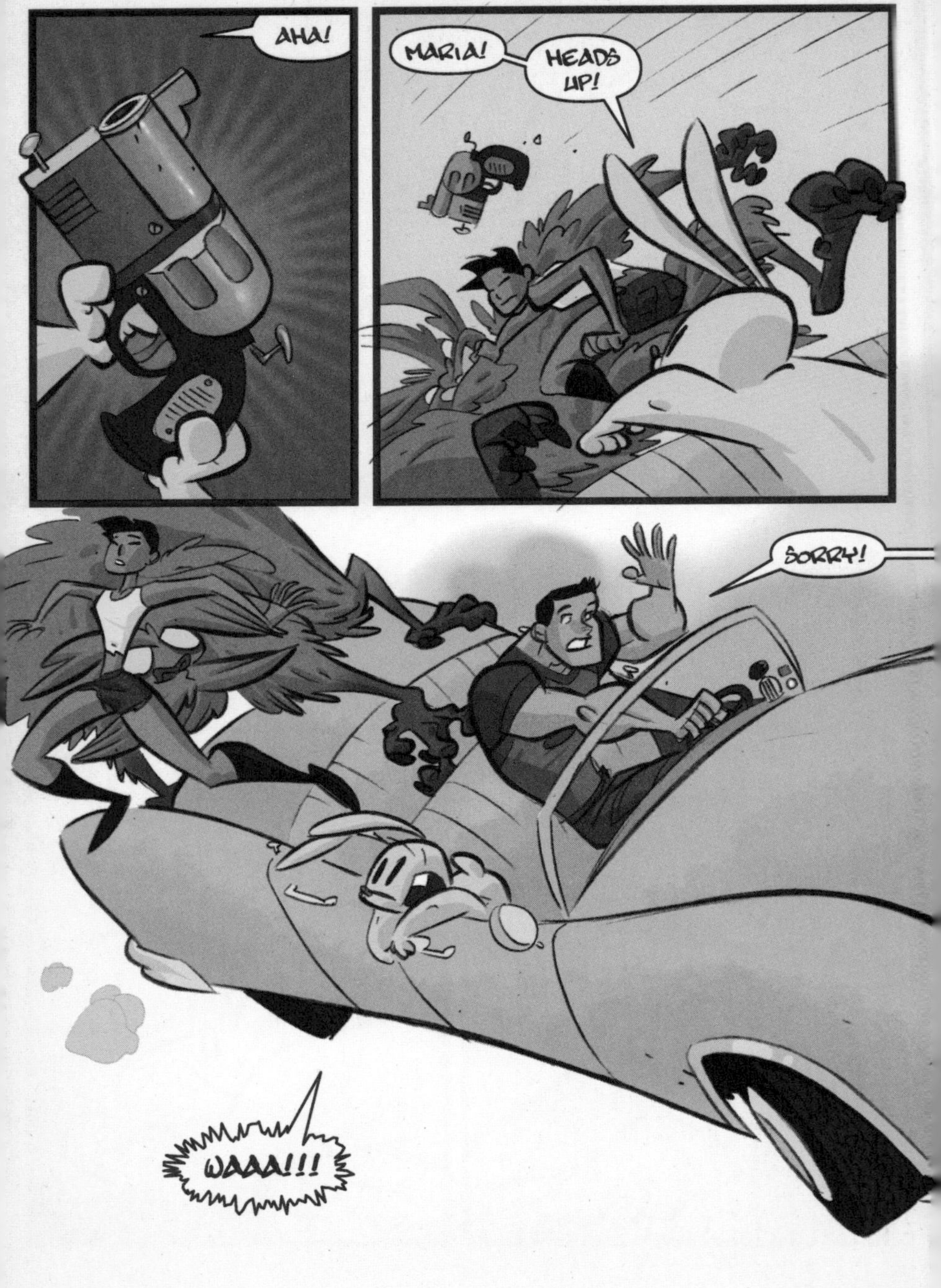
AHA!
MARIA!
HEADS UP!
SORRY!
WAAA!!!

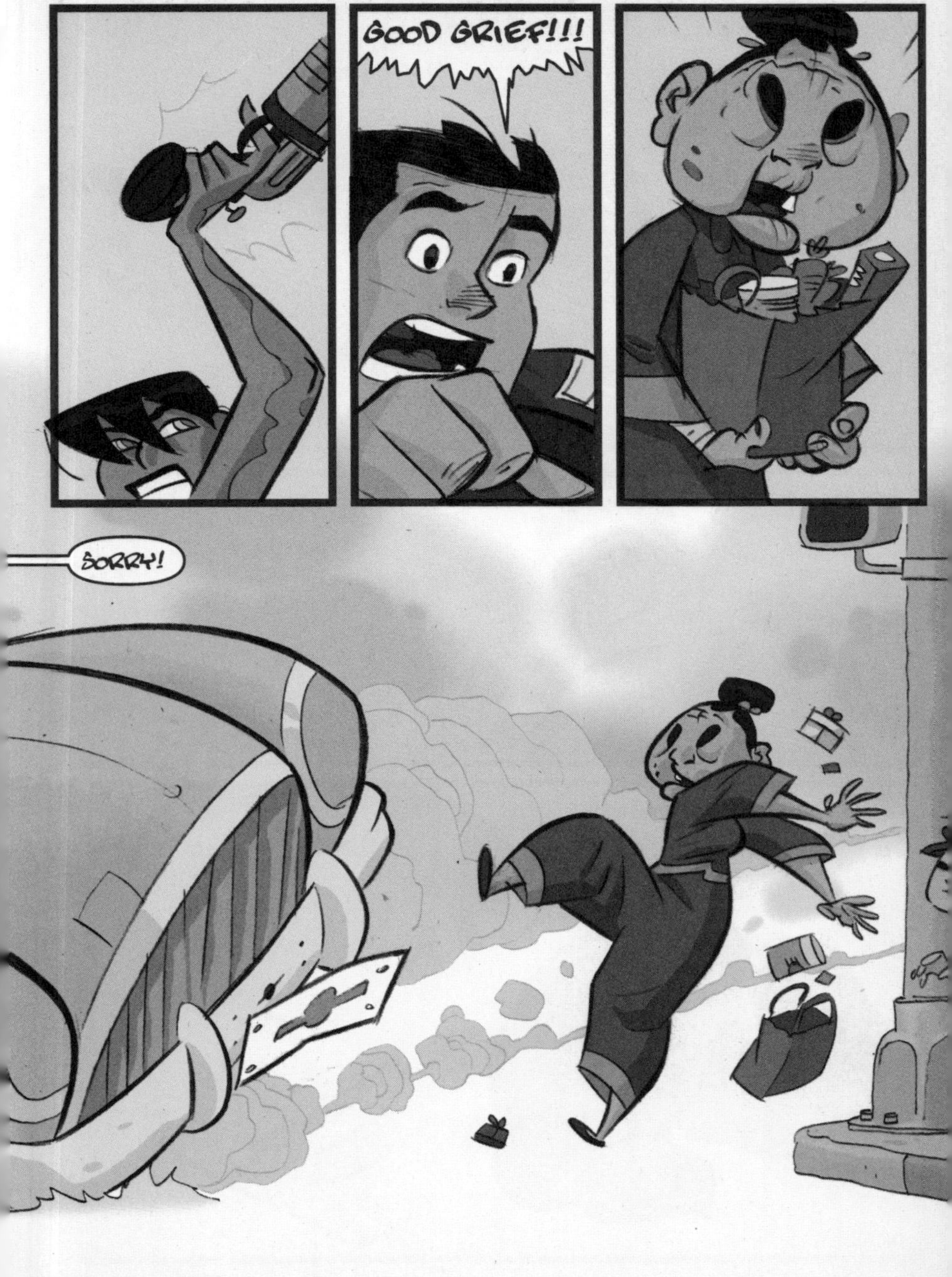
GOOD GRIEF!!!
SORRY!

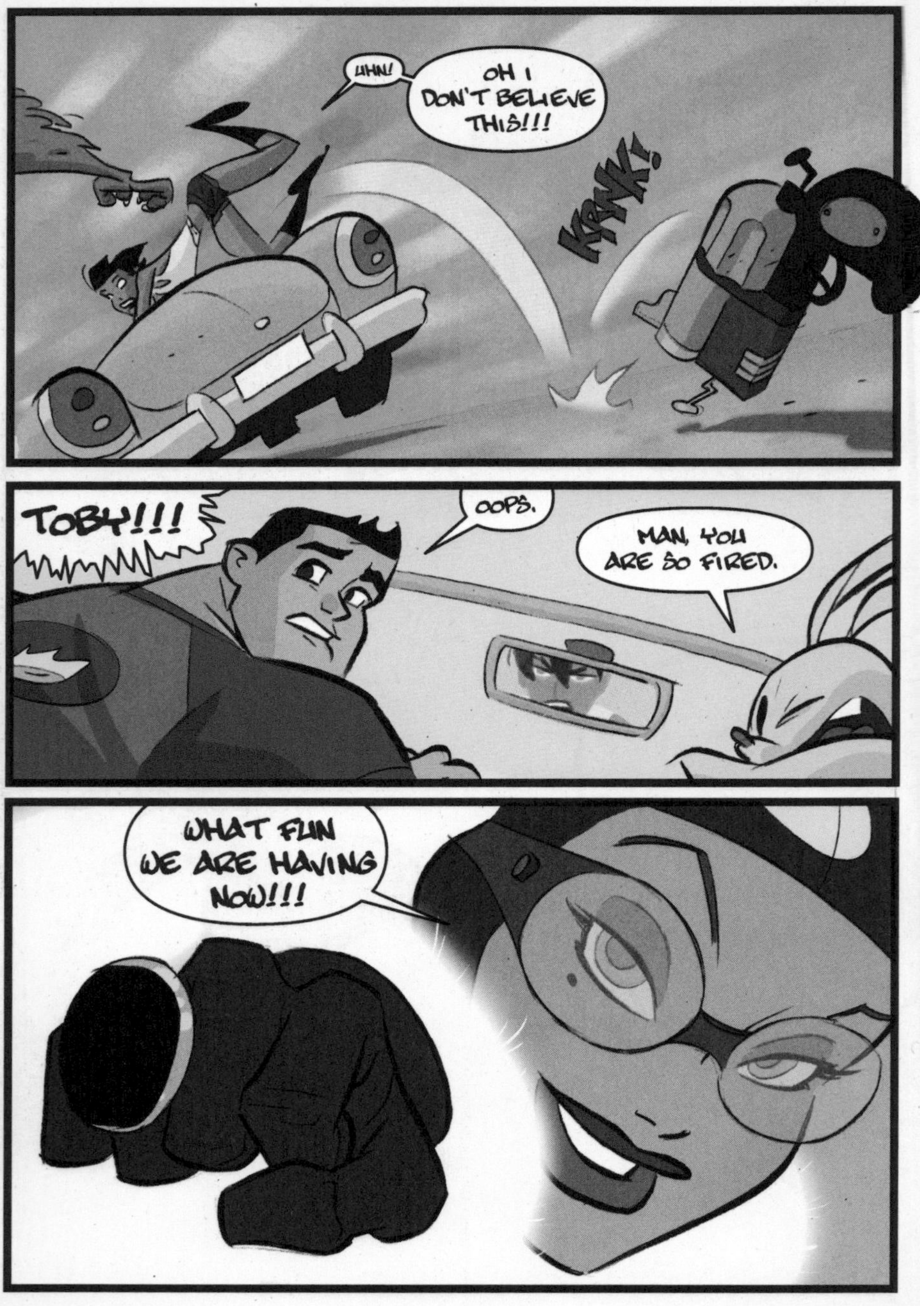
UHN!
OH I DON'T BELIEVE THIS!!!
KRUNK!
TOBY!!!!
OOPS.
MAN, YOU ARE SO FIRED.
WHAT FUN WE ARE HAVING NOW!!!

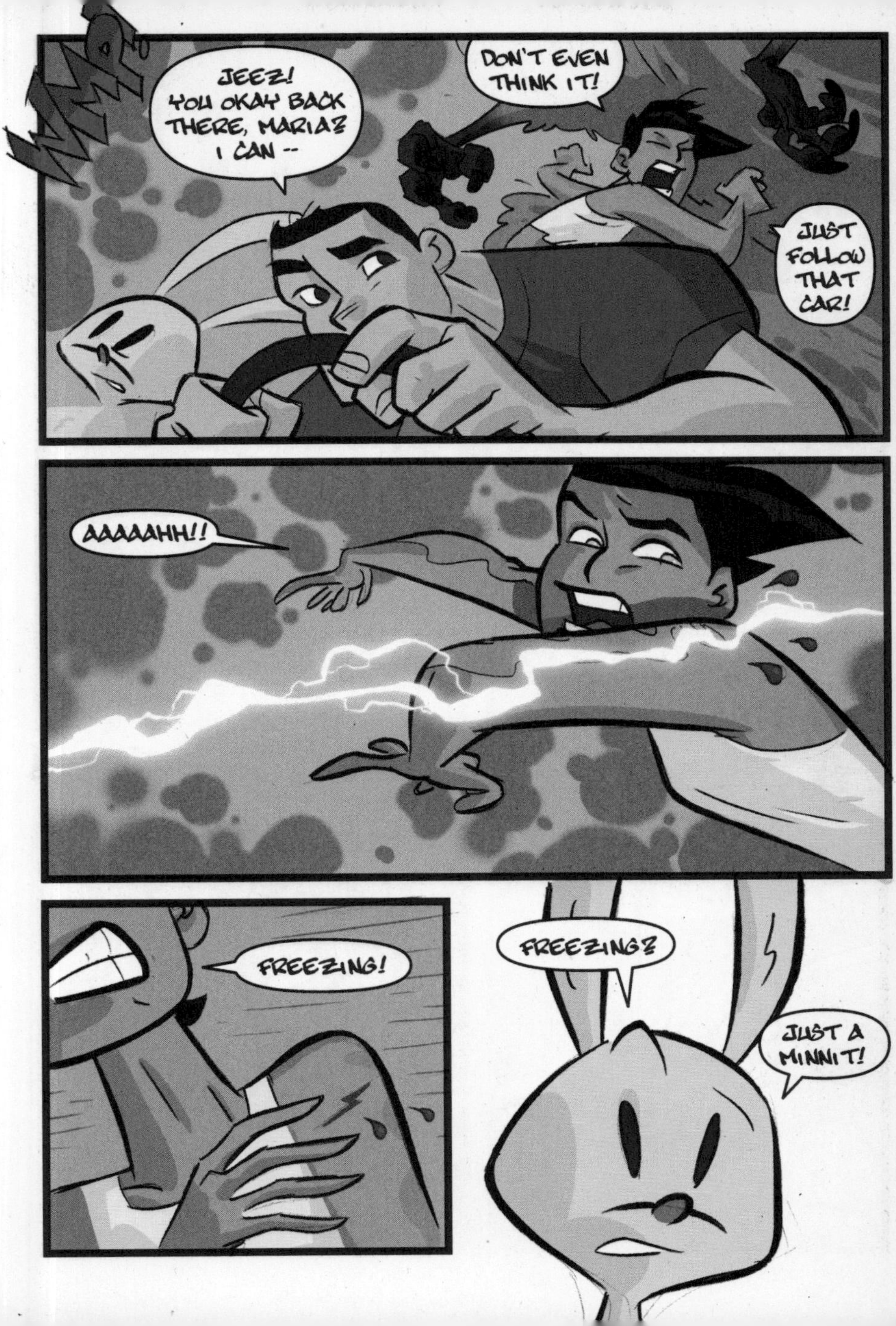
WMP!
JEEZ! YOU OKAY BACK THERE, MARIA? I CAN --
DON'T EVEN THINK IT!
JUST FOLLOW THAT CAR!
AAAAAHH!!
FREEZING!
FREEZING?
JUST A MINNIT!

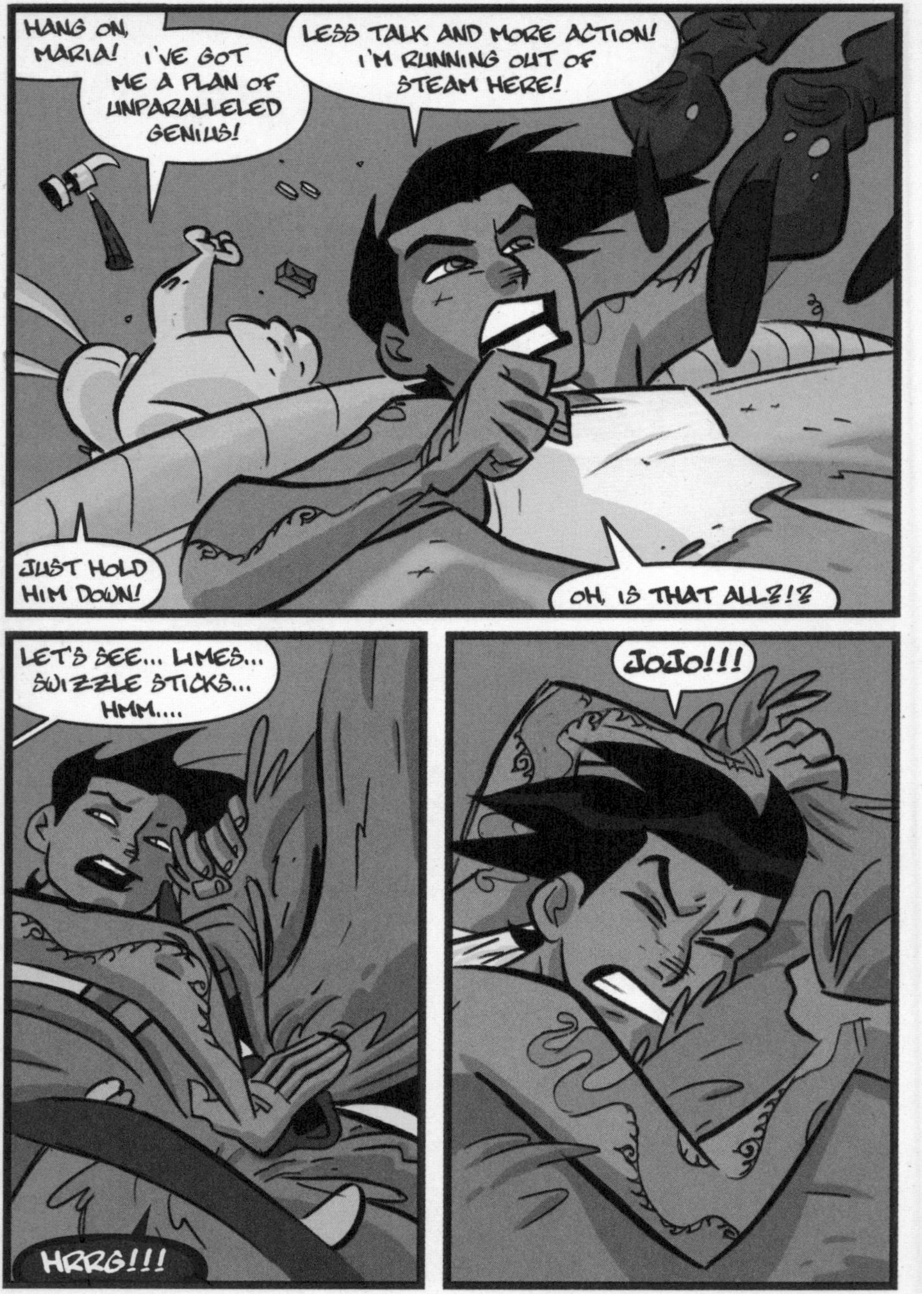
HANG ON, MARIA! I'VE GOT ME A PLAN OF UNPARALLELED GENIUS!
LESS TALK AND MORE ACTION! I'M RUNNING OUT OF STEAM HERE!
JUST HOLD HIM DOWN!
OH, IS THAT ALL?!?
LET'S SEE... LIMES... SWIZZLE STICKS... HMM....
HRRG!!!
JOJO!!!

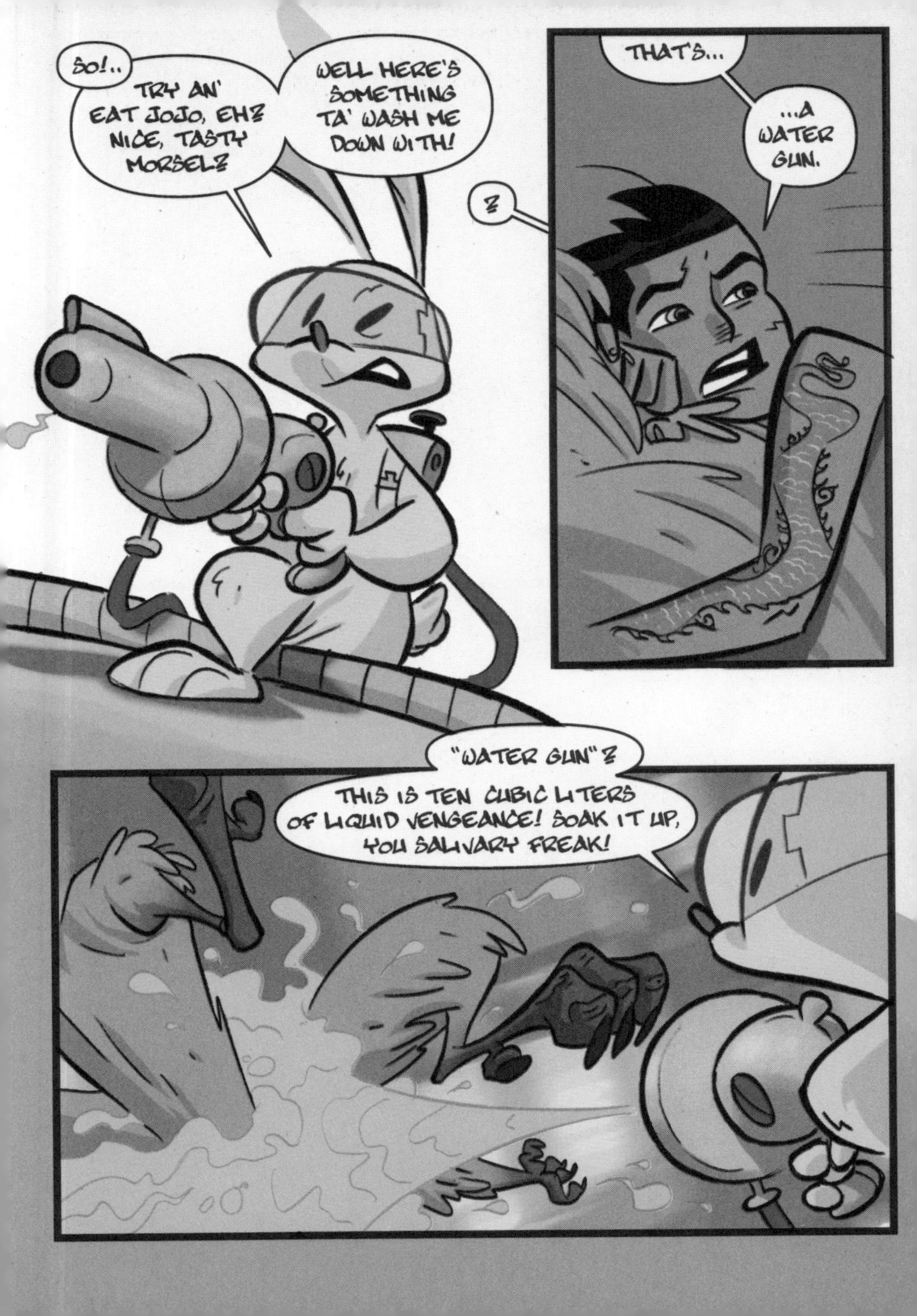
SO!.. TRY AN' EAT JOJO, EH? NICE, TASTY MORSEL?
WELL HERE'S SOMETHING TA' WASH ME DOWN WITH!
THAT'S...
?
...A WATER GUN.
"WATER GUN"? THIS IS TEN CUBIC LITERS OF LIQUID VENGEANCE! SOAK IT UP, YOU SALIVARY FREAK!

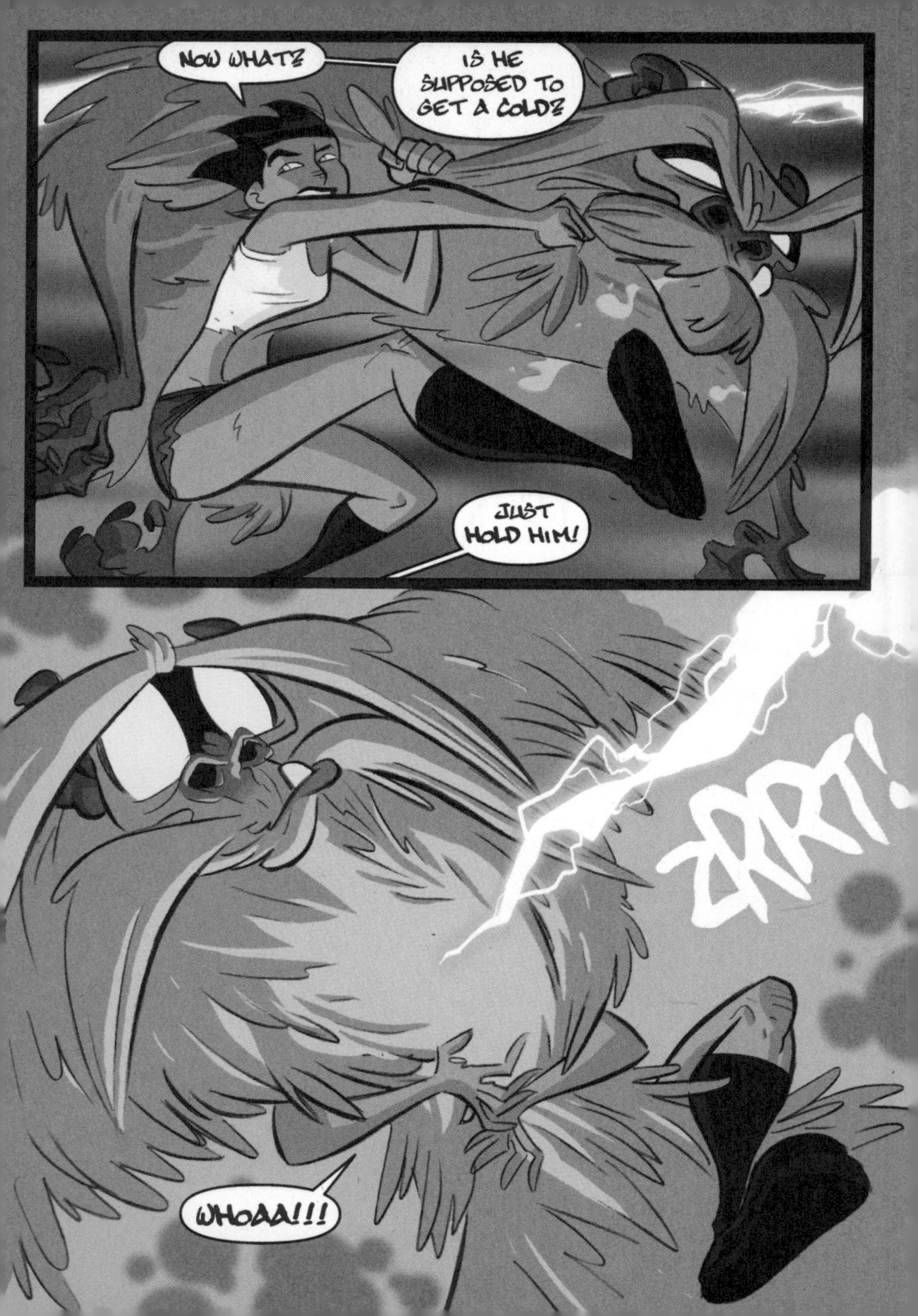
NOW WHAT?
IS HE SUPPOSED TO GET A COLD?
JUST HOLD HIM!
ZZRRT!
WHOAA!!!

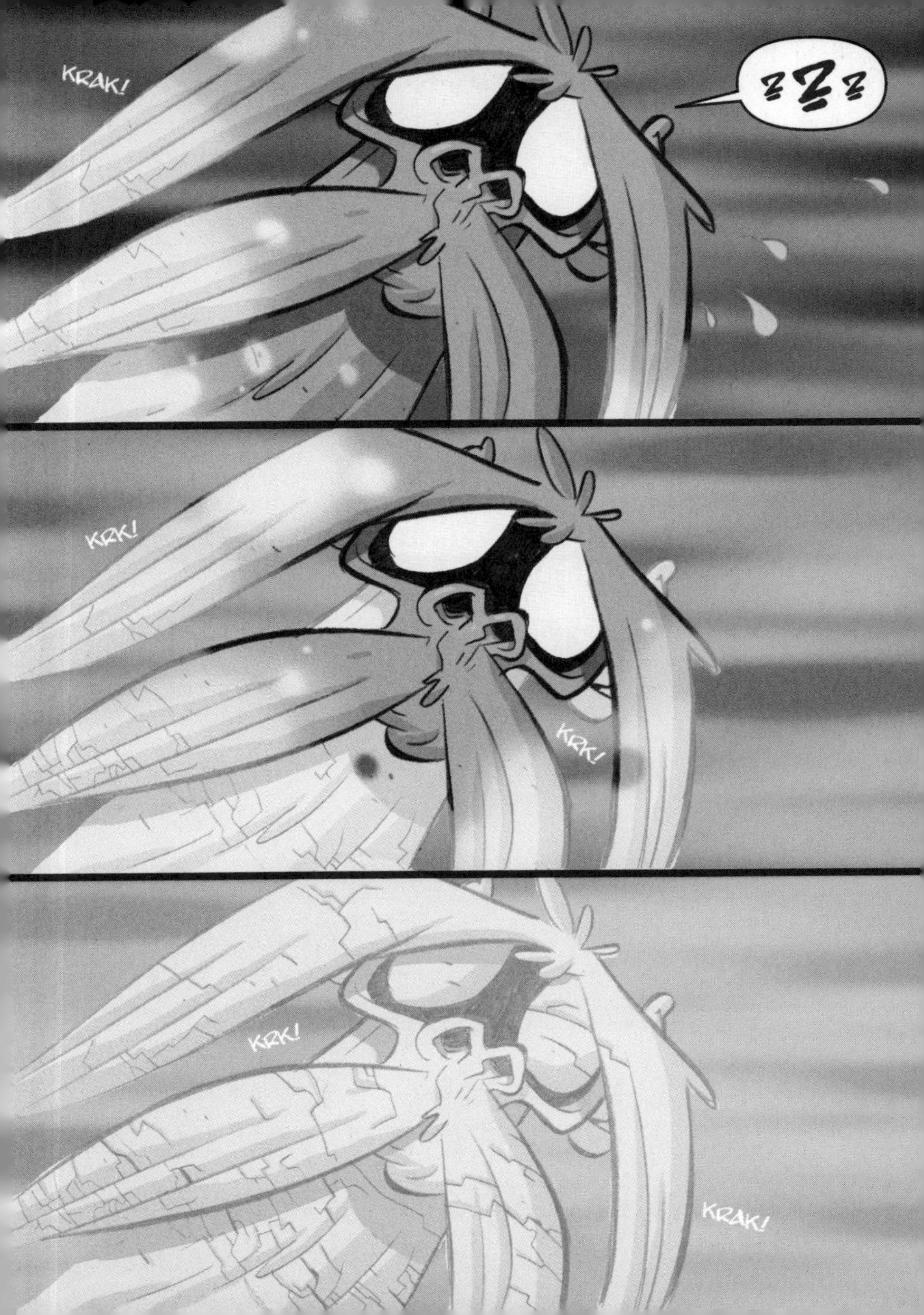
KRAK!
? Z ?
KRK!
KRK!
KRK!
KRAK!

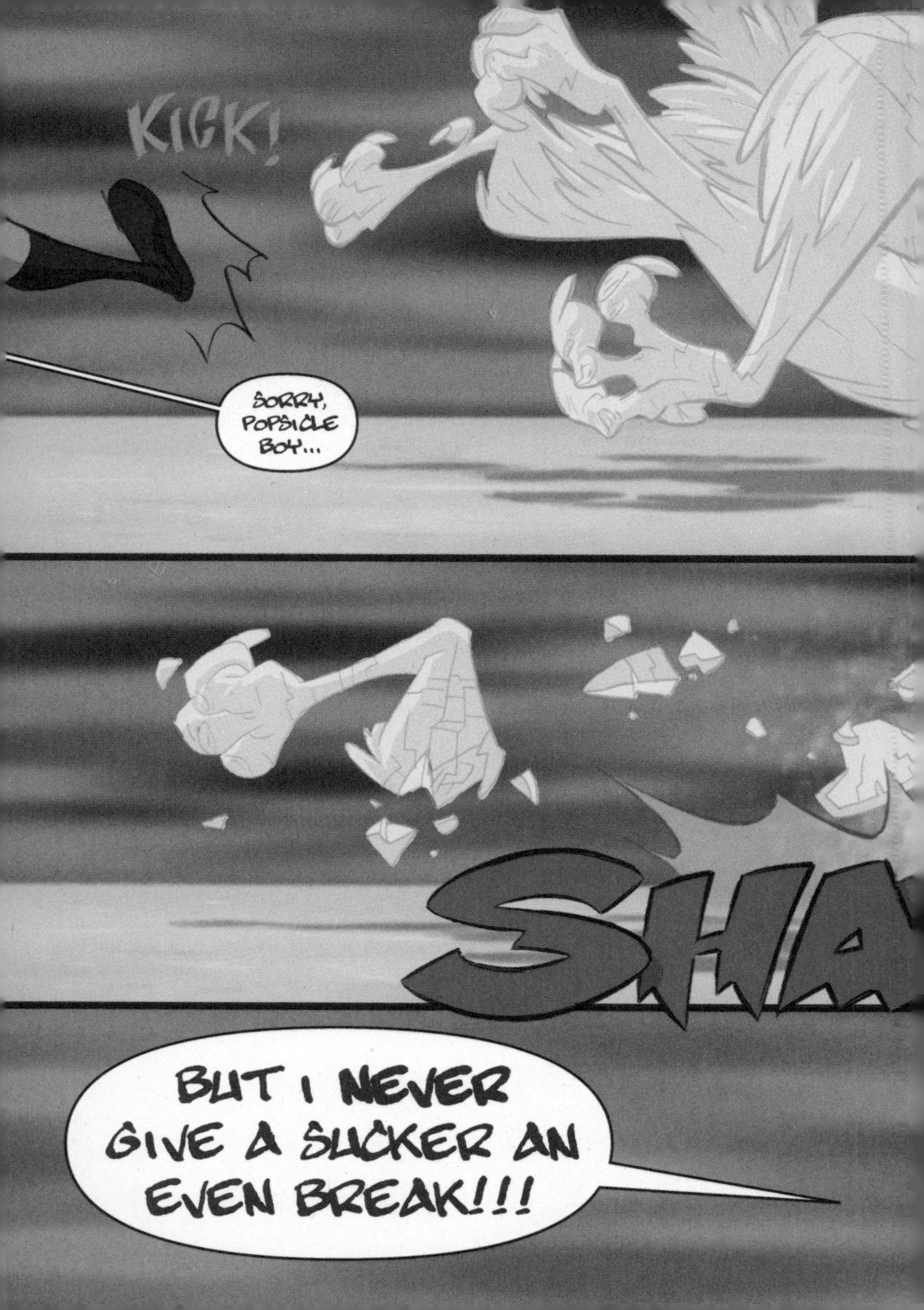
KICK!
SORRY, POPSICLE BOY...
SHA
BUT I NEVER GIVE A SUCKER AN EVEN BREAK!!!

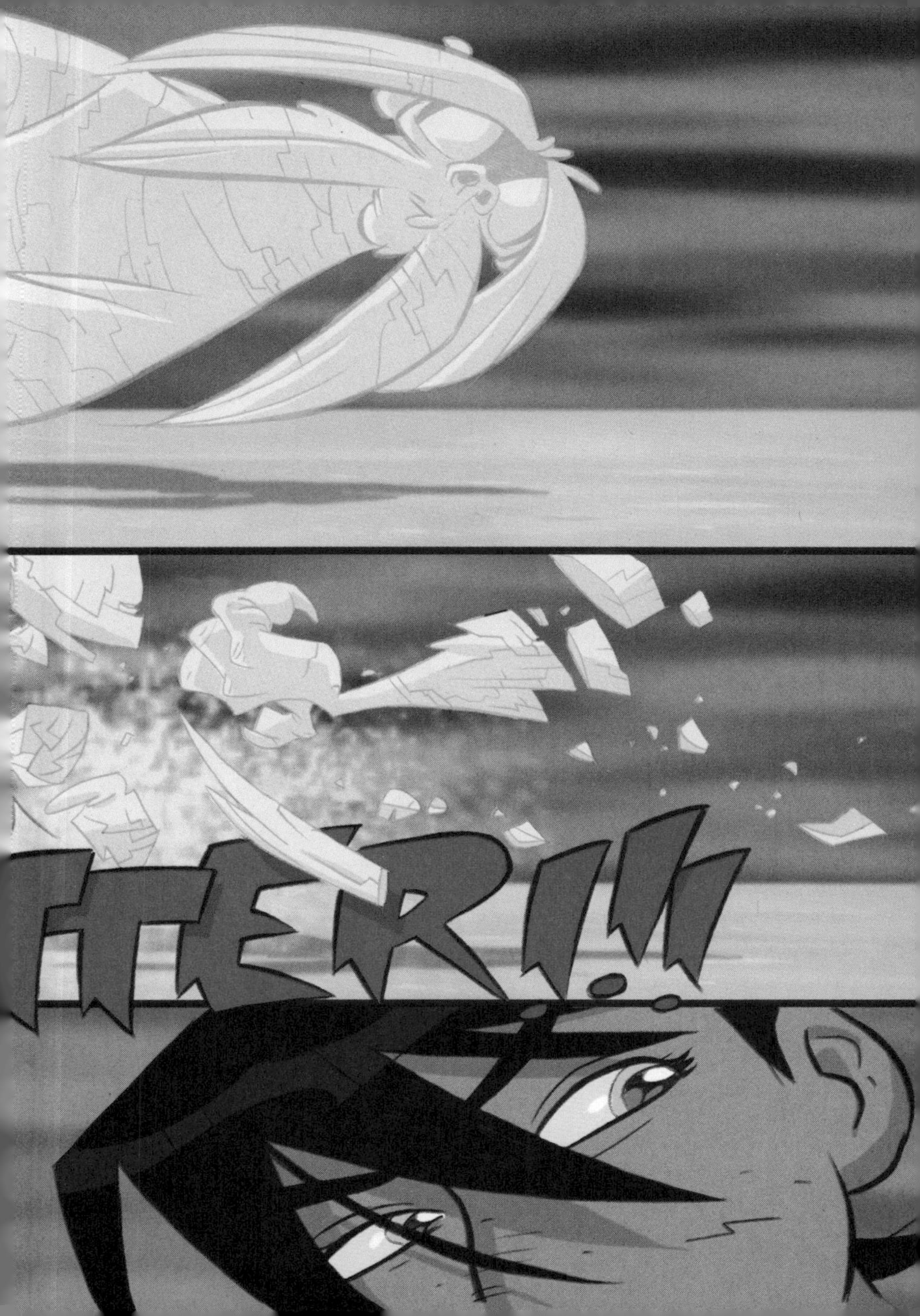

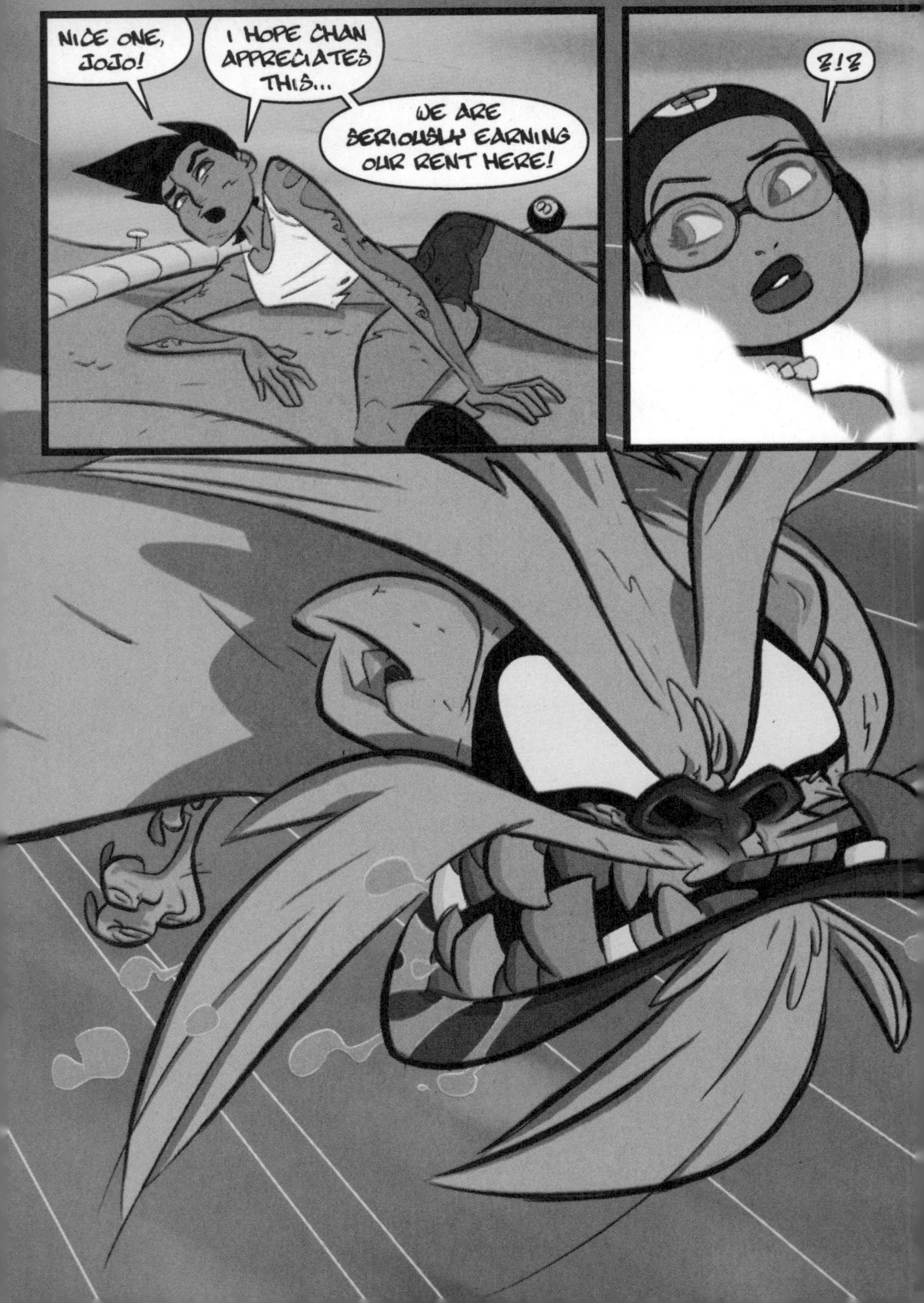
NICE ONE, JOJO!
I HOPE CHAN APPRECIATES THIS...
WE ARE SERIOUSLY EARNING OUR RENT HERE!
?!?

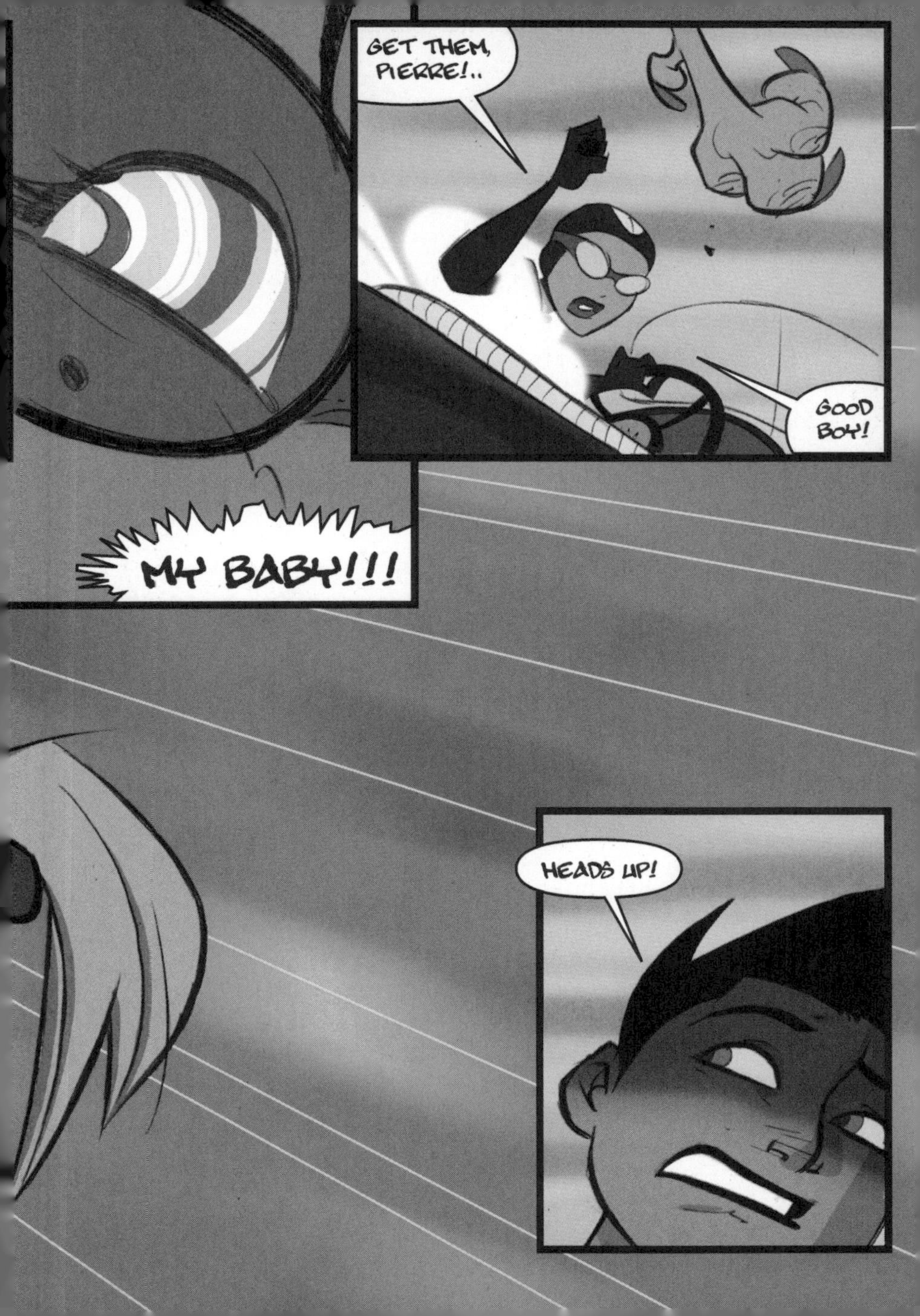
GET THEM, PIERRE!..
GOOD BOY!
MY BABY!!!!
HEADS UP!

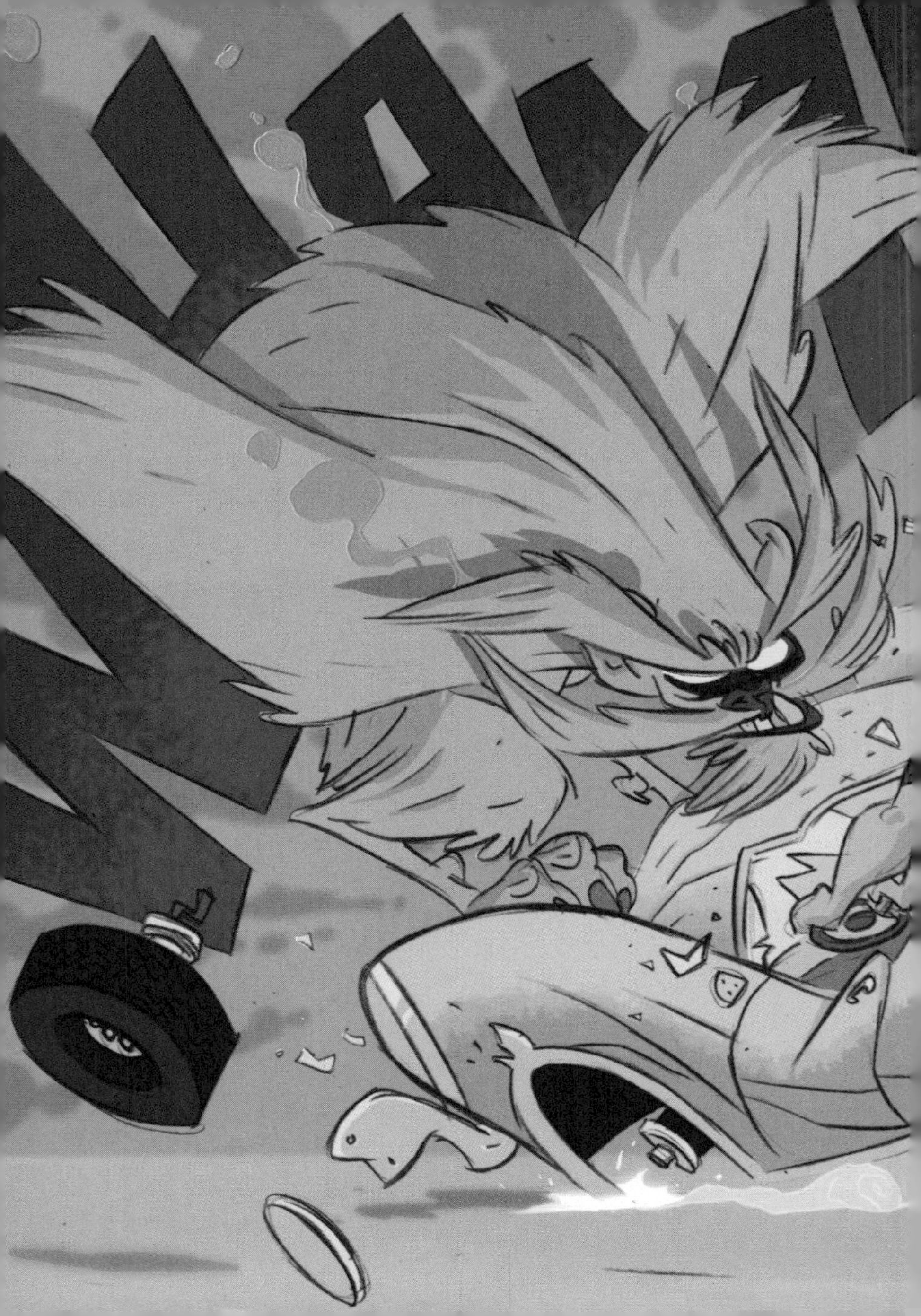

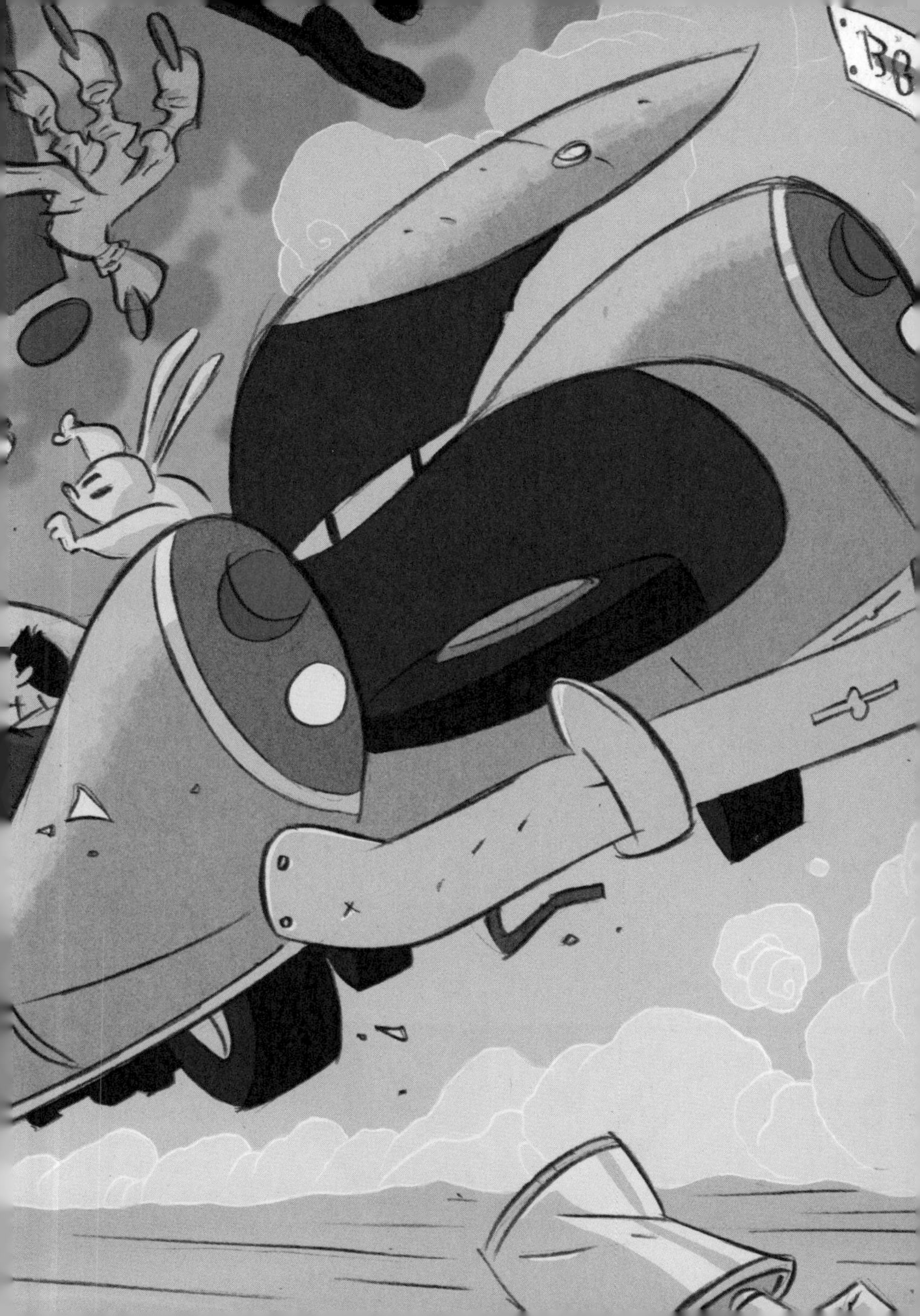

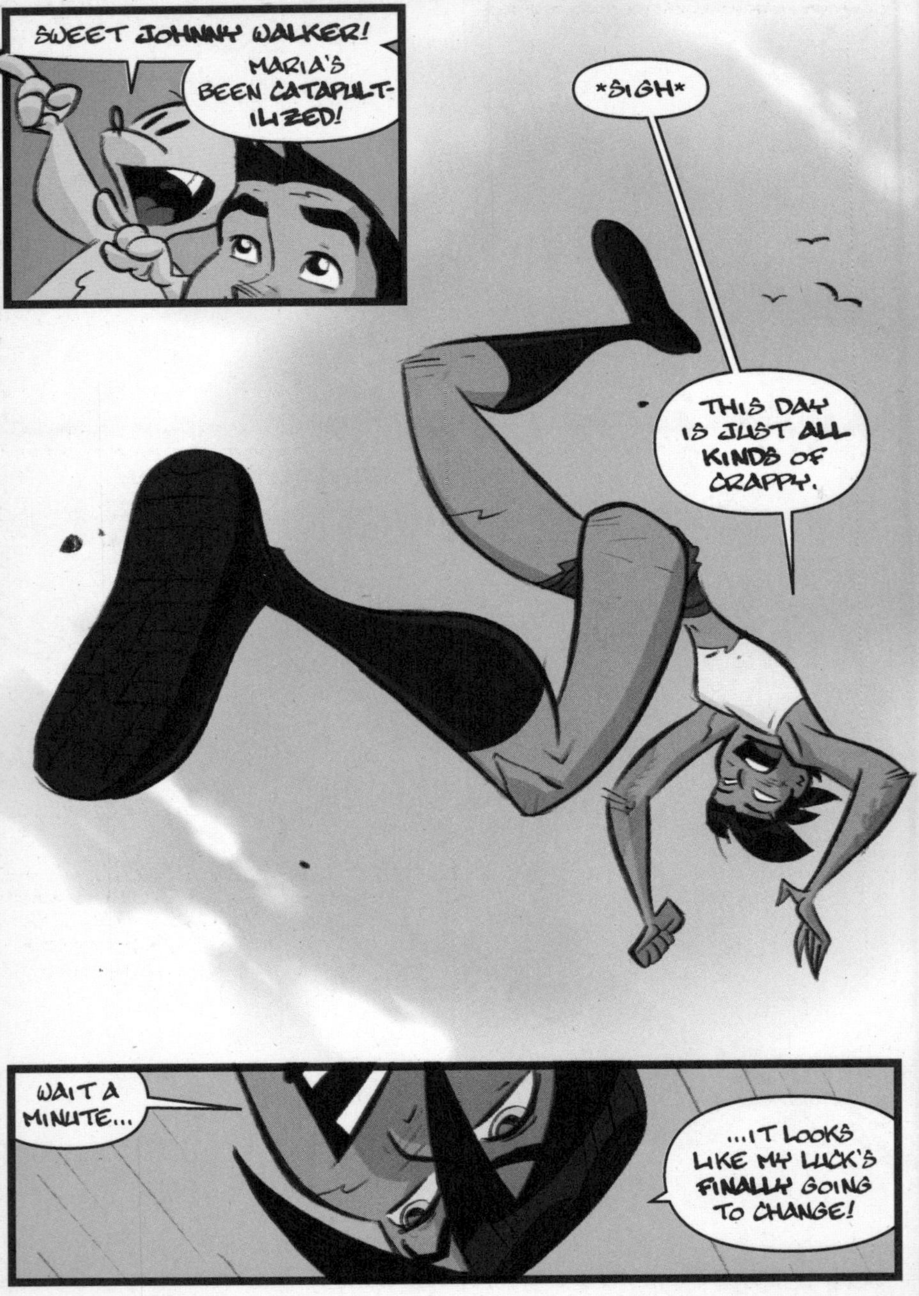
SWEET JOHNNY WALKER!
MARIA'S BEEN CATAPULT-ILIZED!
SIGH
THIS DAY IS JUST ALL KINDS OF CRAPPY.
WAIT A MINUTE...
...IT LOOKS LIKE MY LUCK'S FINALLY GOING TO CHANGE!

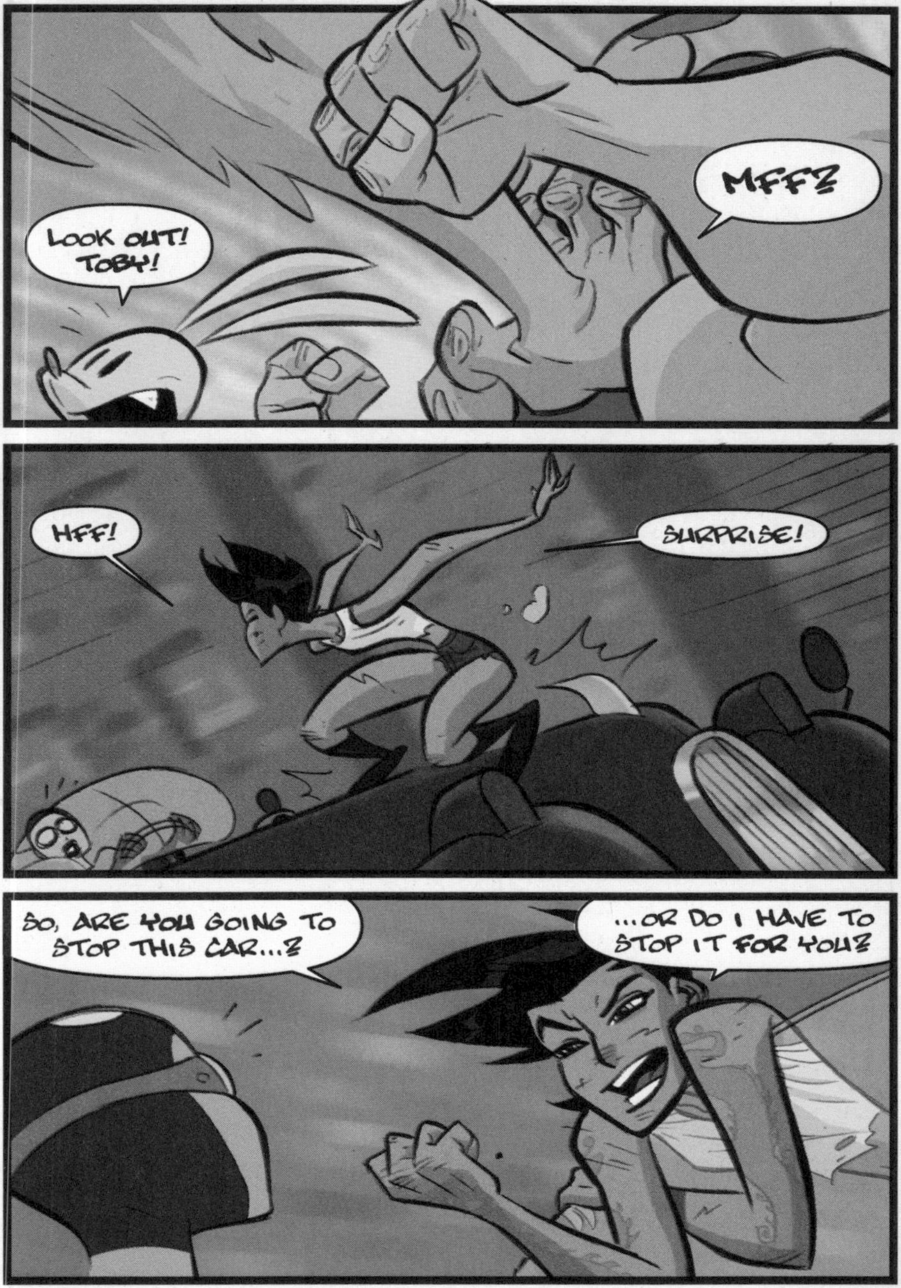

LOOK OUT! TOBY!
MFF?
HFF!
SURPRISE!
SO, ARE YOU GOING TO STOP THIS CAR...?
...OR DO I HAVE TO STOP IT FOR YOU?

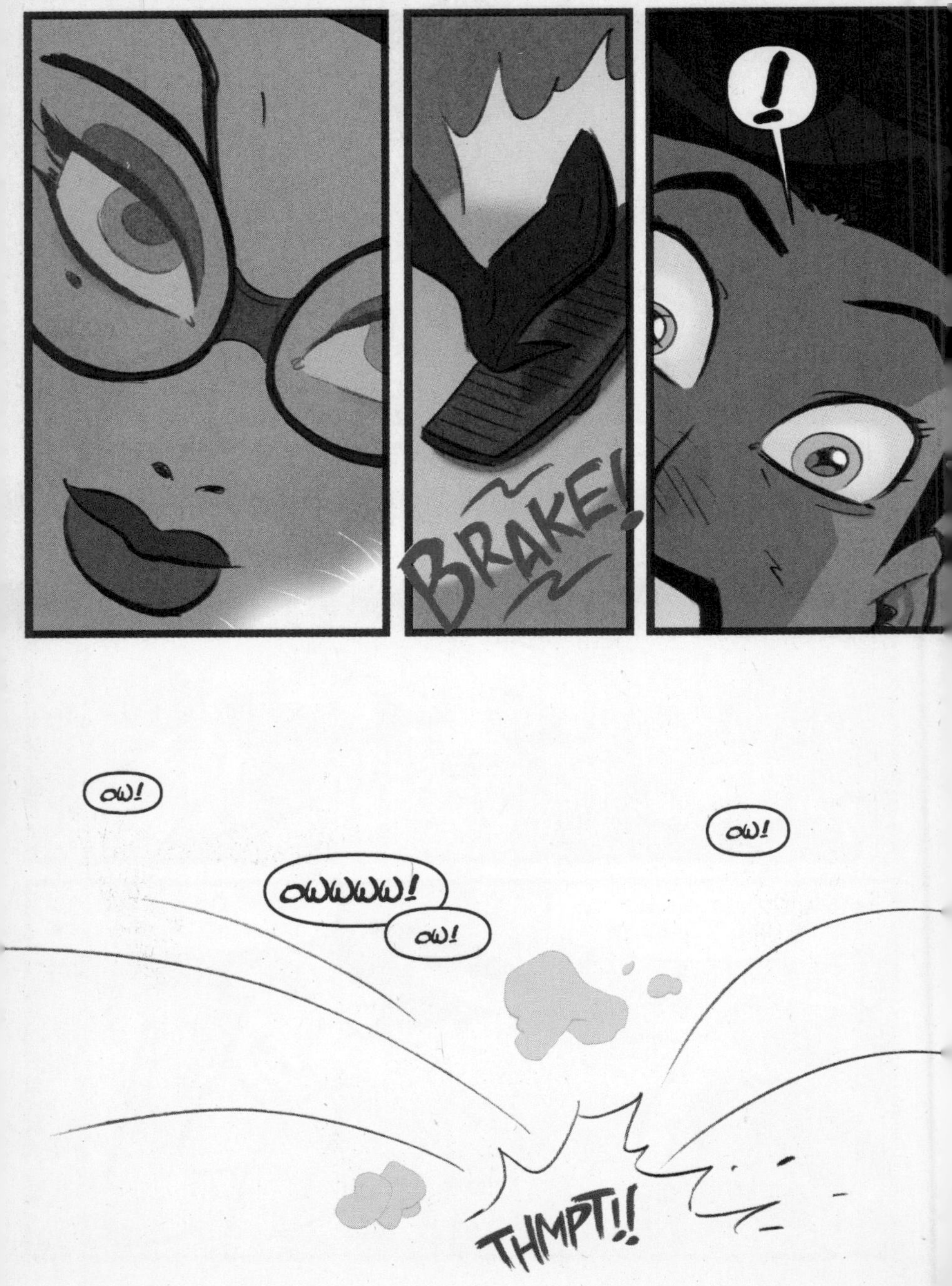

BRAKE!
!
OW!
OWWWW!
OW!
OW!
THMPT!!

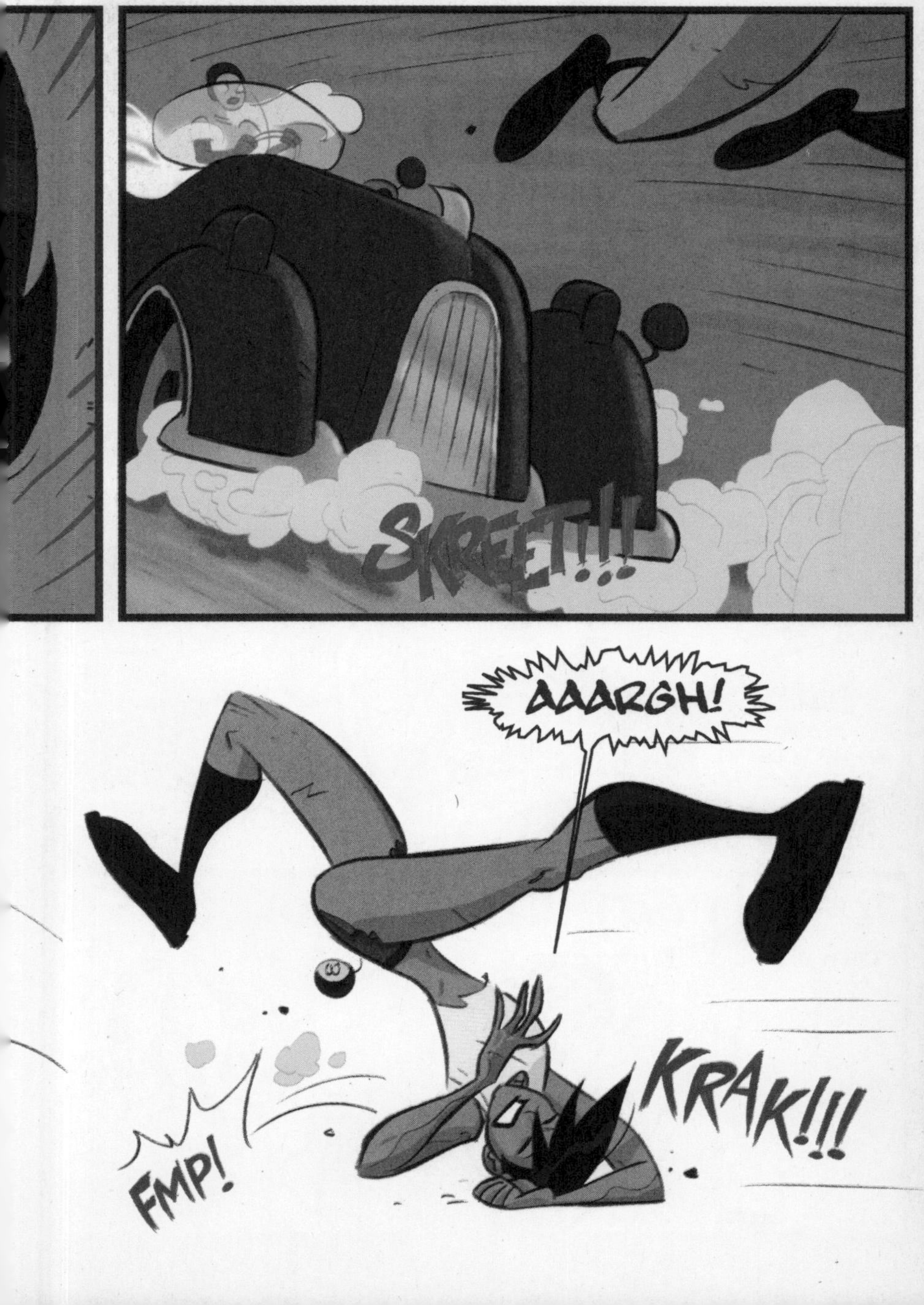
SKREEET!!!
AAARGH!
FMP!
KRAK!!!

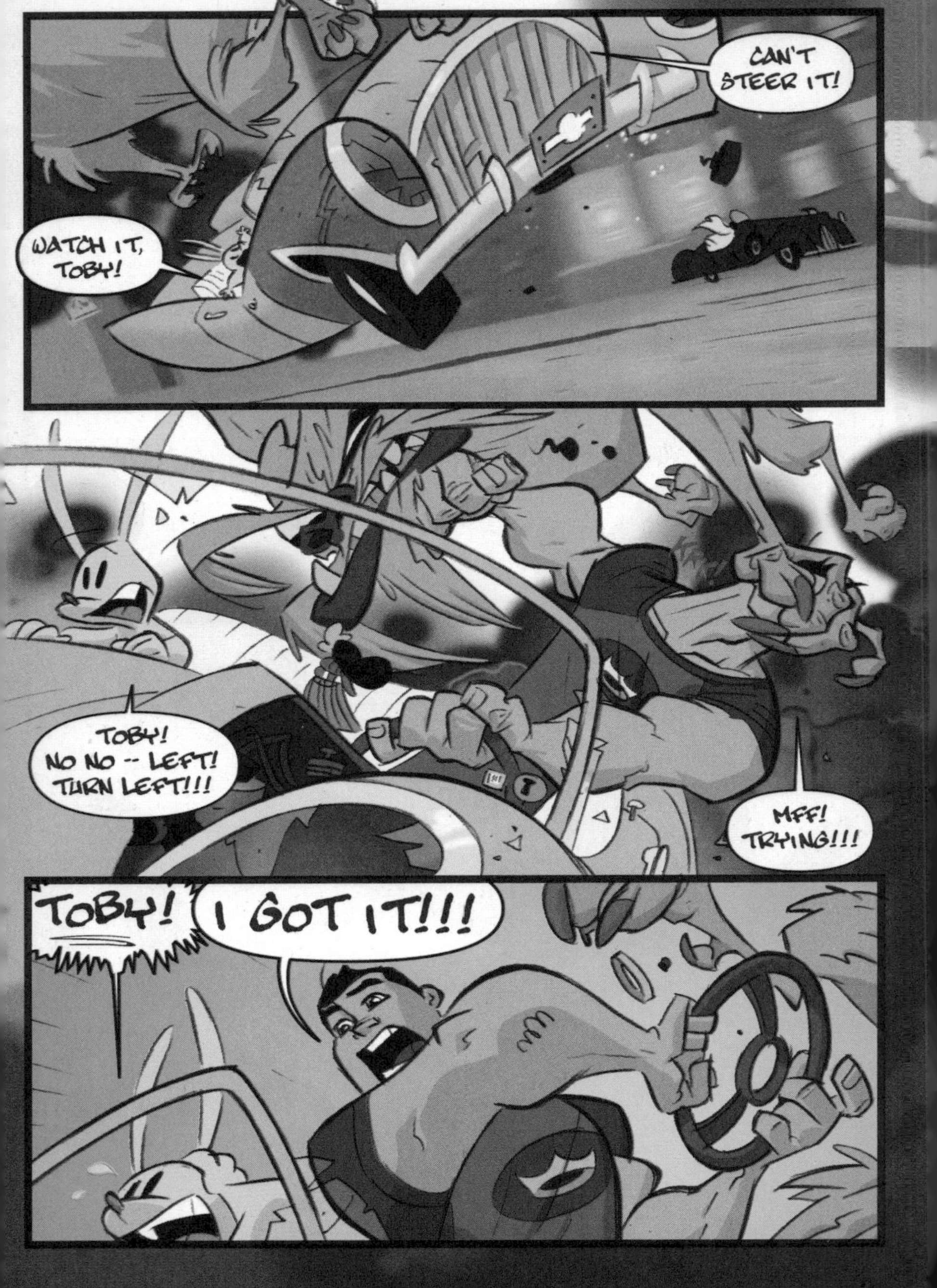
CAN'T STEER IT!
WATCH IT, TOBY!
TOBY! NO NO -- LEFT! TURN LEFT!!!
MFF! TRYING!!!
TOBY!
I GOT IT!!!

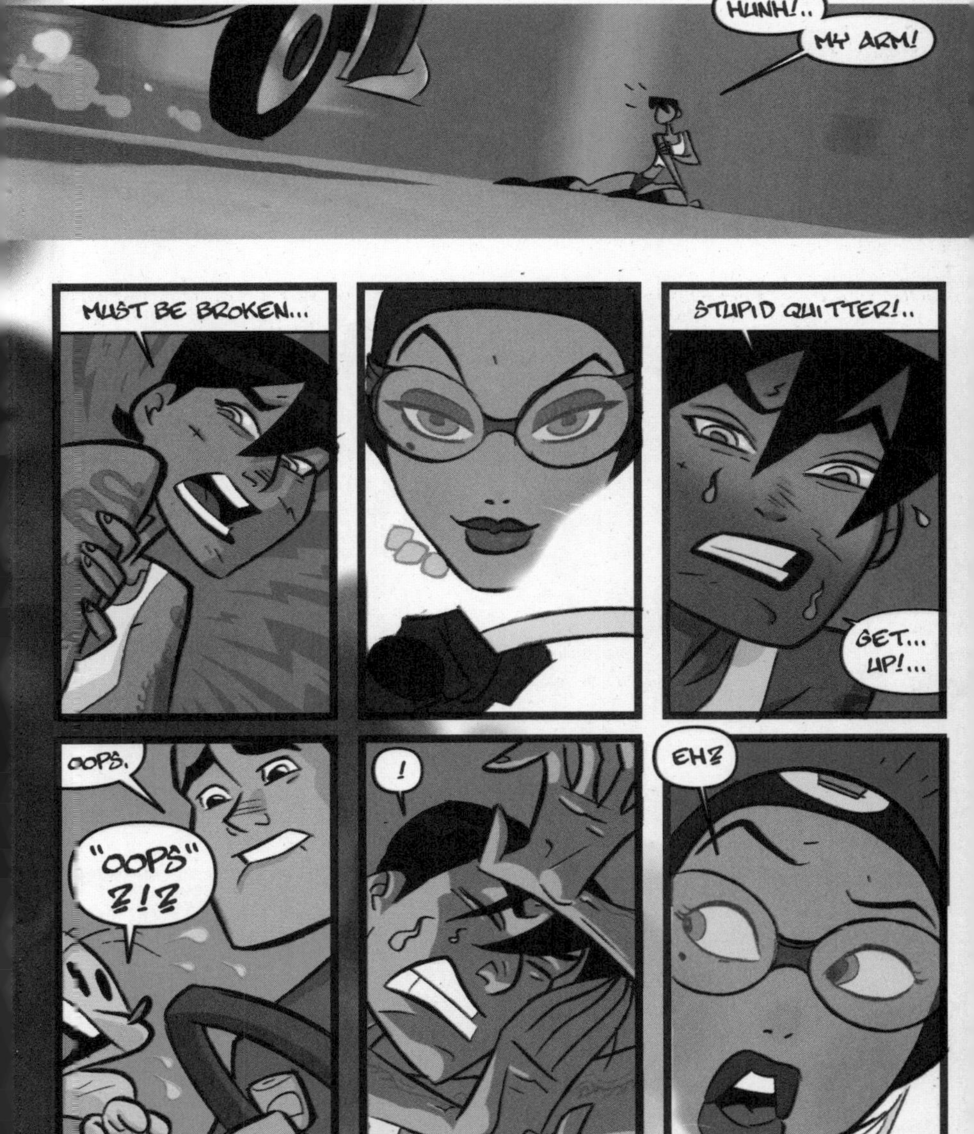
HUNH!..
MY ARM!
MUST BE BROKEN...
STUPID QUITTER!..
GET... UP!...
OOPS.
"OOPS" ?!?
!
EH?

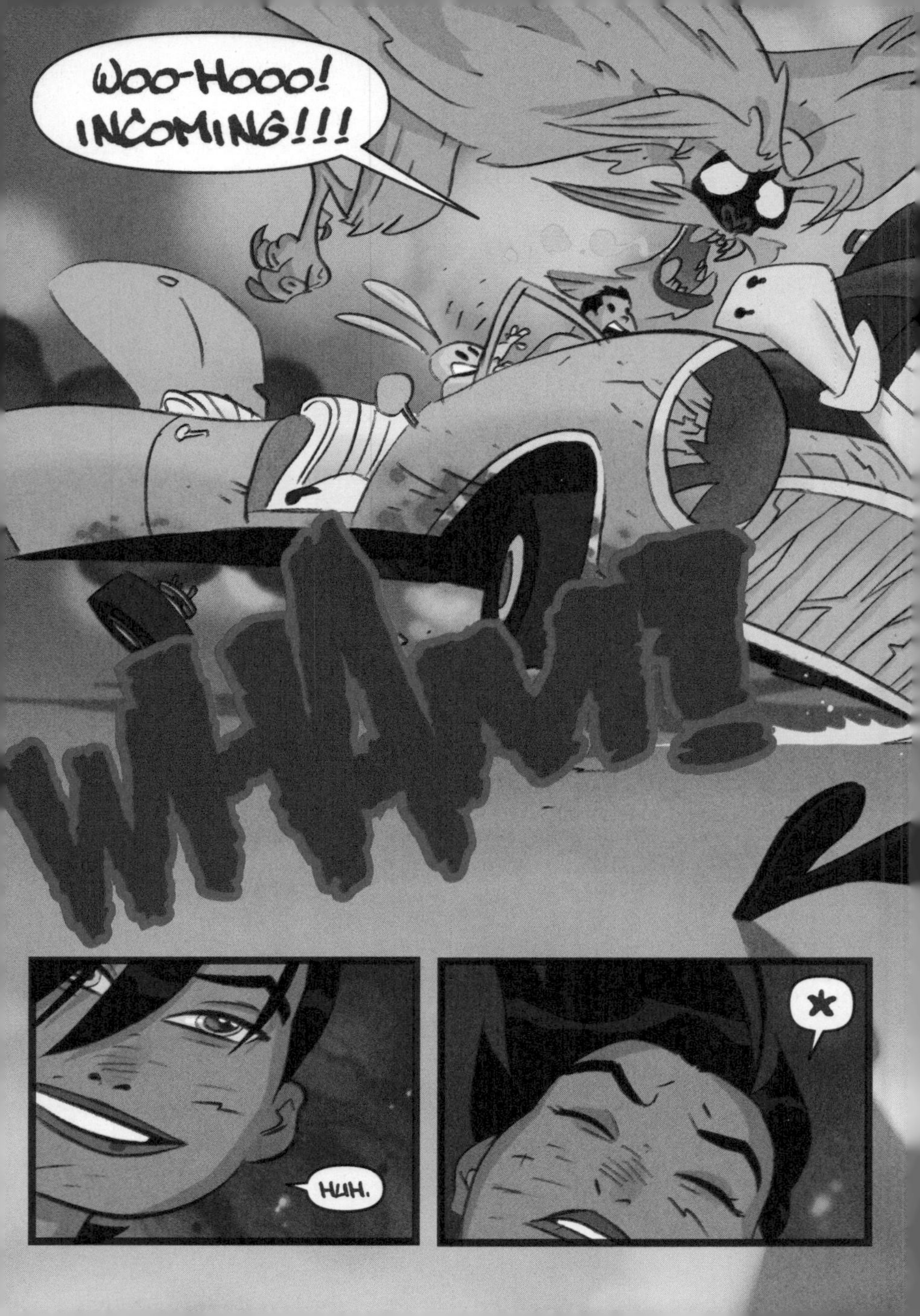
WOO-HOOO! INCOMING!!!!
WHAM!
HUH.
*

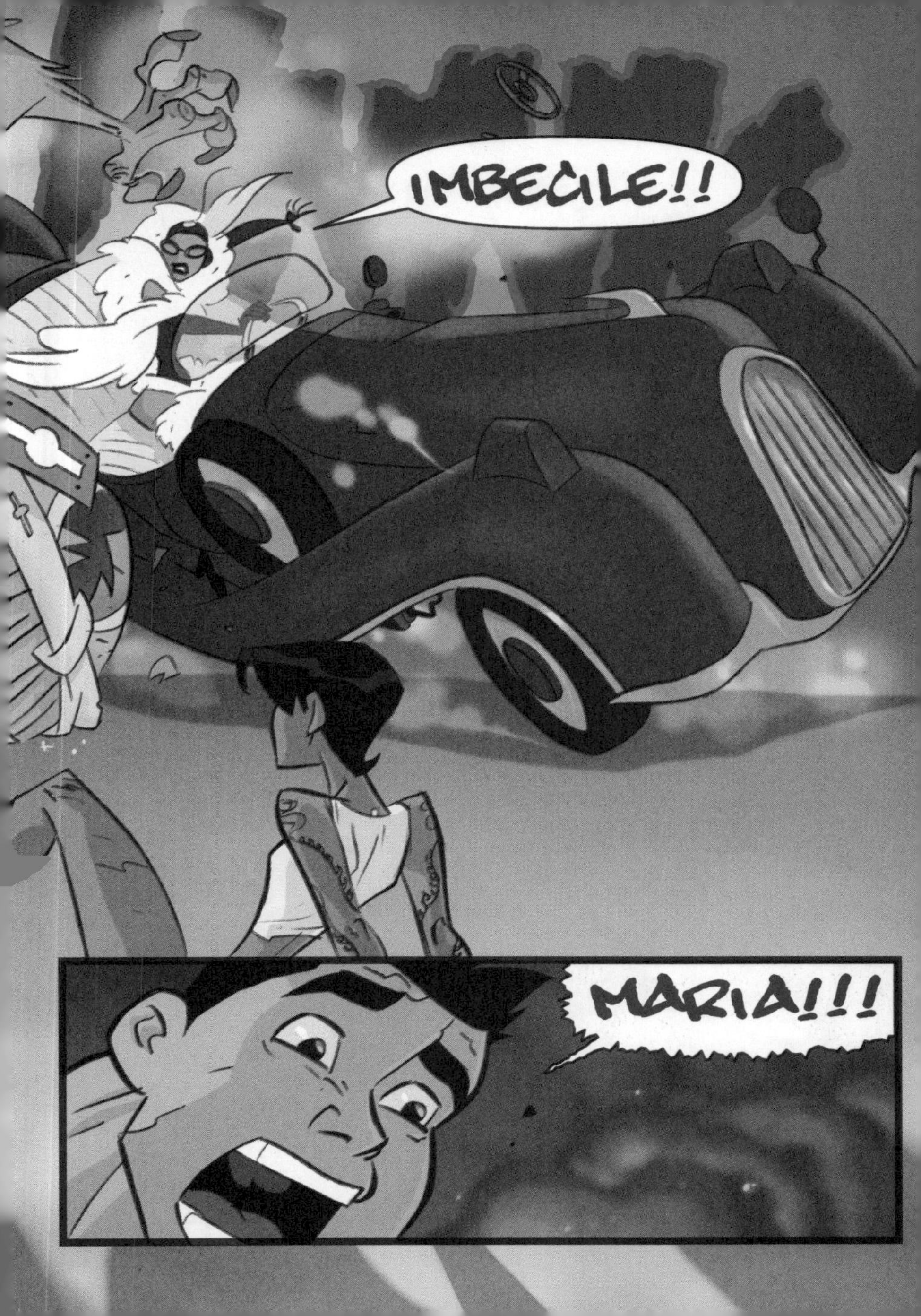
IMBECILE!!
MARIA!!!

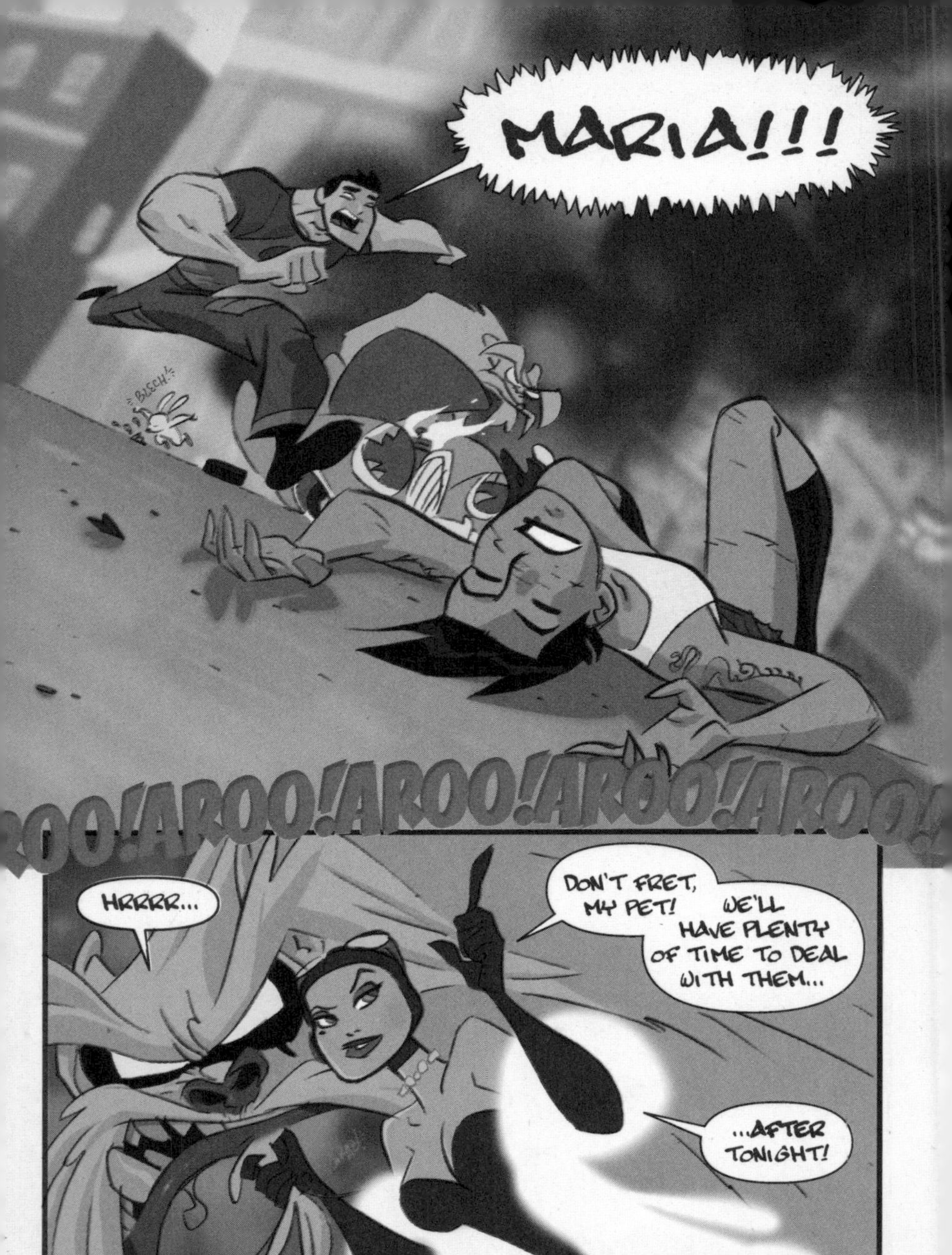
MARIA!!!
BISCH!
ROO! AROO! AROO! AROO! AROO!
HRRRR...
DON'T FRET, MY PET! WE'LL HAVE PLENTY OF TIME TO DEAL WITH THEM...
...AFTER TONIGHT!

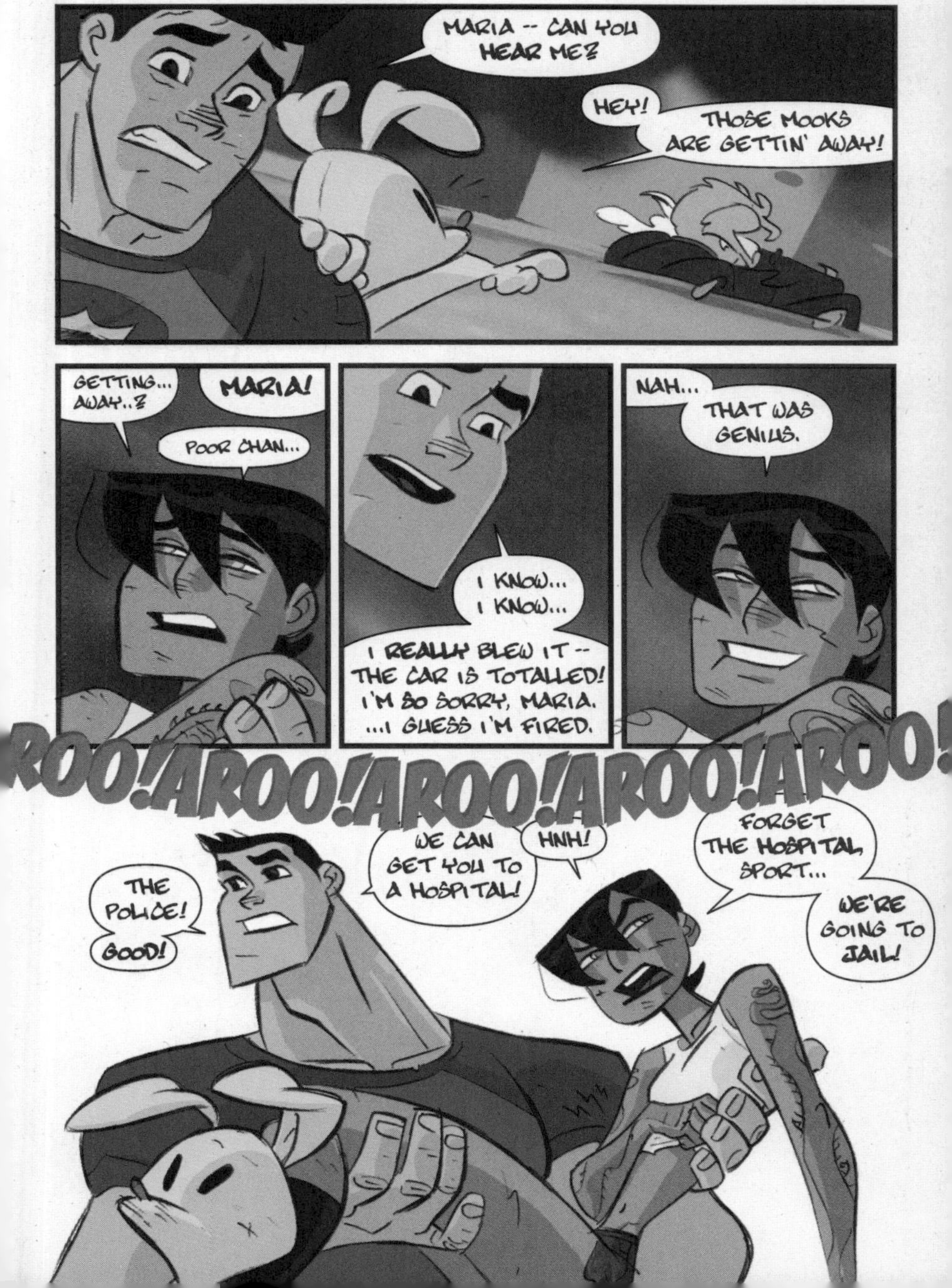
MARIA -- CAN YOU HEAR ME?
HEY!
THOSE MOOKS ARE GETTIN' AWAY!
GETTING... AWAY..?
MARIA!
POOR CHAN...
I KNOW... I KNOW...
I REALLY BLEW IT -- THE CAR IS TOTALLED! I'M SO SORRY, MARIA. ...I GUESS I'M FIRED.
NAH...
THAT WAS GENIUS.
ROO! AROO! AROO! AROO! AROO!
THE POLICE!
GOOD!
WE CAN GET YOU TO A HOSPITAL!
HNH!
FORGET THE HOSPITAL, SPORT...
WE'RE GOING TO JAIL!

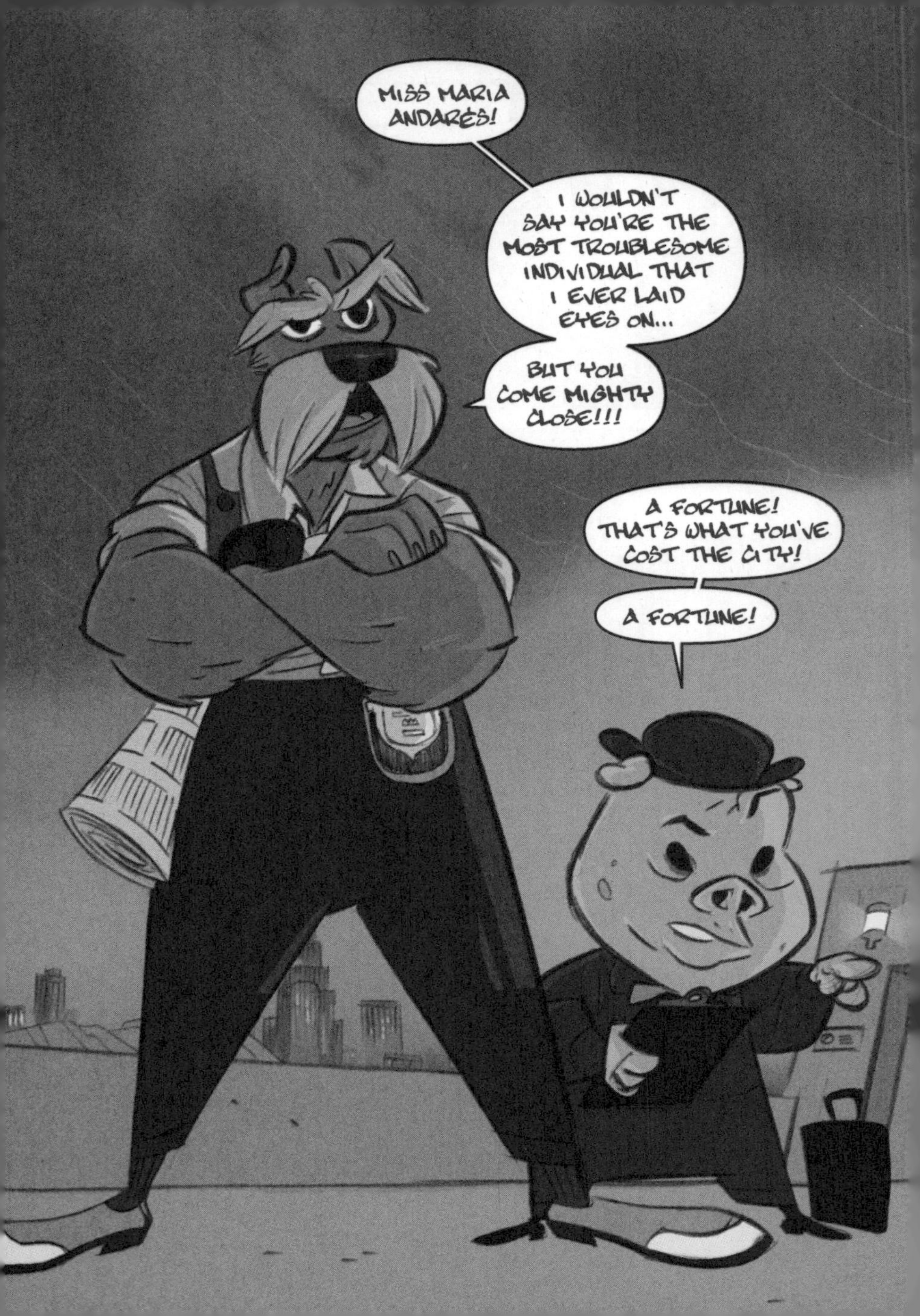
MISS MARIA ANDARÉS!
I WOULDN'T SAY YOU'RE THE MOST TROUBLESOME INDIVIDUAL THAT I EVER LAID EYES ON...
BUT YOU COME MIGHTY CLOSE!!!
A FORTUNE! THAT'S WHAT YOU'VE COST THE CITY!
A FORTUNE!

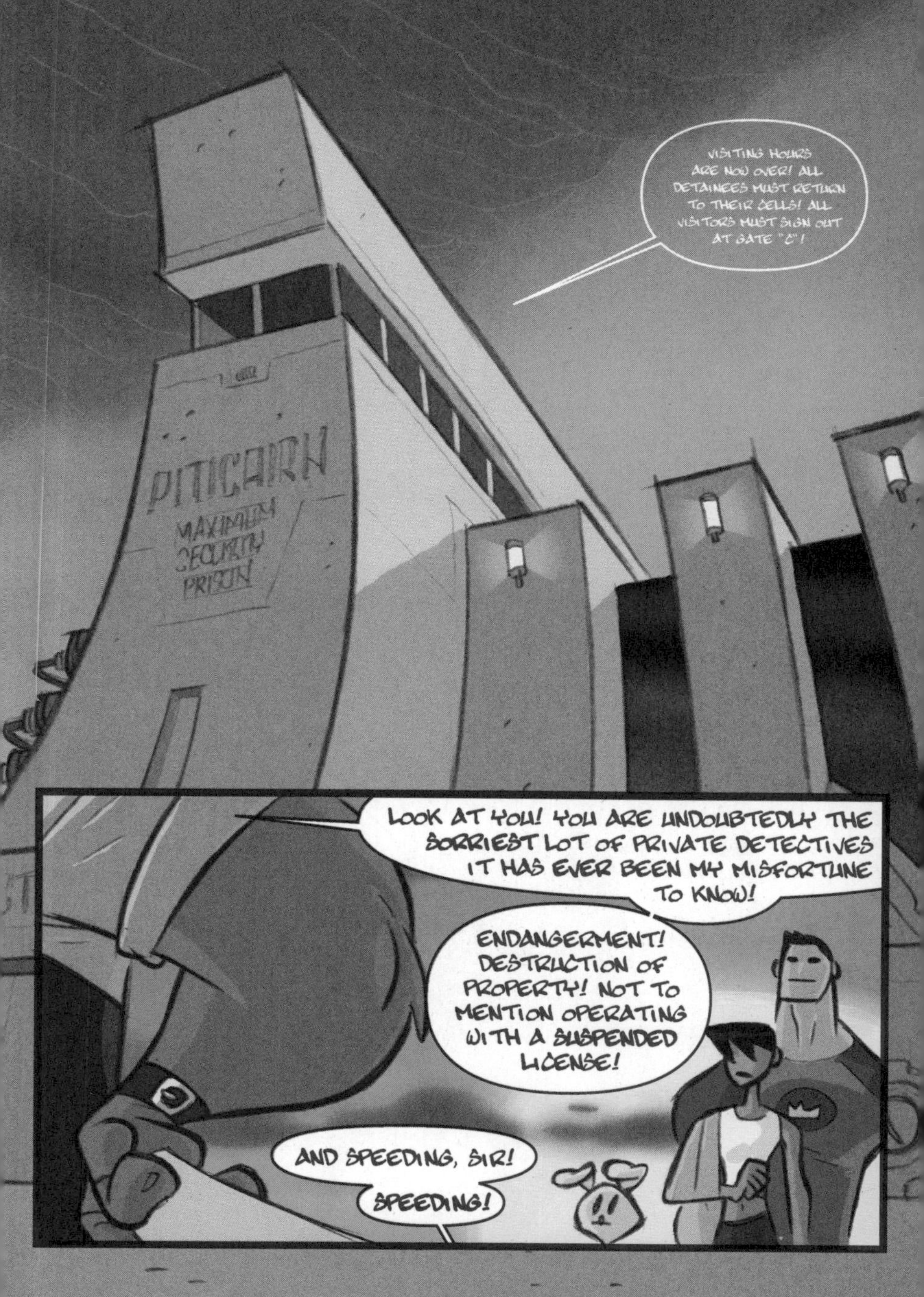
VISITING HOURS ARE NOW OVER! ALL DETAINEES MUST RETURN TO THEIR CELLS! ALL VISITORS MUST SIGN OUT AT GATE "C"!
PITCAIRN
MAXIMUM SECURITY PRISON
LOOK AT YOU! YOU ARE UNDOUBTEDLY THE SORRIEST LOT OF PRIVATE DETECTIVES IT HAS EVER BEEN MY MISFORTUNE TO KNOW!
ENDANGERMENT! DESTRUCTION OF PROPERTY! NOT TO MENTION OPERATING WITH A SUSPENDED LICENSE!
AND SPEEDING, SIR!
SPEEDING!

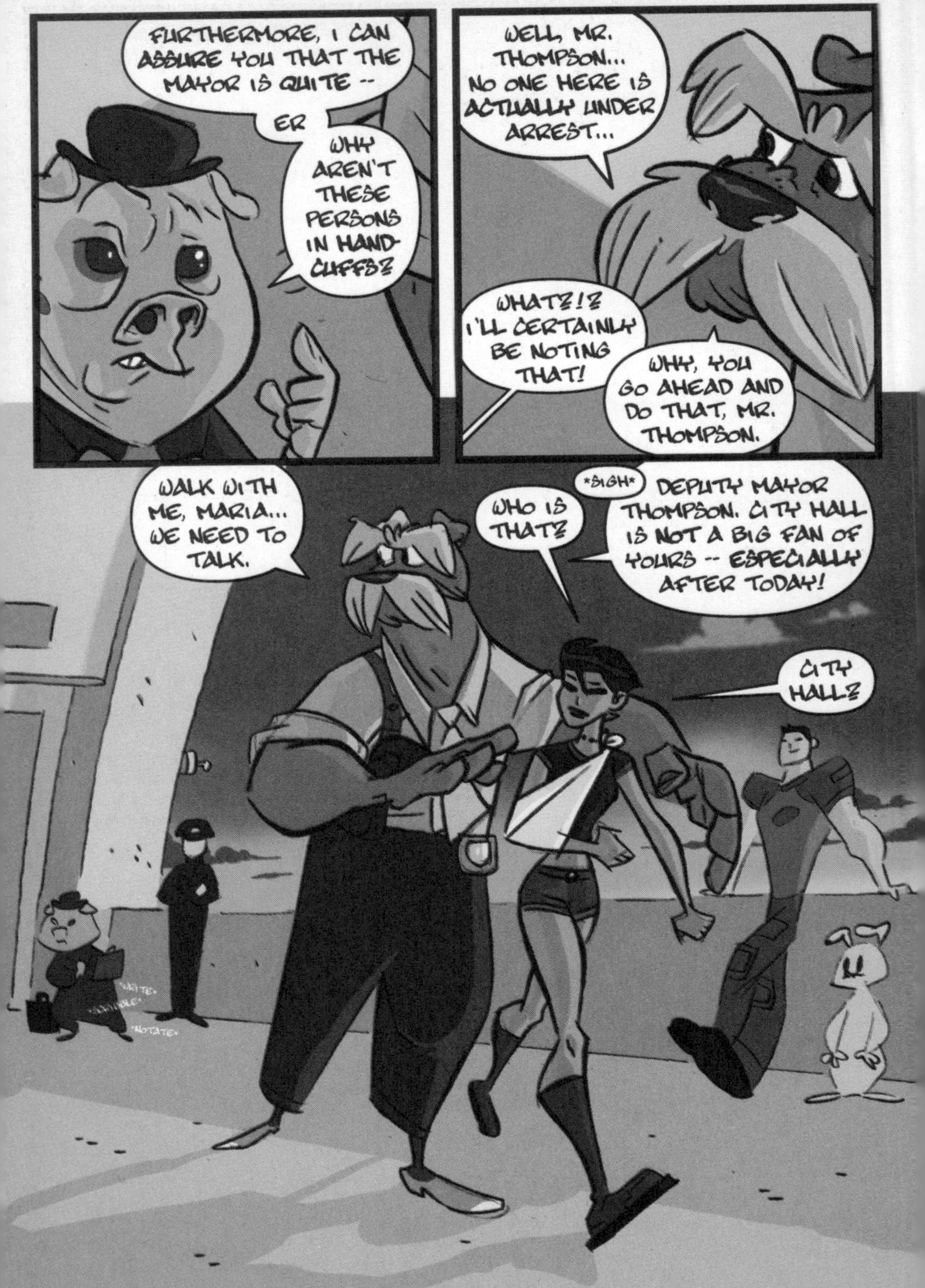
FURTHERMORE, I CAN ASSURE YOU THAT THE MAYOR IS QUITE --
ER
WHY AREN'T THESE PERSONS IN HAND-CUFFS?
WELL, MR. THOMPSON... NO ONE HERE IS ACTUALLY UNDER ARREST...
WHAT?!? I'LL CERTAINLY BE NOTING THAT!
WHY, YOU GO AHEAD AND DO THAT, MR. THOMPSON.
WALK WITH ME, MARIA... WE NEED TO TALK.
WHO IS THAT?
SIGH
DEPUTY MAYOR THOMPSON. CITY HALL IS NOT A BIG FAN OF YOURS -- ESPECIALLY AFTER TODAY!
CITY HALL?
WRITE
NOTATE

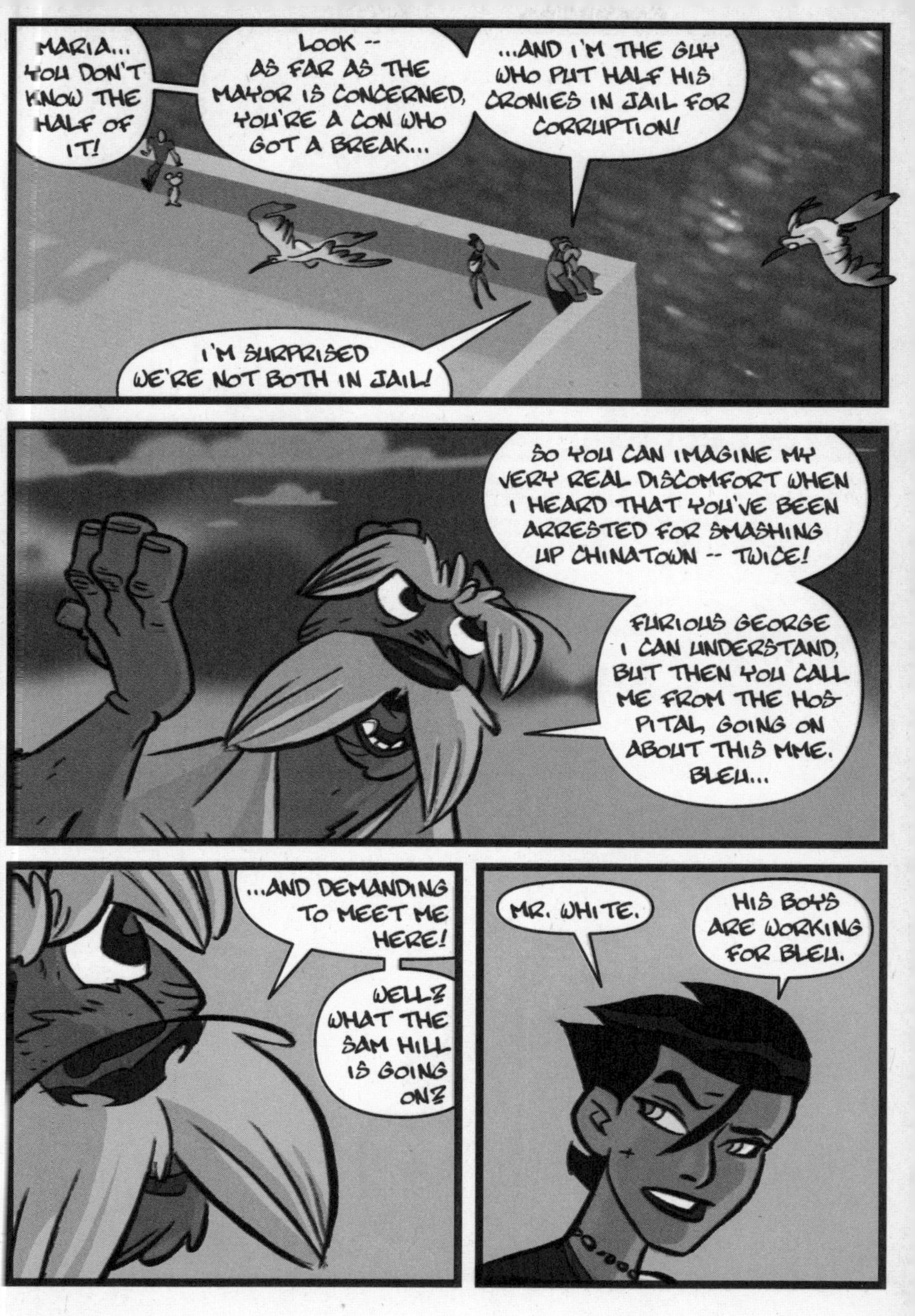
MARIA... YOU DON'T KNOW THE HALF OF IT!
LOOK -- AS FAR AS THE MAYOR IS CONCERNED, YOU'RE A CON WHO GOT A BREAK...
...AND I'M THE GUY WHO PUT HALF HIS CRONIES IN JAIL FOR CORRUPTION!
I'M SURPRISED WE'RE NOT BOTH IN JAIL!
SO YOU CAN IMAGINE MY VERY REAL DISCOMFORT WHEN I HEARD THAT YOU'VE BEEN ARRESTED FOR SMASHING UP CHINATOWN -- TWICE!
FURIOUS GEORGE I CAN UNDERSTAND, BUT THEN YOU CALL ME FROM THE HOS-PITAL, GOING ON ABOUT THIS MME. BLEU...
...AND DEMANDING TO MEET ME HERE!
WELL? WHAT THE SAM HILL IS GOING ON?
MR. WHITE.
HIS BOYS ARE WORKING FOR BLEU.

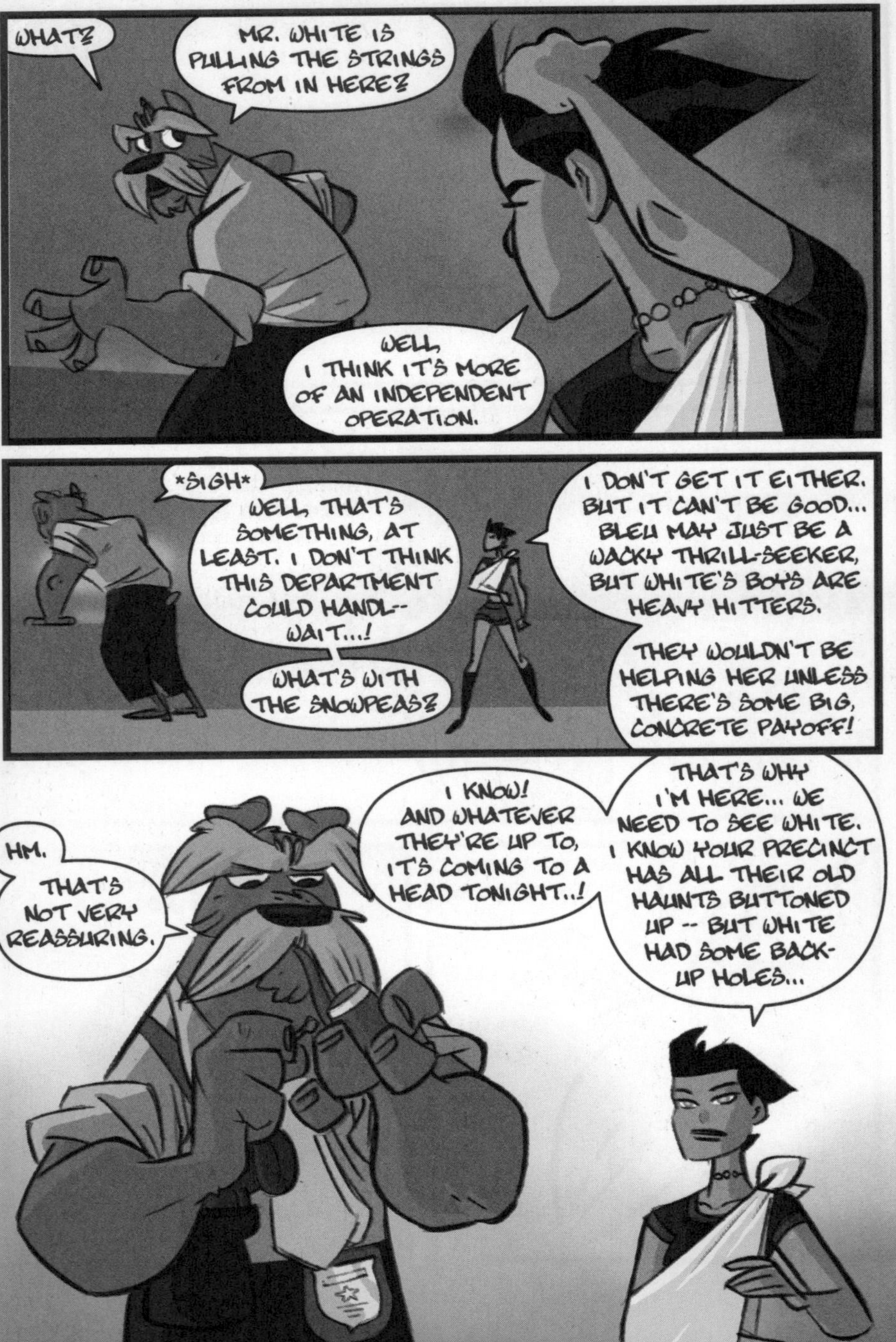
WHAT?
MR. WHITE IS PULLING THE STRINGS FROM IN HERE?
WELL, I THINK IT'S MORE OF AN INDEPENDENT OPERATION.
SIGH WELL, THAT'S SOMETHING, AT LEAST. I DON'T THINK THIS DEPARTMENT COULD HANDL-- WAIT...!
WHAT'S WITH THE SNOWPEAS?
I DON'T GET IT EITHER. BUT IT CAN'T BE GOOD... BLEU MAY JUST BE A WACKY THRILL-SEEKER, BUT WHITE'S BOYS ARE HEAVY HITTERS.
THEY WOULDN'T BE HELPING HER UNLESS THERE'S SOME BIG, CONCRETE PAYOFF!
HM. THAT'S NOT VERY REASSURING.
I KNOW! AND WHATEVER THEY'RE UP TO, IT'S COMING TO A HEAD TONIGHT..!
THAT'S WHY I'M HERE... WE NEED TO SEE WHITE. I KNOW YOUR PRECINCT HAS ALL THEIR OLD HAUNTS BUTTONED UP -- BUT WHITE HAD SOME BACK-UP HOLES...

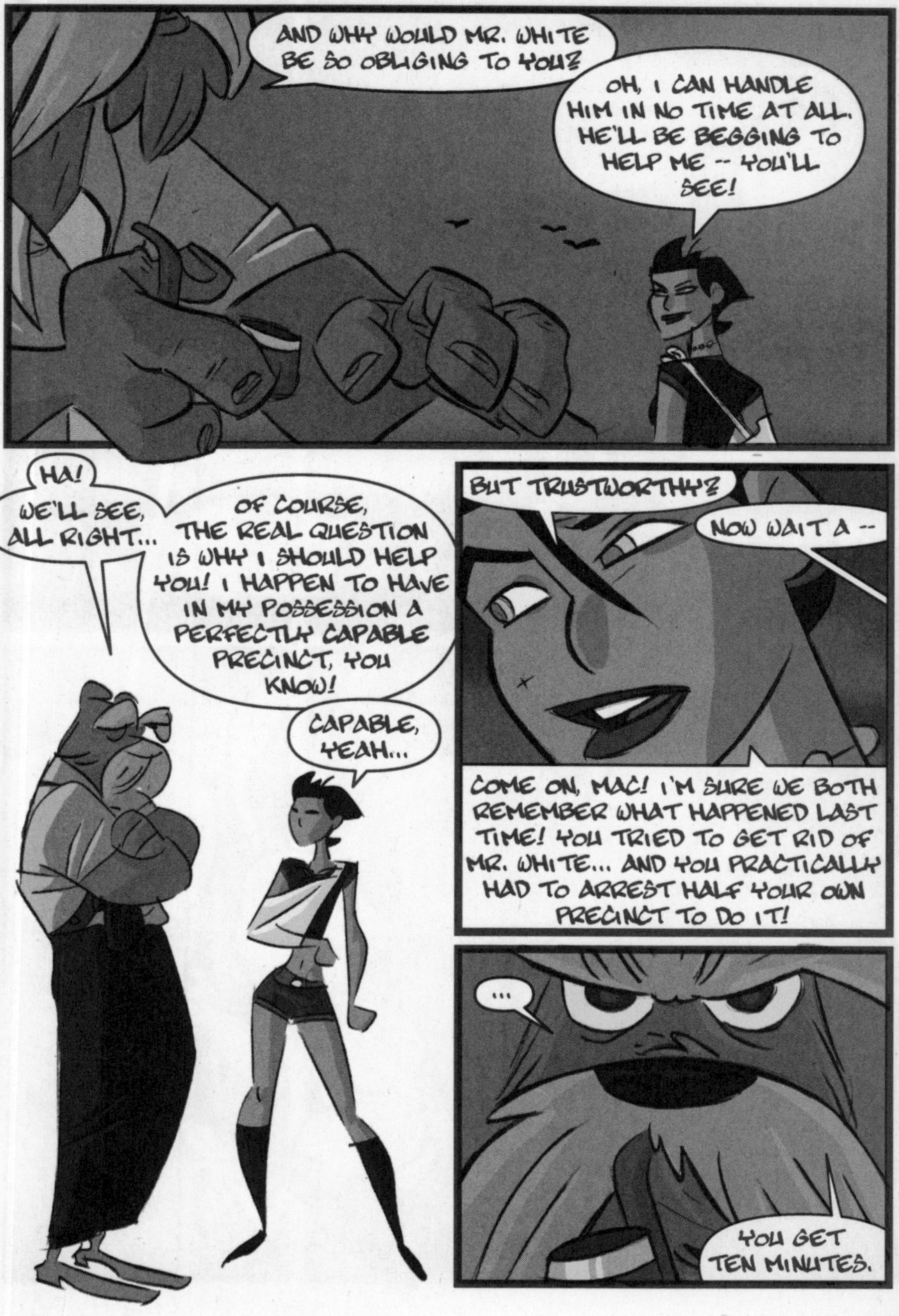

AND WHY WOULD MR. WHITE BE SO OBLIGING TO YOU?
OH, I CAN HANDLE HIM IN NO TIME AT ALL. HE'LL BE BEGGING TO HELP ME -- YOU'LL SEE!
HA!
WE'LL SEE, ALL RIGHT...
OF COURSE, THE REAL QUESTION IS WHY I SHOULD HELP YOU! I HAPPEN TO HAVE IN MY POSSESSION A PERFECTLY CAPABLE PRECINCT, YOU KNOW!
CAPABLE, YEAH...
BUT TRUSTWORTHY?
NOW WAIT A --
COME ON, MAC! I'M SURE WE BOTH REMEMBER WHAT HAPPENED LAST TIME! YOU TRIED TO GET RID OF MR. WHITE... AND YOU PRACTICALLY HAD TO ARREST HALF YOUR OWN PRECINCT TO DO IT!
...
YOU GET TEN MINUTES.

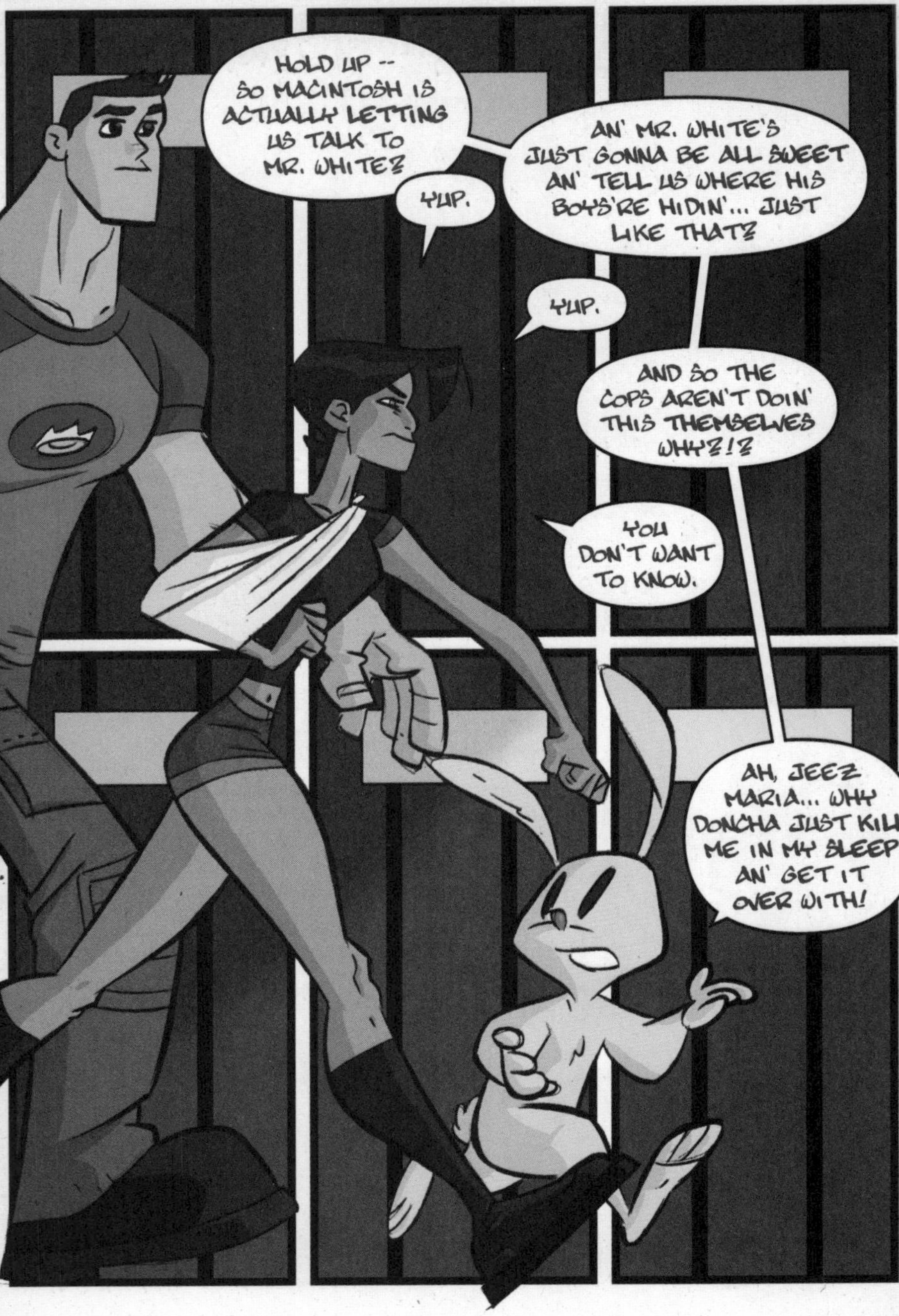
HOLD UP -- SO MACINTOSH IS ACTUALLY LETTING US TALK TO MR. WHITE?
YUP.
AN' MR. WHITE'S JUST GONNA BE ALL SWEET AN' TELL US WHERE HIS BOYS'RE HIDIN'... JUST LIKE THAT?
YUP.
AND SO THE COPS AREN'T DOIN' THIS THEMSELVES WHY?!?
YOU DON'T WANT TO KNOW.
AH, JEEZ MARIA... WHY DONCHA JUST KILL ME IN MY SLEEP AN' GET IT OVER WITH!

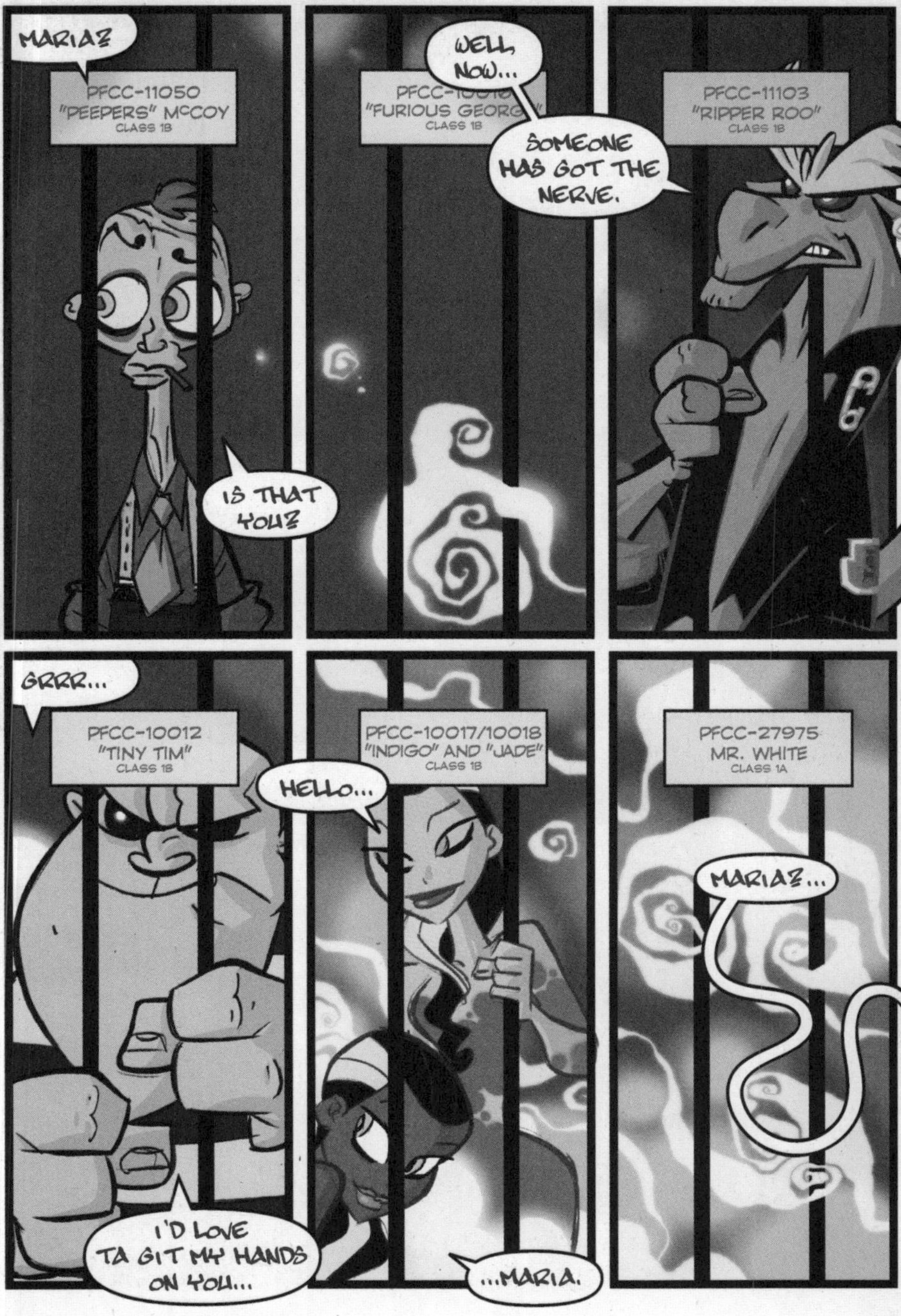
MARIA?
PFCC-11050 "PEEPERS" McCOY CLASS 1B
IS THAT YOU?
WELL, NOW...
SOMEONE HAS GOT THE NERVE.
"FURIOUS GEORG" CLASS 1B
PFCC-11103 "RIPPER ROO" CLASS 1B
GRRR...
PFCC-10012 "TINY TIM" CLASS 1B
I'D LOVE TA GIT MY HANDS ON YOU...
PFCC-10017/10018 "INDIGO" AND "JADE" CLASS 1B
HELLO...
...MARIA.
PFCC-27975 MR. WHITE CLASS 1A
MARIA?...

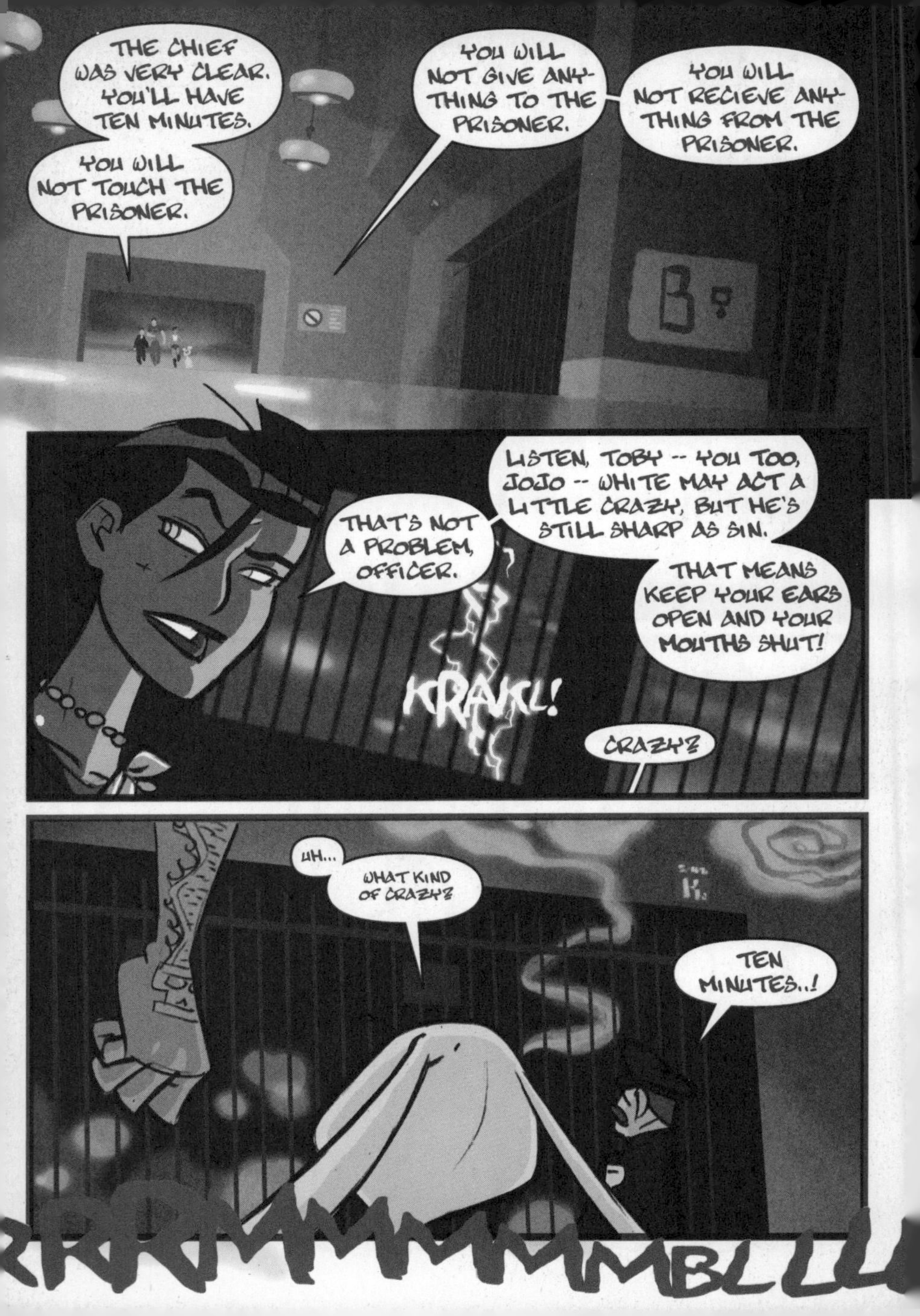

THE CHIEF WAS VERY CLEAR. YOU'LL HAVE TEN MINUTES.
YOU WILL NOT TOUCH THE PRISONER.
YOU WILL NOT GIVE ANY-THING TO THE PRISONER.
YOU WILL NOT RECIEVE ANY-THING FROM THE PRISONER.
LISTEN, TOBY -- YOU TOO, JOJO -- WHITE MAY ACT A LITTLE CRAZY, BUT HE'S STILL SHARP AS SIN.
THAT'S NOT A PROBLEM, OFFICER.
THAT MEANS KEEP YOUR EARS OPEN AND YOUR MOUTHS SHUT!
KRAKL!
CRAZY?
UH...
WHAT KIND OF CRAZY?
TEN MINUTES..!
RRRMMMMMMBLLL

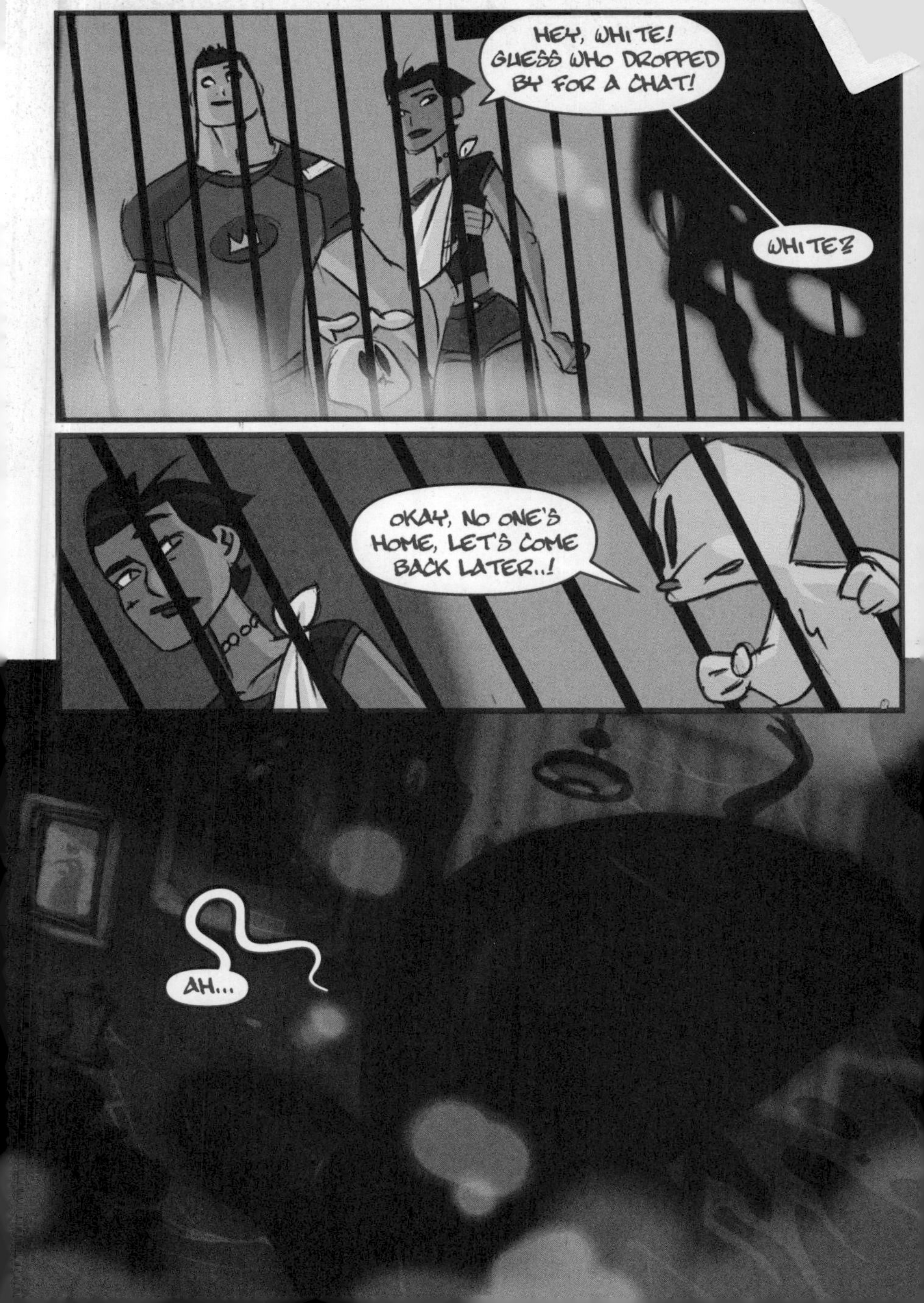
HEY, WHITE!
GUESS WHO DROPPED BY FOR A CHAT!
WHITE?
OKAY, NO ONE'S HOME, LET'S COME BACK LATER..!
AH...

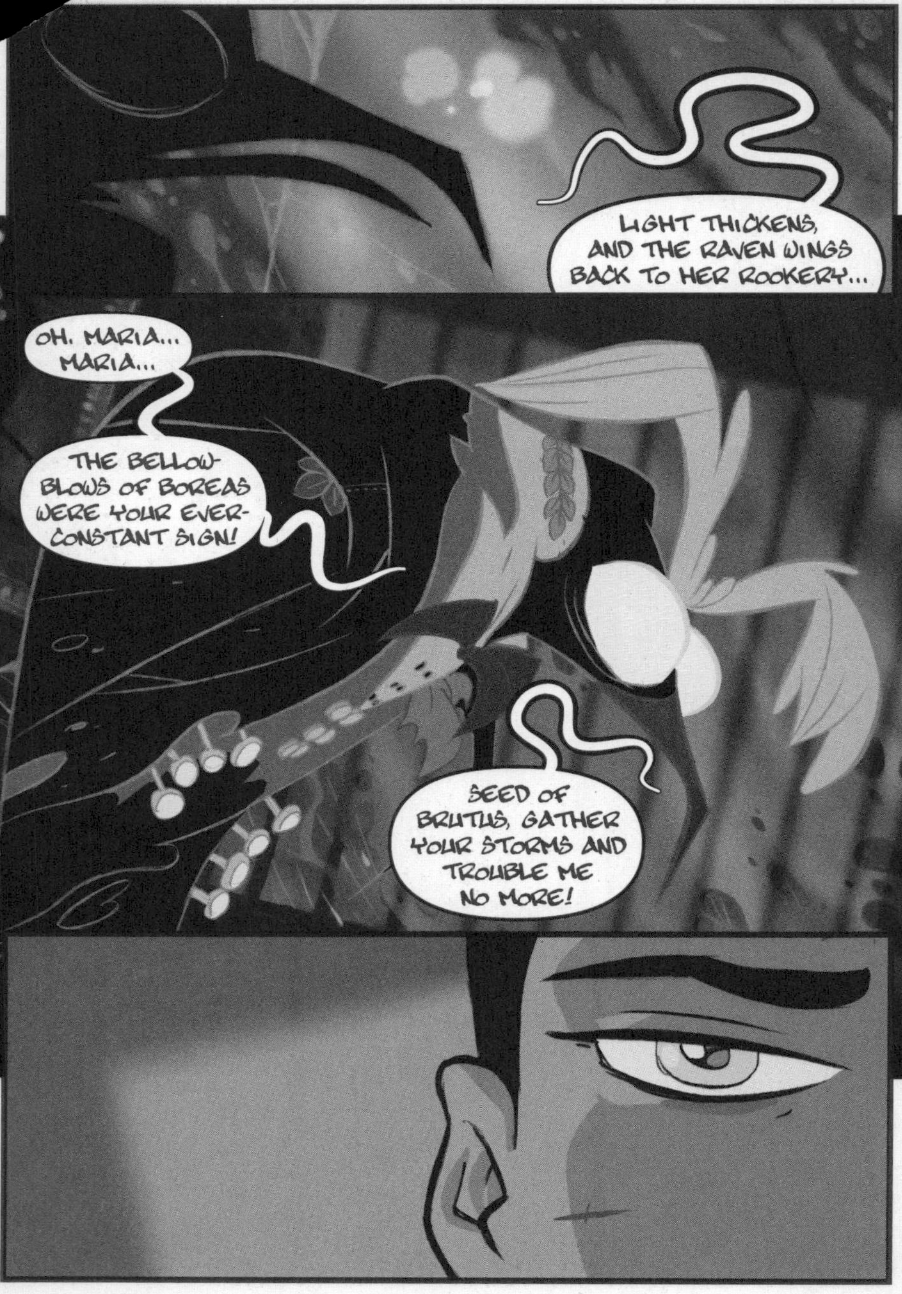
LIGHT THICKENS, AND THE RAVEN WINGS BACK TO HER ROOKERY...
OH, MARIA... MARIA...
THE BELLOW-BLOWS OF BOREAS WERE YOUR EVER-CONSTANT SIGN!
SEED OF BRUTUS, GATHER YOUR STORMS AND TROUBLE ME NO MORE!

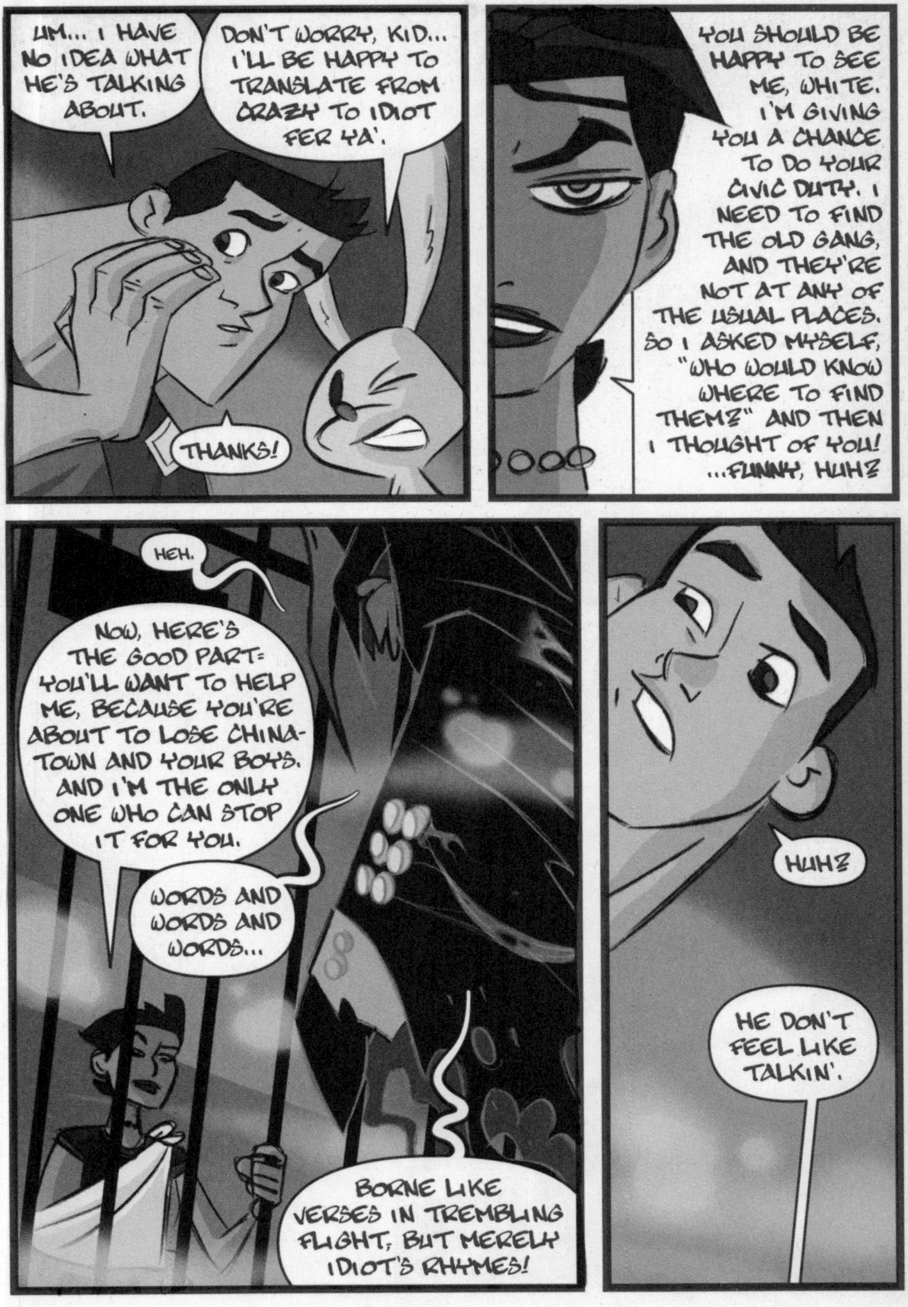
UM... I HAVE NO IDEA WHAT HE'S TALKING ABOUT.
DON'T WORRY, KID... I'LL BE HAPPY TO TRANSLATE FROM CRAZY TO IDIOT FER YA'.
THANKS!
YOU SHOULD BE HAPPY TO SEE ME, WHITE. I'M GIVING YOU A CHANCE TO DO YOUR CIVIC DUTY. I NEED TO FIND THE OLD GANG, AND THEY'RE NOT AT ANY OF THE USUAL PLACES. SO I ASKED MYSELF, "WHO WOULD KNOW WHERE TO FIND THEM?" AND THEN I THOUGHT OF YOU! ...FUNNY, HUH?
HEH.
NOW, HERE'S THE GOOD PART: YOU'LL WANT TO HELP ME, BECAUSE YOU'RE ABOUT TO LOSE CHINA-TOWN AND YOUR BOYS. AND I'M THE ONLY ONE WHO CAN STOP IT FOR YOU.
WORDS AND WORDS AND WORDS...
BORNE LIKE VERSES IN TREMBLING FLIGHT, BUT MERELY IDIOT'S RHYMES!
HUH?
HE DON'T FEEL LIKE TALKIN'.

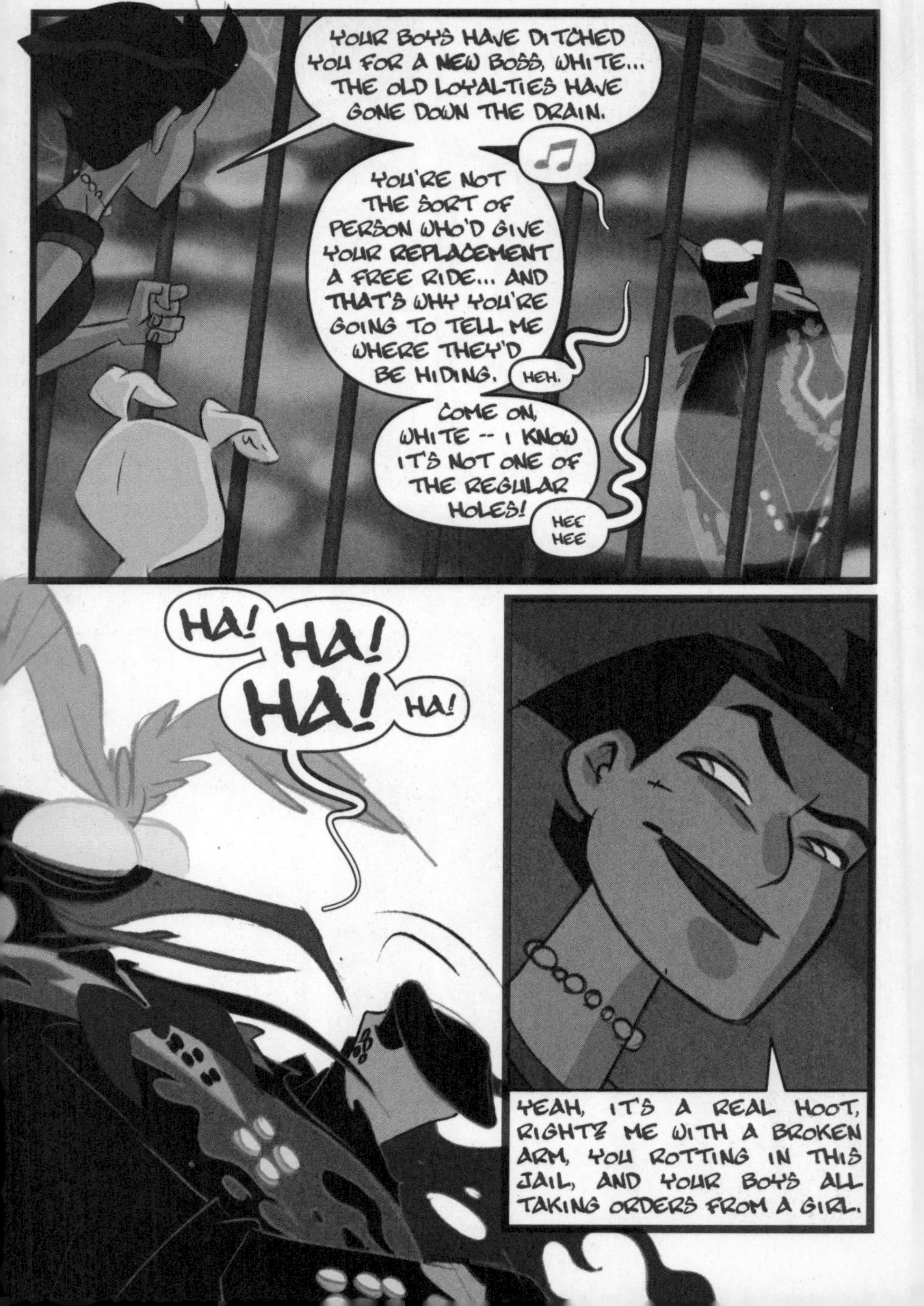
YOUR BOYS HAVE DITCHED YOU FOR A NEW BOSS, WHITE... THE OLD LOYALTIES HAVE GONE DOWN THE DRAIN.
♫
YOU'RE NOT THE SORT OF PERSON WHO'D GIVE YOUR REPLACEMENT A FREE RIDE... AND THAT'S WHY YOU'RE GOING TO TELL ME WHERE THEY'D BE HIDING.
HEH.
COME ON, WHITE -- I KNOW IT'S NOT ONE OF THE REGULAR HOLES!
HEE HEE
HA! HA! HA! HA!
YEAH, IT'S A REAL HOOT, RIGHT? ME WITH A BROKEN ARM, YOU ROTTING IN THIS JAIL, AND YOUR BOYS ALL TAKING ORDERS FROM A GIRL.

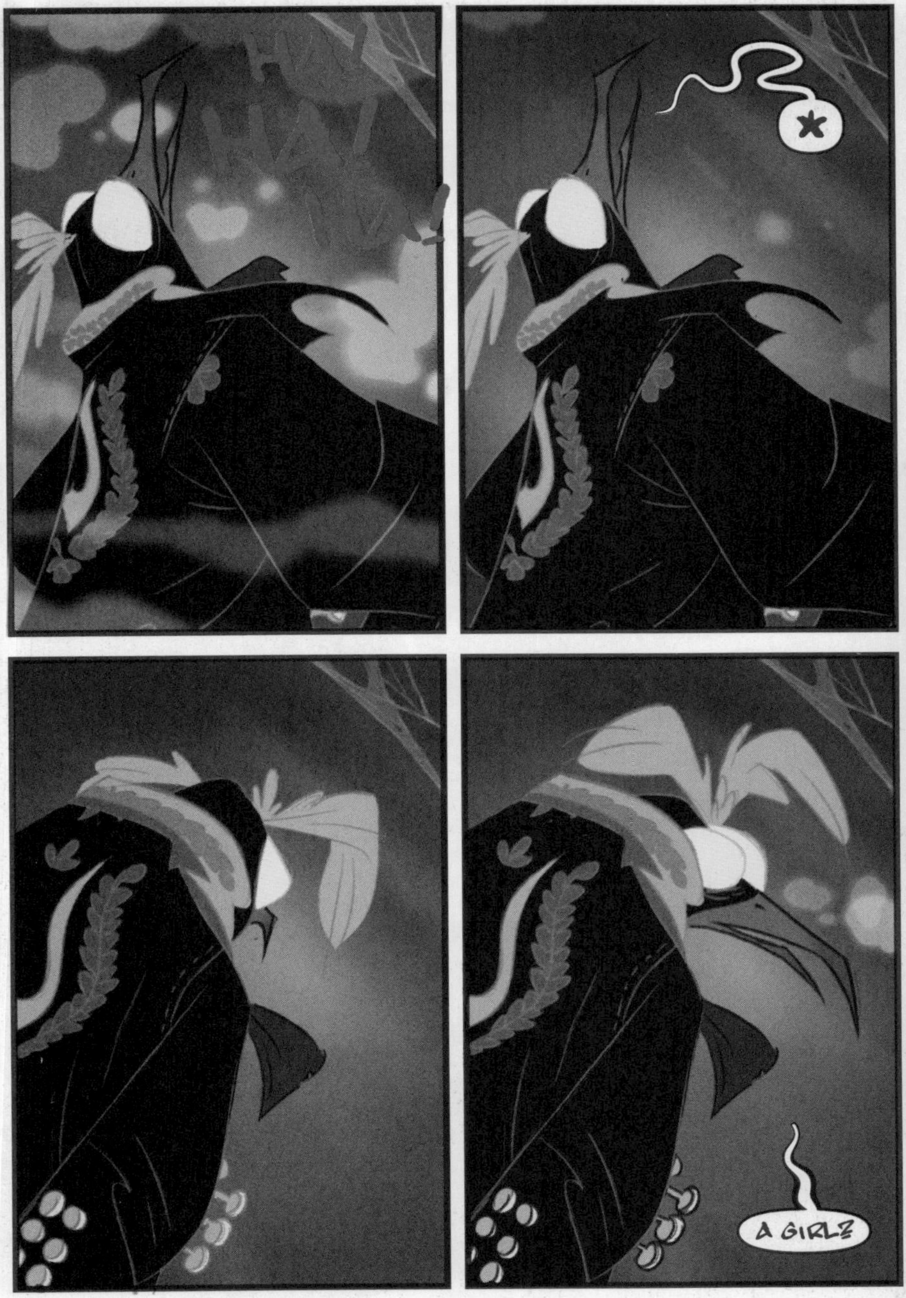
HA! HA! HA!
*
A GIRL?

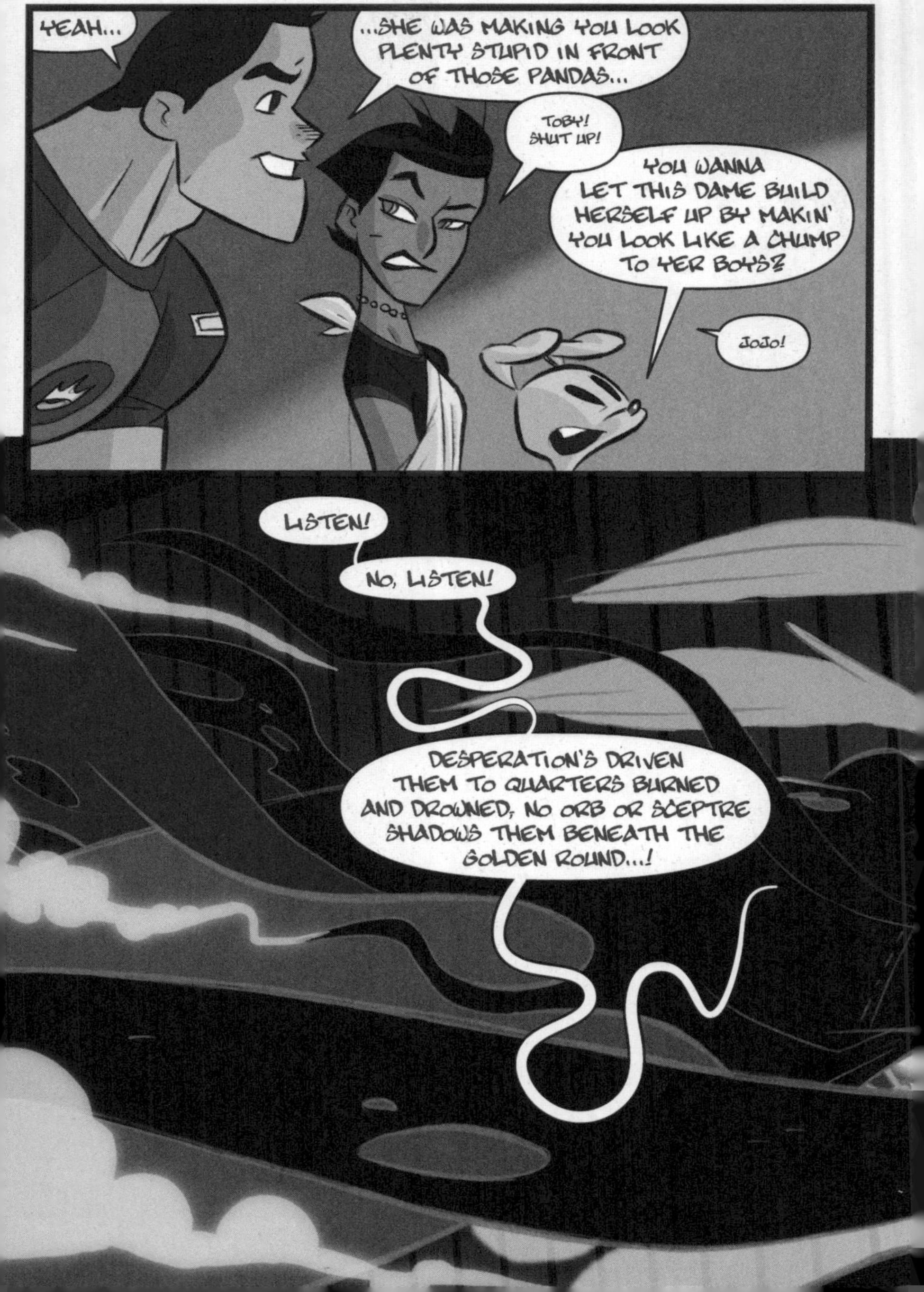
YEAH...
...SHE WAS MAKING YOU LOOK PLENTY STUPID IN FRONT OF THOSE PANDAS...
TOBY! SHUT UP!
YOU WANNA LET THIS DAME BUILD HERSELF UP BY MAKIN' YOU LOOK LIKE A CHUMP TO YER BOYS?!
JOJO!
LISTEN!
NO, LISTEN!
DESPERATION'S DRIVEN THEM TO QUARTERS BURNED AND DROWNED; NO ORB OR SCEPTRE SHADOWS THEM BENEATH THE GOLDEN ROUND...!

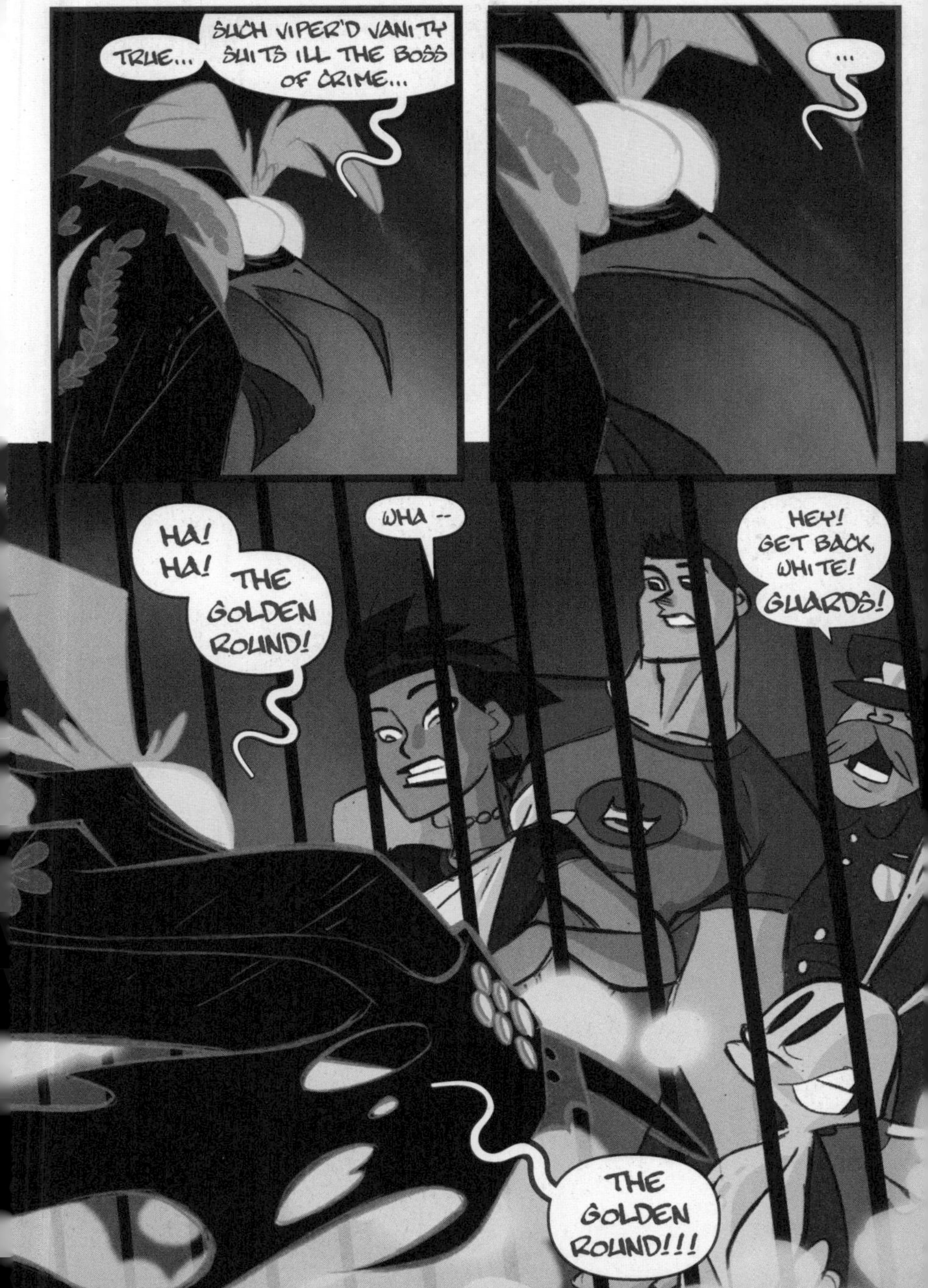
TRUE...
SUCH VIPER'D VANITY SUITS ILL THE BOSS OF CRIME...
...
HA! HA! THE GOLDEN ROUND!
WHA --
HEY! GET BACK, WHITE! GUARDS!
THE GOLDEN ROUND!!!

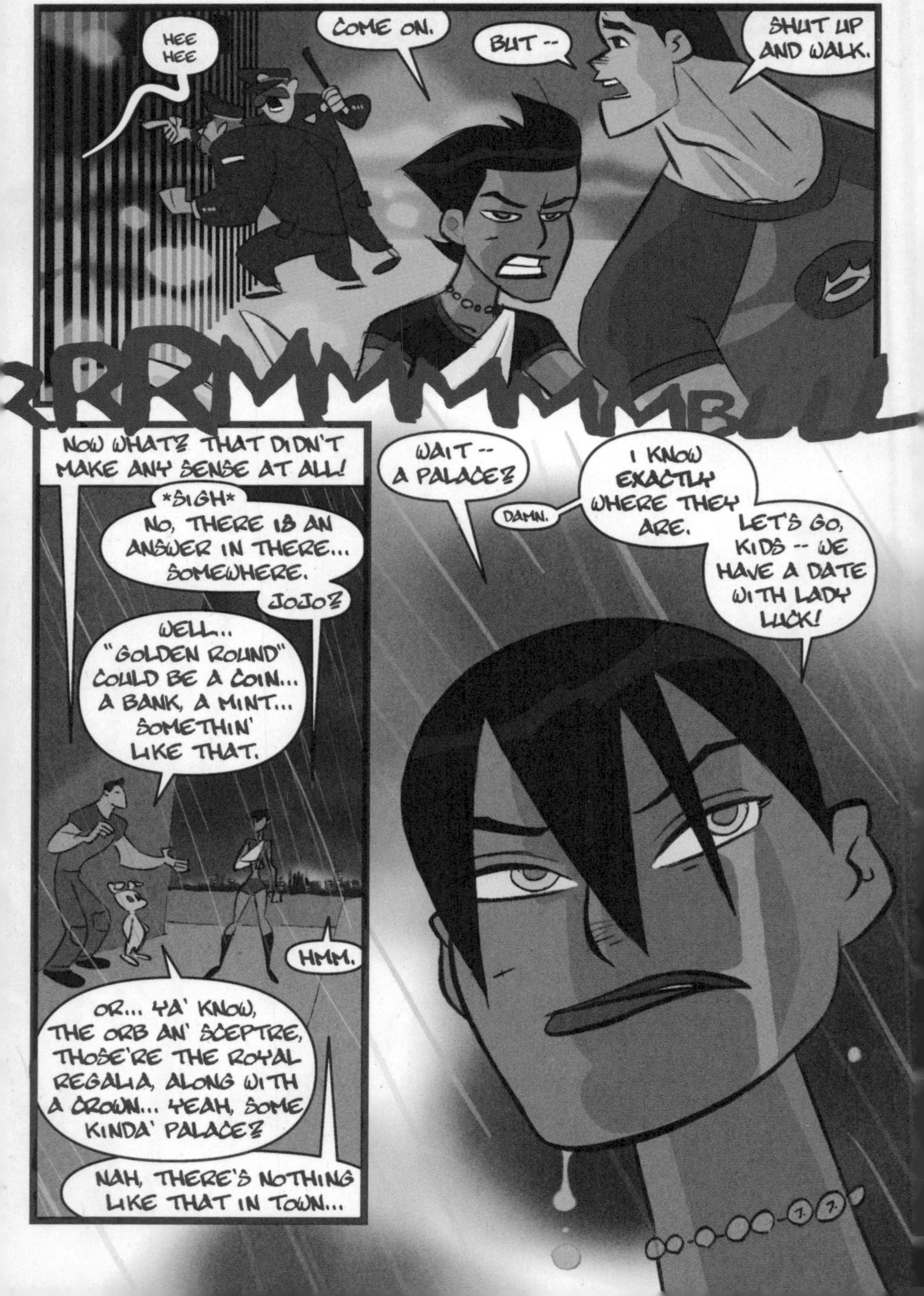
HEE HEE
COME ON.
BUT --
SHUT UP AND WALK.
RRRMMMMMMBLLL
NOW WHAT? THAT DIDN'T MAKE ANY SENSE AT ALL!
SIGH NO, THERE IS AN ANSWER IN THERE... SOMEWHERE.
JOJO?
WELL... "GOLDEN ROUND" COULD BE A COIN... A BANK, A MINT... SOMETHIN' LIKE THAT.
HMM.
OR... YA' KNOW, THE ORB AN' SCEPTRE, THOSE'RE THE ROYAL REGALIA, ALONG WITH A CROWN... YEAH, SOME KINDA' PALACE?
NAH, THERE'S NOTHING LIKE THAT IN TOWN...
WAIT -- A PALACE?
DAMN.
I KNOW EXACTLY WHERE THEY ARE.
LET'S GO, KIDS -- WE HAVE A DATE WITH LADY LUCK!

NEXT ISSUE...

THE DARE DETECTIVES FACE BLEU'S GANG AND RECEIVE "THE ROYALE TREATMENT"!

WHAT..? YOU GOT A BETTER TITLE? YEAH, I DIDN'T THINK SO.

ANYWAY... I HOPE YOU HAD AS MUCH FUN READING THIS ISSUE AS I DID CREATING IT! I'VE DRAWN ALL SORTS OF CHARACTERS AND STORIES BEFORE, BUT THIS IS THE FIRST TIME I'VE CREATED SOMETHING FROM SCRATCH.

IN THE PROCESS, A LOT OF MATERIAL WAS CHANGED OR DELETED, ESPECIALLY TO FIT THIS STORY INTO TWO ISSUES. HERE ARE SOME OF MY INITIAL CONCEPT SKETCHES, ALONG WITH DESIGNS FOR ENDERBY CITY'S CHINATOWN.

ENJOY!

AN EARLIER VERSION OF UNCLE CHAN, FIDDLING WITH HIS RADIO.

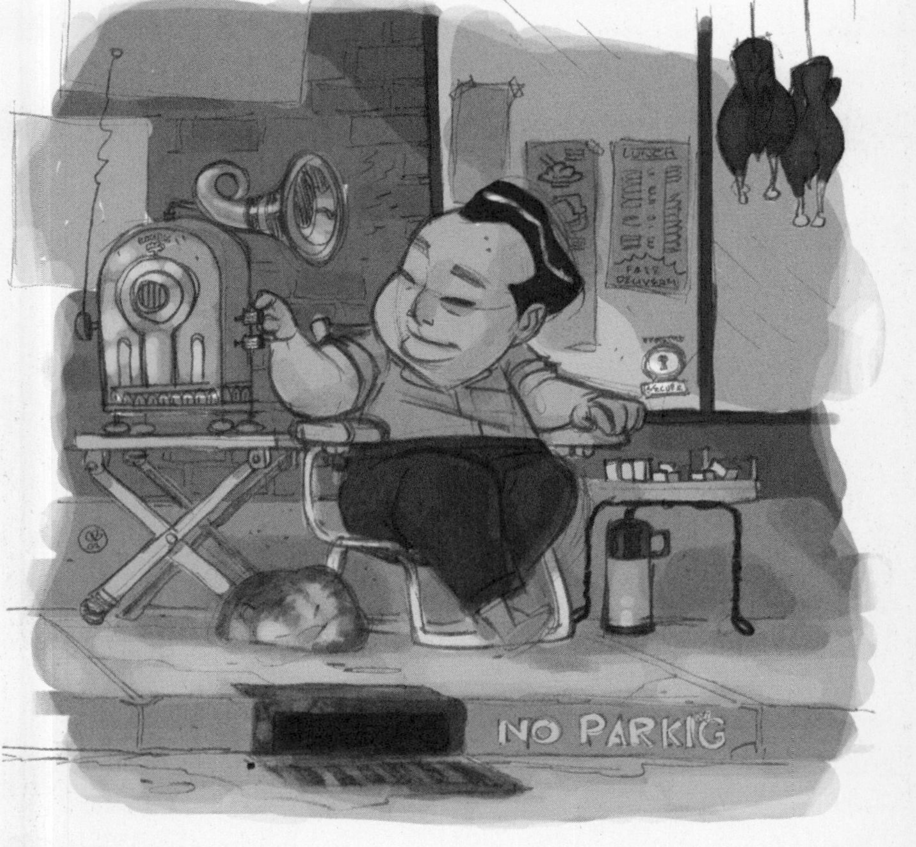
NO PARKIG

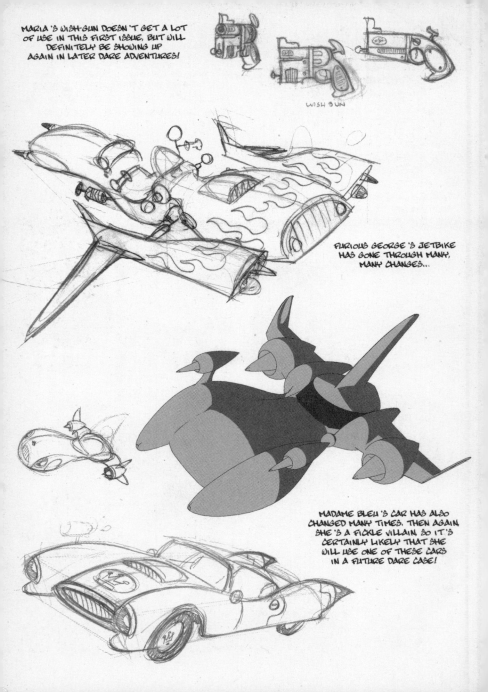

MARIA'S WISH-GUN DOESN'T GET A LOT OF USE IN THIS FIRST ISSUE, BUT WILL DEFINITELY BE SHOWING UP AGAIN IN LATER DARE ADVENTURES!

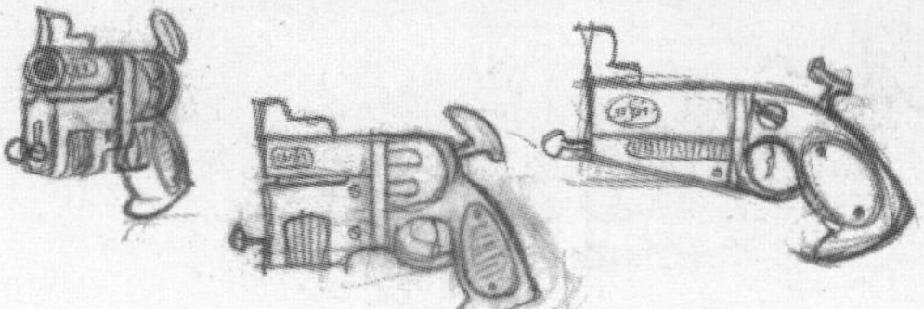

WISH GUN

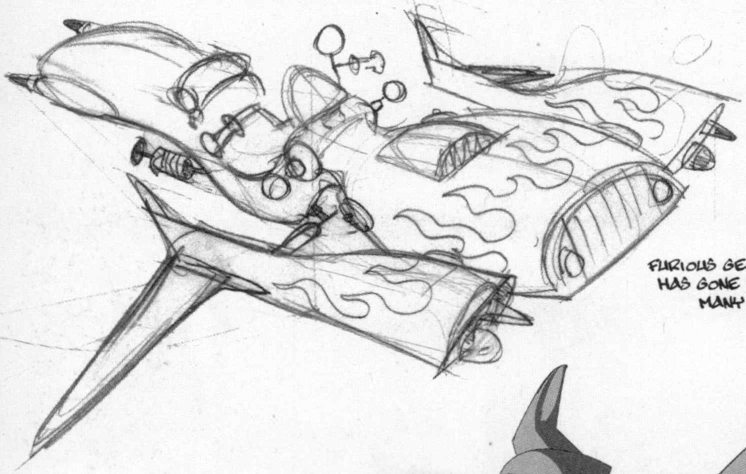

FURIOUS GEORGE'S JETBIKE HAS GONE THROUGH MANY, MANY CHANGES...

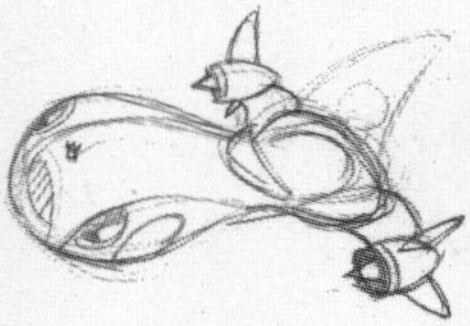

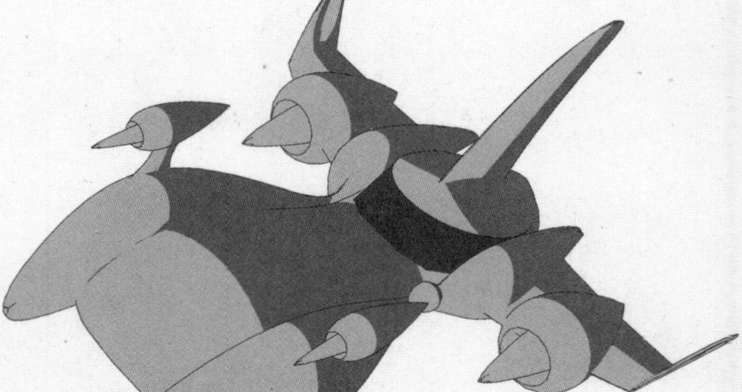

MADAME BLEU'S CAR HAS ALSO CHANGED MANY TIMES. THEN AGAIN, SHE'S A FICKLE VILLAIN, SO IT'S CERTAINLY LIKELY THAT SHE WILL USE ONE OF THESE CARS IN A FUTURE DARE CASE!

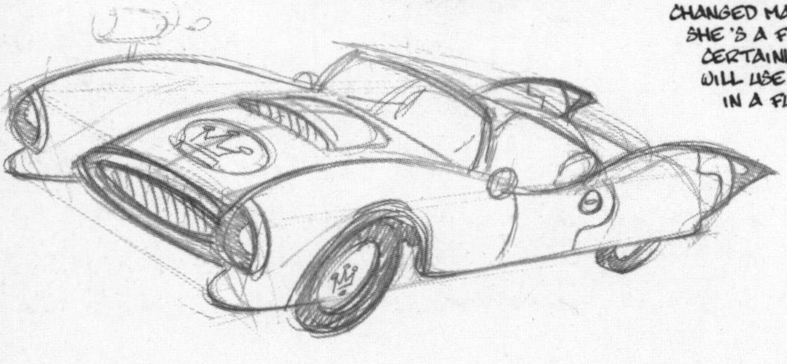

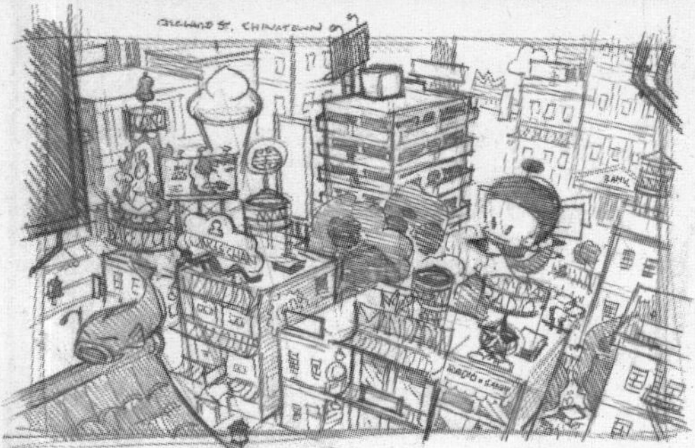
ORCHARD ST. CHINATOWN

(LEFT) SOMETIMES I DO TEENY TINY SKETCHES TO WORK OUT THE BASIC "LOOK" OF A SCENE OR PROP. HERE IS A THUMBNAIL OF CHINATOWN'S ORCHARD STREET, WHERE THE DARE DETECTIVES LIVE.

(RIGHT) ORIGINALLY MARIA HAD AN AMULET OF KUAN YIN, THE CHINESE GODDESS OF MERCY.

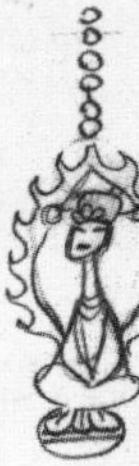

(RIGHT) ONE OF MY FAVORITE DARE THUMBNAILS... ALTHOUGH IT HAS PRACTICALLY NOTHING TO DO WITH "THE SNOWPEA PLOT", IT HELPED ME IN THE EARLIEST STAGES OF DEVELOPING THE ALLEY SCENE IN THIS ISSUE.

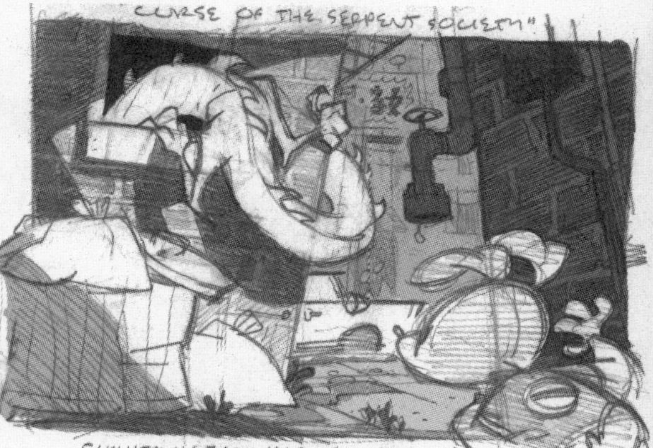
CURSE OF THE SERPENT SOCIETY"
CHINATOWN BACK ALLEY (FIREFLY CLUB?)

(BELOW) ANOTHER KUAN YIN. BY THE MING DYNASTY, SHE HAD BECOME ONE OF THE MOST POPULAR DIVINITIES IN CHINESE CULTURE, AND TODAY PORCELAIN FIGURES OF HER CAN BE FOUND IN RESTAURANTS, CURIO SHOPS AND SHRINES THROUGHOUT CHINATOWN.

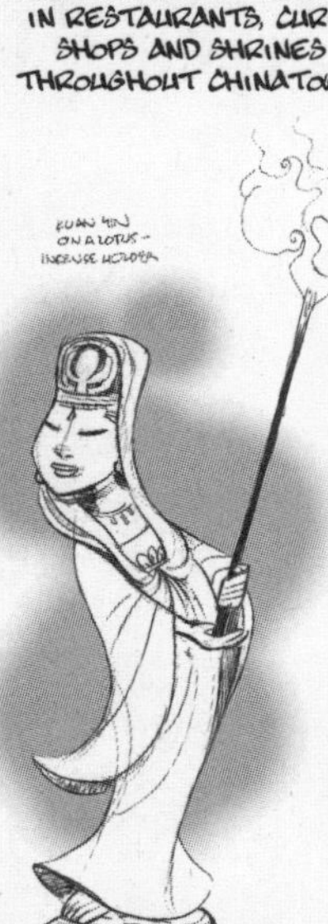
KUAN YIN ON A LOTUS - INCENSE HOLDER

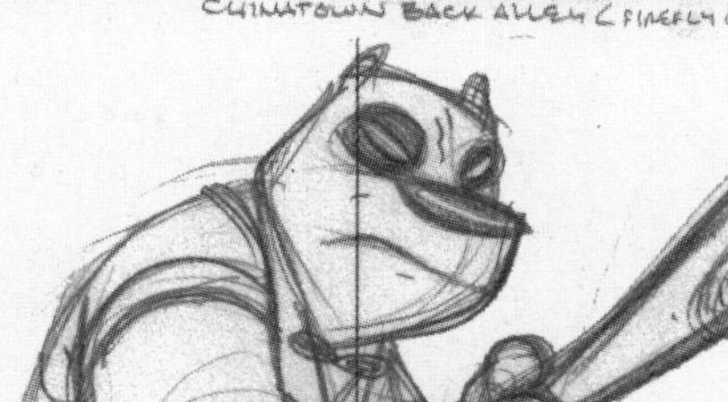
NO SNOWPEAS.

(ABOVE) WHITE'S GANG WERE ORIGINALLY PENGUINS, BUT THAT DIDN'T WORK SO WELL FOR ACTION SCENES, AS PENGUINS HAVE NO HANDS. THIS WAS MY FIRST SKETCH OF THE REPLACEMENT PANDA GOONS.

(RIGHT) ANOTHER THUMBNAIL, THIS ONE OF UNCLE CHAN'S NOODLETOWN (AND DARE'S APARTMENT ABOVE). I WAS GETTING BOGGED DOWN IN DETAILS, HERE I WANTED TO CONCENTRATE ON A SIMPLE BUT INTERESTING SHAPE.

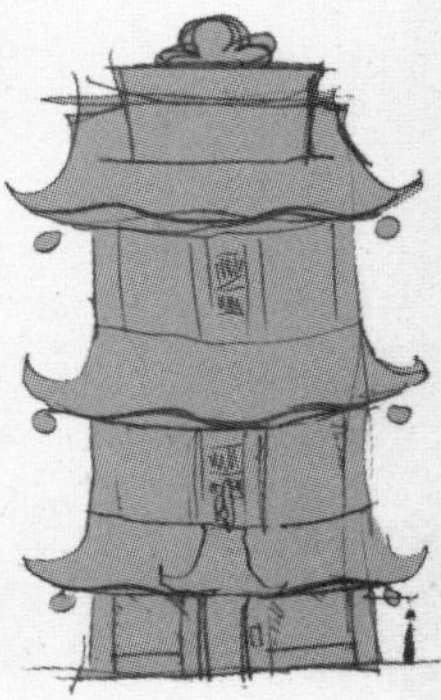

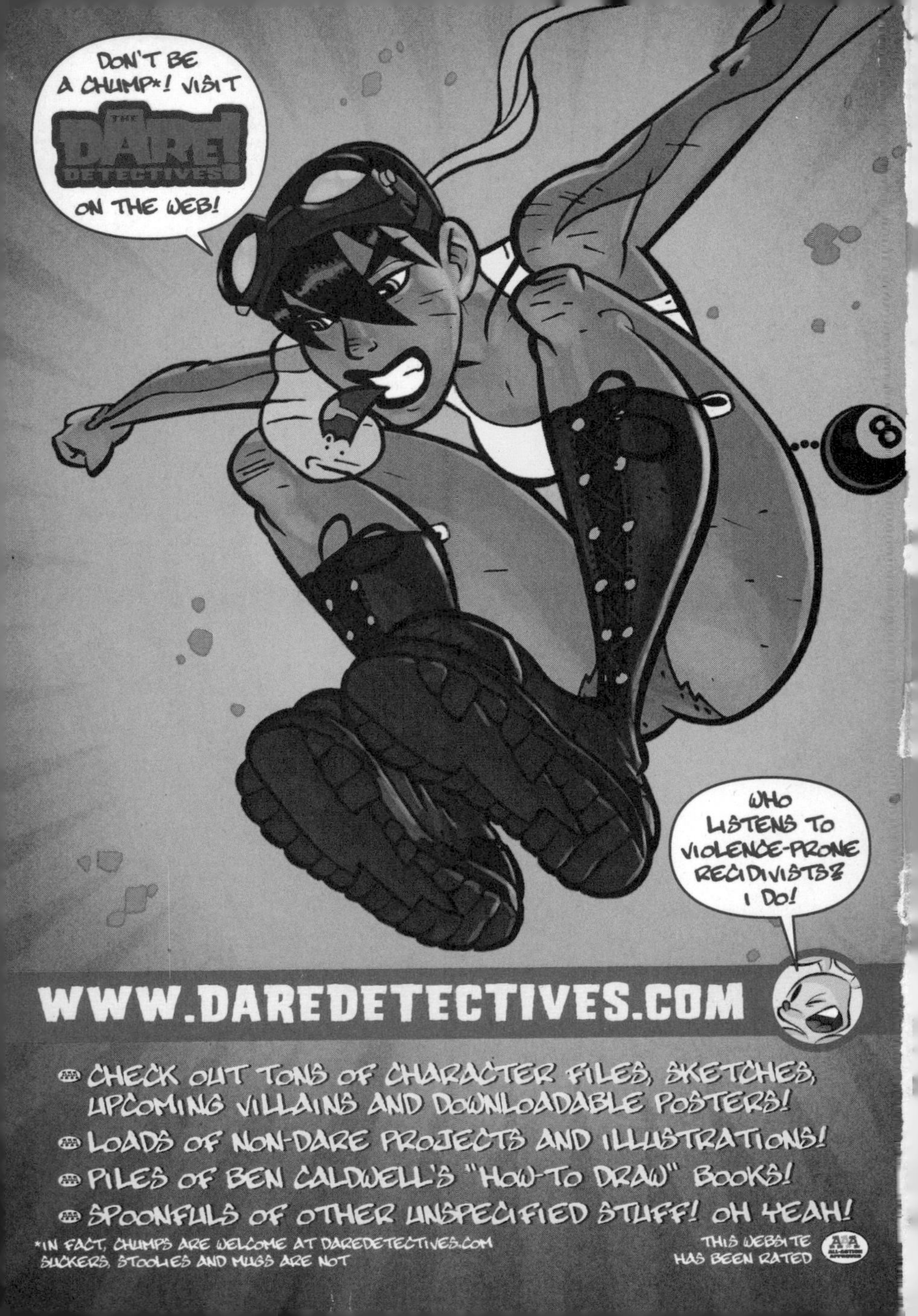
DON'T BE A CHUMP*! VISIT
THE DARE! DETECTIVES
ON THE WEB!
WHO LISTENS TO VIOLENCE-PRONE RECIDIVISTS? I DO!
WWW.DAREDETECTIVES.COM
CHECK OUT TONS OF CHARACTER FILES, SKETCHES, UPCOMING VILLAINS AND DOWNLOADABLE POSTERS!
LOADS OF NON-DARE PROJECTS AND ILLUSTRATIONS!
PILES OF BEN CALDWELL'S "HOW-TO DRAW" BOOKS!
SPOONFULS OF OTHER UNSPECIFIED STUFF! OH YEAH!
*IN FACT, CHUMPS ARE WELCOME AT DAREDETECTIVES.COM SUCKERS, STOOLIES AND MUGS ARE NOT
THIS WEBSITE HAS BEEN RATED